Computer Networks and Communications

Computer Networks and Communications

Edited by

Adele Kuzmiakova

ARCLER
PRESS

www.arclerpress.com

Computer Networks and Communications

Adele Kuzmiakova

Arcler Press
224 Shoreacres Road
Burlington, ON L7L 2H2
Canada
www.arclerpress.com
Email: orders@arclereducation.com

ISBN: 978-1-77407-746-7 (Hardcover)

ABOUT THE EDITOR

Adele Kuzmiakova is a computational engineer focusing on solving problems in machine learning, deep learning, and computer vision. Adele attended Cornell University in New York, United States for her undergraduate studies. She studied engineering with a focus on applied math. While at Cornell, she developed close relationships with professors, which enabled her to get involved in academic research to get hands-on experience with solving computational problems. She was also selected to be Accel Roundtable on Entrepreneurship Education (REE) Fellow at Stanford University and spent 3 months working on entrepreneurship projects to get a taste of entrepreneurship and high-growth ventures in engineering and life sciences. The program culminated in giving a presentation on the startup technology and was judged by Stanford faculty and entrepreneurship experts in Silicon Valley. After graduating from Cornell, Adele worked as a data scientist at Swiss Federal Institute of Technology in Lausanne, Switzerland where she focused on developing algorithms and graphical models to analyze chemical pathways in the atmosphere. Adele also pursued graduate studies at Stanford University in the United States where she entered as a recipient of American Association of University Women International Fellowship. The Fellowship enabled her to focus on tackling important research problems in machine learning and computer vision. Some research problems she worked on at Stanford include detecting air pollution from outdoor public webcam images. Specifically, she modified and set up a variety of pre-trained architectures, such as DehazeNet, VGG, and ResNet, on public webcam images to evaluate their ability to predict air quality based on the degree of haze on pictures. Other deep learning problems Adele worked on include investigating the promise of second-order optimizers in deep learning and using neural networks to predict sequences of data in energy consumption. Adele also places an emphasis on continual education and served as a Student Leader in PyTorch scholarship challenge organized by Udacity. Her roles as the Student Leader were helping students debug their code to train neural networks with PyTorch and providing mentorship on technical and career aspects. Her hobbies include skiing, playing tennis, cooking, and meeting new people.

TABLE OF CONTENTS

LIST OF FIGURES

having to set this infrastructure up would be very expensive. It is also expensive to transport and bury cables in the ground. In addition, acquiring the required permits is also quite expensive

Figure 8.8. Above are some of the uses of the radio frequency spectrum. This system allows for many different devices to communicate without affecting the intercommunication of other types of devices

Figure 8.9. Wide Area Wireless Data Services is wide area network that works by providing internet services to large separate areas that have coverage or cells through a wireless connection

Figure 8.10. Above are some of the pros and cons of Wi-Fi. One of the greatest concerns is security. Cyber hacking has led many issues such as identity theft, spreading of malware, stealing private information for malicious intent, etc

Figure 8.11. Above is a summary of the advantages and disadvantages of the Home RF system. This system is much more secure when compared to Wi-Fi. In addition, it also supports multimedia and the internet

Figure 8.12. One of main advantages of Bluetooth is that it is very efficient due to its wireless nature. However, its greatest disadvantage is that is can easily be hacked, making is not secure for private information

Figure 8.13. Above is a scatternet with three piconet within it. There is a good illustration of how the master and the slaves relate

Figure 8.14. This is the difference between an access point creating a pure wireless network and extending a wired network to wireless devices

Figure 8.15. This is an illustration of the difference in functionality of the Ad-hoc mode and the Infrastructure mode. The Infrastructure mode requires an access point to connect to different devices

Figure 8.16. These are the seven layers of the OSI model

LIST OF ABBREVIATIONS

ACK	acknowledgment letter
AMLS	advanced mini link system
ANSC	American National Standardization Committee
BGP	border gate-pass protocol
BLE	Bluetooth low energy
BR/EDR	basic ratio/enhanced data rate
CBP	contention-based protocol
CICS	client information control system
CRC	cyclical redundancy check
CS	computer networks
CSMA/CD	carrier sensor multiple access and collision detection
CSU/DSU	channel service unit/ data service unit
CVD	chemical vapor deposition
DDS	digital data service
DHCP	dynamic host configuration-protocol
DoD	Department of Defense
DTE	data terminal equipment
ECL	emitter-couples logic
ECMA	European Computer Manufacturing Association
EDR	enhanced data ratio
EEE's	Institute of Electrical and Electronics Engineers
EIA	Electronic Industries Alliance
FCS	frame check sequence
FDDI	fiber data-distribution interface
FHSS	frequency-hopping spread spectrum
GDT	ground data terminal
GPS	global positioning system

HA	highly accessible
IETF	internet engineering taskforce
IP	internet-protocol
ISDN	Integrated Services Digital Network
ISO	International Standardization Organization
ISP	Internet Service Provider
IT	information-technology
LAN	local area networks
LFSR	linear feedback shifting register
LLC	logical link control
LSP	label switched path
M2DLS	mini microdata link system
MAC	medium access control
MAN	Metropolitan Area Network
MIC	media interaction connector
MPLS	multiprotocol label switching
MS	Microsoft
NAK	not acknowledged
NIC	networking interface card
ONIE	open network install environment
OS	operating system
OSI	open structure interconnections
PAN	personal area network
PCs	personal computers
PID	program identification number
PSTN	Public Switched Telephone Network
QoS	quality of services
RR	round-robin
RSVP	resource reservation protocol
SDN	software-defined networking
SFD	start of the frame delimiter
SIG	special interest group
SONET	synchronous optical network
TFTP	trivial file transfer protocol

TPID	tag protocol identifier
USB	universal serial bus
UTP	unshielded twisted pair
VPNs	virtual private networks
VR	virtual reality
WAN	wide area networks
WPA	Wi-Fi protected accessibility
WWANs	wide area wireless data services

PREFACE

In recent times, the internet has continued to grow, allowing the world to witness the arrival of new technology almost every day. In fact, the society considers the Web as the major means of accessing and viewing information, all due to the many different projects in computer networking and data communication. These projects have worked to produce communication protocols that define the network messages formats, application programs such as browsers, and prototype networks. This has led to capitalizing on the ubiquity of the telephone network that is used globally, which provided the underlying physical infrastructure that was used to build the internet.

In the creation of computer networks data communication has proven to be very essential. Before networks were invented, data had to be carried physically from a device to another. Digital networks have not only made this much easier, but they have also allowed us to transfer data much faster. The entire computer industry has been driven by this ability, including innovations of software and also the formation of the internet as a means of communication for use by both the public and professionals. As the industry continues to grow, so does the number of people connecting to these networks, which results in an exponential increase of the scope.

This volume on computer networks and data communications provides a wide range of knowledge on all the aspects involved in this topic. It contains ten chapters providing insights on the manner in which we are able to maintain the main characteristics of a communication system: communication between two or more people, the ability to exchange ideas, the ability to communicate directly or indirectly, the ability to utilize both words and symbols, and finally avoiding errors occur during the process of transmission.

The ten chapters discuss different specific topics: The first chapter will explore an introduction to computer networking and communication, which will provide a better understanding on the main definitions that are used throughout the book. The second chapter will discuss the fundamentals of data and signals which will describe the characteristics of both data and signals. The third chapter will explore media: conducted and wireless. The fourth chapter will discuss making connections which will describe the different types of connections available. The fifth chapter will explore multiplexing and manners in which signals are combined. The sixth chapter will explore error detection, and error control. It will provide an overview on how, errors occur during the transmission of signals, what causes them and how they can be avoided. The seventh chapter will discuss Local Area Network (LAN). The eighth chapter will discuss the different wireless networks and their pros and cons. The ninth chapter will investigate challenges in computer networking and communication. Lastly, the tenth chapter will study the trends of computer networking.

These ten chapters were written in a manner that will provide the readers with a good understanding of all the aspects of computer networks and data communication. The volume has been written in an understandable way to focus on the understanding of the broader aspects.

We hope that this volume will guide all readers towards the understanding and development of communication networks and data communication.

CHAPTER

1

Introduction to Computer Networking and Communication

CONTENTS

1.1. INTRODUCTION

A computer network refers to a group of computers linked together to share data and resources. Currently, the most popular resource that's being used today is the internet connection. Examples of shared resources are printers and file servers. The Web itself is regarded as a form of computer network. Computers are connected on a network through nodes. The linkage between computers is possible through cabling, most importantly the Ethernet cable, and wirelessly via radio waves. Interconnected workstations can share resources, including the Internet, file servers and printers so long as they are connected to the main computer.

Figure 1.1. The internet is a networking technology that connects computers from all over the world.

Source: *https://favpng.com/png_view/computer-computer-network-internet-networking-hardware-computer-hardware-png/H3b2rccp.*

Historically, computer networks are subdivided into topologies, referring to a system of connecting computers. Among the most widely used topologies today is the collapsed ring, mainly because of the Ethernet network protocol's success. This network mode supports the Internet, Wide Area Networks (WAN) and Local Area Networks (LAN).

The star topology refers to a network design whereby the central node stretches a cable to every computer found on the network. For a star network, normally computers are linked independently to the core of the network. In case when the cable is damaged, then other computers will still continue to operate without any problems. Its only downside is that star topology needs lots of wiring.

Another alternative is bus topology, whereby one cable connects all workstations and the data purposed for the final node through the network should run through every connected computer. In case when the cable is destroyed, all computers attached down the line won't reach the network. Meaning the advantage of bus topology network is its reduced use of cabling.

A comparable topology is known as ring. For this design, workstations are linked together from a single cable, however, the final nodes also are attached to each other. Signals pass through the network up to the end recipient. In case when the network node isn't configured well, or it's down momentarily for another cause, the signal shall make several attempts to locate its destination.

As for collapsed ring topology, it's where the primary node is a networked instrument known as a switch, hub, or router. The device features a ring topology inside and has plugins for cabling. Next, every workstation has a self-operating cable that directly plugs into the instrument. Many present-day offices have some form of cabling closet, which is simply a space with a switch instrument that links the network. Every workstation in the office is attached to the wiring closet and switch. Particularly if a networking plug is next to a desk, where the plug is attached through a connective cable onto the wiring closet.

1.2. LOCAL AREA NETWORK (LAN)

A local-area network or LAN refers to a computer network which spans a fairly small space. Oftentimes, the LAN is restricted to one room, building or cluster of buildings, though, one LAN may be attached to other LANs across any distance through phone networks and radio waves. A grid of LANs joined in this format is known as wide-area network or WAN. The main point of divergence between WAN and LAN is that wide area network covers a somewhat vast geographical area. Normally, a WAN comprises of two or several local-area networks which are linked through public networks.

Majority of LANs are connected to workstations and PCs. Every node (single computer) in a LAN is also capable of accessing and implementing data anywhere across the LAN. It means that most users are able to share otherwise costly devices, such as data and laser printers. Additionally, they might use LAN to network with each other through sending emails or participating in chat sessions. The LANs can transmit information at very quick rates though the distances are restricted and there is also a cap on the amount of computers which can be connected to one LAN (White, 2015).

Every LAN relays data in virtual format through serial transmission cables. Furthermore, synchronous programming is typically used since it allows for comparatively high transfusion speeds, through transferring sets of characters per time. A normal data block contains 80 characters, which is heralded by a synchronization chain and trailed by a stop sequence.

Furthermore, the synchronization sequence often makes the receiver to adjust its clock comparatively with the one for the transmitter. There are two key principles for synchronous, serial data broadcasting which are RS485 and RS422. They are now officially printed by the ANSI Telecoms Industry Association, or Electronic Industries Alliance (EIA) consisting of the codes ANSI/TIA/EIA-485 and ANSI/TIA/EIA-422-B.

LANs have a unique value in the assessment and management of systems with a wide number of different sensors, actuators, and switch units distributed over a vast area. Certainly, for such immense instrumentation systems, the local area network forms the only practical transmission model with regards to performance and rate.

On the other hand, parallel data buses that convey data in analog system, suffer from signal tempering and noise pickup through large distances (White, 2015).

Nevertheless, the invention of instrumentation systems isn't without glitches. Careful design of the computer network is needed to avert data corruption whenever several appliances on the network seek to access it concurrently or add information within the data bus simultaneously.

This issue can be solved by developing a convenient network protocol which ensures that connected devices don't access the network together, therefore avoiding data corruption. With LAN, the electronic path may assume the context of either copper electrodes or fiber-optic wiring.

Copper conductors are a less costly option and permit for transmission speeds of around 10 Mbit/s, through a basic pair of twisted cables or the co-axial cable. Nevertheless, fiber-optic cords are favored in most networks for various reasons. In addition to the high-resistance of these signals to noise, fiber-optic relay system can also transfer information at rates of about 240 Mbit/s. The decline in wave attenuation during transfusion also means that exceedingly longer transmission expenses are possible without any repeaters involved.

For example, permissible distances between the repeaters for fiber-optic systems are estimated as 1 kilometer for a half-duplex set-up and roughly 3.5 kilometers for a whole-duplex operation. Furthermore, the bandwidth connecting fiber-optic transmissions is considerably higher compared to electrical transfusion. Some cost savings may be realized by using synthetic fiber-optic cables, however, these can't generally be applied over vast distances more than 30 meters since signal attenuation might be exceedingly high (Robertazzi, 2017).

There are diverse protocols used for local-area networks (LAN), though these are dependent on 1 of 3 network structures called star networks, ring networks and bus networks. Typically, LANs operate within one building or site, plus can transfer data across large distances of up to around 500 meters, without any signal weakening issues.

For transmission over vast distances, phone lines are normally added to the network. Moreover, intelligent instruments are connected to the phone line. This line is used for information transmission through a modem, which alters the signal to form a frequency-tuned analog form. Once this form is achieved, it is possible to be transferred over a public switched phone network, or through private-lines leased from telephone firms. The latter option refers to special lines that allow for greater data-transmission rates (Robertazzi, 2017).

1.3. PERSONAL AREA NETWORK

A personal area network, also known as PAN, is created when several computers or mobile phones network with each other wirelessly across a short expanse, normally less than around 30-feet. Typically, these networks are wireless and consists of data transmission between portable devices or to a central server being the network that permits additional linking to the Web. Advances in the field of PANs are mainly managed through the IEEE 802.15 operations group.

1.3.1. Bluetooth

Bluetooth is a short-distance cordless networking system that allows appliances like smartphones, peripherals, and workstations to convey data or voice cordlessly over a short expanse. The goal of Bluetooth is replacing the wires that normally link devices, while ensuring interactions between them are protected.

The name "Bluetooth" is believed to be borrowed from an ancient Danish King who ruled during the 10th century and was called Harald Bluetooth, remembered for uniting warring regional territories. Similarly, Bluetooth technology joins together a wide range of devices spanning different sectors through a uniting communication standard (Robertazzi, 2017).

Originally created in 1994, Bluetooth technology was meant to be a cordless replacement for cables. The innovation uses a similar 2.4GHz frequency similar to other wireless innovations at home or the office, for example Wi-Fi routers and cordless handsets. It forms a 10-meter radius cordless network, known as piconet or PAN, that is capable of networking between 2 to 8 devices at a go. The short-range network permits you to dispatch a file directly to user in another room, who also has Bluetooth switched on for their device. With this technology, there is no need to connect unsightly cables all over the room.

Bluetooth consists of two forms, which are Bluetooth low energy (BLE) and basic ratio/enhanced data rate (BR/EDR). The latter is commonly used for streaming information applications, while BLE performs control and monitoring roles including single-way beacons, whereby low-energy usage for extended battery life is required (Robertazzi, 2017).

Model of operation: This technology uses a unique connectivity method called frequency-hopping spread spectrum (FHSS), whereby data is subdivided into chunks and transferred through a carrier which skips from one unsystematic frequency to another.

Information is passed at a rate of 1-Mbps through FSK. Furthermore, an enhanced data ratio (EDR) model of Bluetooth is available that transmits data at greater speeds of around 3 Mbps. Even the latest versions can deliver data ratios as big as 24 Mbps, besides much higher rates may be attainable in future renditions of the standard. This standard is managed courtesy of Bluetooth's Special Interest Group or (SIG).

Among the basic attributes of Bluetooth technology is that it is able to form tiny networks known as piconets. This is achieved by connecting two Bluetooth appliances together. One acts as a primary controller, with the ability to link up to 7 other Bluetooth slave appliances. When the PAN is established, different connected devices are capable of exchange data with each other utilizing the master (Robertazzi, 2017).

Currently, the most popular Bluetooth application is the cordless headset used for smartphones. It can also be found in a few wireless networks between laptops and smartphones. The technology is also widely applied in some PC peripheral devices, such as PC-to-printer networks.

Compared to Wi-Fi, Bluetooth uses less power, which makes the technology far less susceptible to encountering interferences with other cordless appliances within a similar 2.4GHz radio wave. Typically, Bluetooth range and transmission rates are lower compared to Wi-Fi (the cordless local area network (LAN) which you could be having in your house) (White, 2015).Some Bluetooth top-speed technology devices are capable of delivering around 24Mbps of data, a ratio that's quicker than 802.11b Wi-Fi standard, however, slower than cordless-a or cordless-g standards. With advancements in technology, nevertheless, Bluetooth speeds have risen considerably.

In particular, Bluetooth 4.0 technology which was officially launched in 2010 now features improved range, low energy consumption and multiuser interoperability. It also has reduced power requirements since appliances connected to Bluetooth v4.0 are modified for reduced battery operation. Additionally, you can operate it using tiny coin-cell batteries, which leads to new prospects for wireless technology. Rather than fearing that switching Bluetooth on can drain your smartphone's battery, for instance, you can have a Bluetooth v4.0 smartphone connected always to your alternative Bluetooth accessories (White, 2015).

Linking to Bluetooth: Most smartphones have Bluetooth radios entrenched in them. Personal computers (PCs) and different other devices which don't have integral radios may be Bluetooth-allowed, through integrating a Bluetooth dongle, such as, the procedure of attaching a pair Bluetooth device commonly known as "pairing."

Normally, devices showcase their presence to each other, while the user chooses the Bluetooth appliance that they wish to link with once its ID or name shows on their device. When the Bluetooth-allowed device multiplies, it becomes key that you understand when and onto which appliance you are connecting. This pairing method may vary based on the appliances involved. For instance, connecting a Bluetooth instrument to your iPad may involve unique steps, different from those used to pair Bluetooth appliances to your vehicle (Robertazzi, 2017).

1.3.2. Wi-Fi

This refers to a group of cordless networking technologies, which run on IEEE 802.11 technology. As recently as 2010, it's estimated that Wi-Fi-based circuit chips shipped roughly 580 million connectivity devices annually. These devices include PCs, smartphones, tablets, desktops, smart TVs, laptops, and virtual cameras. Wi-Fi utilizes different modules of IEEE 802 protocol group, plus is developed to interwork easily with its cabled counterpart Ethernet. Linked devices can network via a virtual access point to one another, and to wired appliances and the Web. The different editions of Wi-Fi are categorized by different IEEE 802.11 protocol measures, with the diverse radio technologies controlling radio bands, plus the maximum extents, and speeds which can be achieved.

Figure 1.2. The Wi-Fi is a wireless computer networking system.

Source: *https://www.ekahau.com/blog/2018/07/09/state-of-wi-fi-report/.*

More importantly, Wi-Fi runs on 2.4 gigahertz UHF and 5 gigahertz SHF-ISM radio bands, which are segmented into various channels. These can be shared across networks though a single transmitter can regionally transfer on a frequency at any given moment. The Wi-Fi's wavebands have comparatively high absorption rates and work ideally for line-of-sight applications. Various common obstructions like home appliances, walls, and pillars can significantly reduce range, though this further helps to reduce interference between varying networks in crowded spaces (Robertazzi, 2017).

Typically, an access point covers a range of roughly 20 meters indoors, even though some contemporary access points say that they can cover up to 150-meter range outdoors. The hotspot coverage may be as limited as one room with walls which jam radio signals, or as big as several square kilometers through using different corresponding access points where roaming is allowed between them. With time, the pace and spectral proficiency of Wi-Fi has improved. By 2019, at close quarters, some editions of Wi-Fi, operating on a suitable hardware, may reach speeds of above 1 Gbit/s or gigabit a second.

Generally, Wi-Fi is more susceptible to attacks compared to cable networks since anybody within the network's range with a virtual network interface controller may attempt access. Thus, to link to a Wi-Fi system, users normally require the SSID/network name and a PIN. The PIN is used for encrypting Wi-Fi packets in order to prevent eavesdroppers (Robertazzi, 2017).

Moreover, Wi-Fi Protected Accessibility or (WPA) refers to a group of technologies developed to protect data moving across Wi-Fi systems and covers solutions for individual and enterprise networks. Considering that the data security field has changed with time, the security functions of WPA equally have incorporated stronger protections and fresh security practices.

Common uses: Wi-Fi technology can be applied to offer local network and Web access to devices which are within the Wi-Fi spectrum, where one or several routers are linked to the Web. The networking of one or several interconnected access spots (hotspots) can spread from a zone as limited as some few rooms, to much larger spaces with multiple square kilometers.

Moreover, coverage in large areas may need a collection of access points having overlapping coverage. Case in point, the public outdoor Wi-Fi system has been used effectively in cordless mesh networks within London. Wi-Fi provides wireless internet connectivity to private homes, companies, and public spaces. Furthermore, Wi-Fi hotspots can be established either completely free or commercially, typically applying a captive portal website for access (Robertazzi, 2017).

Companies, supporters, authorities, and institutions typically provide free or paid hotspots for attracting clients to their premises. Routers typically have a virtual subscriber line modem or cabling modem, including a Wi-Fi access spot, and are normally established in homes as well as buildings, to offer Web access and internetworking services for the structure.

Equally, battery-run routers may consist of a cellular Web radio modem or even Wi-Fi access point. Once subscribed to the cellular information carrier, these systems allow adjacent Wi-Fi units to access the Web through 2G, 3G and 4G networks applying the tethering method. Most Smartphone's also have an integral function of this kind, including those that are centered on BlackBerry, Android, Windows Phone, iOS (iPhone), Symbian, and Bada systems,

Even though carriers typically disable the function, or charge a different fee to allow it, particularly for clients with limitless data plans. "Web packs" offer standalone amenities of this form also, but without using a smartphone; for instance, the WiBro-and MiFi-branded appliances. Moreover, there are laptops with cellular modem cards which may also serve as portable Web Wi-Fi access points. Most traditional college campuses in developed countries provide at least provisional Wi-Fi coverage (Robertazzi, 2017).

The first ever campus-wide cordless Internet network was developed by Carnegie-Mellon University, where it was known as Wireless Andrew. The network was exclusively used at their Pittsburgh campus during 1993, before Wi-Fi branding came up. By 1997, the university's Wi-Fi zone became fully operational. Nowadays, many universities partner in providing Wi-Fi accessibility to learners and employees through their Eduroam global authentication infrastructure.

During the early 2000s, various cities around the globe announced plans to build citywide Wi-Fi systems. There are multiple successful examples; like the city of Mysore in India which became the country's first Wi-Fi-accessible city in 2004. In America, the cities of Florida, Sunnyvale, St. Cloud and California established themselves as the first municipalities in U.S. to provide citywide no-cost Wi-Fi in 2005.

South Korea has even taken it further, where officials are planning to install well over 10,000 sites across the city, including in outdoor public places, large streets and highly populated residential zones. Seoul city intends to grant Wi-Fi installation leases to LG Telecom, KT, and SK Telecom broadband companies. Together, these companies hope to invest around $44 million into the project that was to be finished by 2015.

Apart from a few small implementations (like home and small office networks), the Wi-Fi implementations have further progressed toward "thin" access spots, where a good part of the web intelligence is housed within a centralized network system, relegating personal accessibility points to the part of "dumb" transceivers. Besides, outdoor applications can use mesh topologies as well (Robertazzi, 2017).

1.4. COMPUTER NETWORK CONFIGURATIONS

The field of computer networking and data infrastructures is a remarkably huge and progressively significant area of practice. Previously considered just the purvey of communications mechanics and technicians, with time CS have grown to include corporate managers, computer programmers, home computer users, system designers and office managers, including other normal citizens.

It is nearly impossible for any typical individual to spend a whole day without using any kind of computer network. Some common places where computer network can be found are banking, education, transportation, telecommunication, and retail sales. It is essential to recognize the general broad aspects of computer networking and information communications. For instance, you must be able to describe some terms including network management, wide area network (WAN) and Telecommunications. Every one of these terminologies is a topic subject under the network computer field (Cowley, 2012).

1.4.1. Convergence

This happens nearly at all stages, such as the convergence of technologies. To keep different parts of the network working mutually and to permit modularity between the sections, it's crucial to utilize a network architecture framework, or communications model, which puts the necessary network segments in layers. Every layer within the model describes what type of services are offered by the software, firmware or even both.

Large software applications work in a way that diverse processes do different tasks, besides the whole can't work without the appropriate functioning of its different parts. The communications software isn't an exception. With steady growth in the application's size, there's increased need for sharing of labor which becomes more important (Cowley, 2012).

Furthermore, it is essential to understand the OSI model including its 7 layers, and the basic functions done at every layer: such as data linking, network, session, presentation, carriage, and application. While the OSI model isn't the primary model used for supporting the Internet, comprehending it is necessary, since a lot of networks and products regularly mention the OSI computer network for definition. It's equally essential to grasp the TCP/IP protocol setup (Internet model) including its four layers which are: network accessibility, network, conveyance, and application. The Web model is the structure used to support every activity happening on the Internet.

1.4.2. Mainframes Networking

To support the varying needs of online transactions, business networks may be designed, modified, operated, and sustained using the combined elements and functions of structural protocols, like TCP/IP and SNA. Typically, z/

OS network capabilities comprise of a fully-equipped communications server that integrates both TCP/IP and SNA protocols, therefore making the workstation a massive server capable of attending to a big number of global clients concurrently.

There are many technology options in existence that can be used to transport, safeguard, protect, as well as encode z/OS hosted corporate sensitive and client confidential data that's exchanged between the mainframe and accredited clients. The needs and specifications of a business transaction often determines the type of technologies used to handle its processes. Data communications specialists in the realm of mainframe computing must understand the function of the computer network in your organization's business goals and corporate infrastructure (Cowley, 2012).

It's also essential to recognize how the most recent networking technologies function with your firm's mainframe computer. In the wider sense of the term, a network is simply an interlinked system of things. In today's fast-paced, interactive area of information-technology (IT), the network is described as the firmware and software that allows processors to share documents and resources while also exchanging data. Based on the overall size or scope of a business, the network can consist of as basic as two personal processors on a regionally connected network, or as multifaceted as the Web, which is a universal system consisting of millions of processors of different types.

In order to send or obtain data from a network, the users interact through different communication devices like telephones, computers, and workstations. Furthermore, network data may pass through an even wider variety of mechanisms: such as communication hardware and software, broadband cable, fiber optics, cordless, and microwave transmission systems, satellite, and telephone wires (Cowley, 2012).

To some degree, the description of a "network" depends on who's really using the network. For example, while voice and data may share a similar network, the IT expert who's hired to maintain the voice traffic may likely perceive the network differently compared to an individual that's hired to maintain information traffic. A telephony specialist or electrical engineer may define the network as "collection of electronic modules and connecting circuitry developed to work in a particular manner," whereas a network developer or architect may say that the network is "a structure of lines or communication channels crisscrossing or interconnected to form an advanced, interconnected system or group or system."

What really is a mainframe: In occasions where speed and security form essential parts of a network, mainframes are applied as the most crucial servers for the network infrastructure. This is a computer which supports multiple applications including input/output devices, so that they can serve several 1000s of users concurrently. What differentiates the mainframe from other types of computers isn't only its processing functions. The mainframe has redundancy functions and system health recognition attributes that allow it to provide holistic availability. Mainframe networking is responsible for today's virtual transaction processing, which increasingly needs support for online transactions spanning a network and might include several companies. Networks are considered to comprise of both intranets, internets, and extranets.

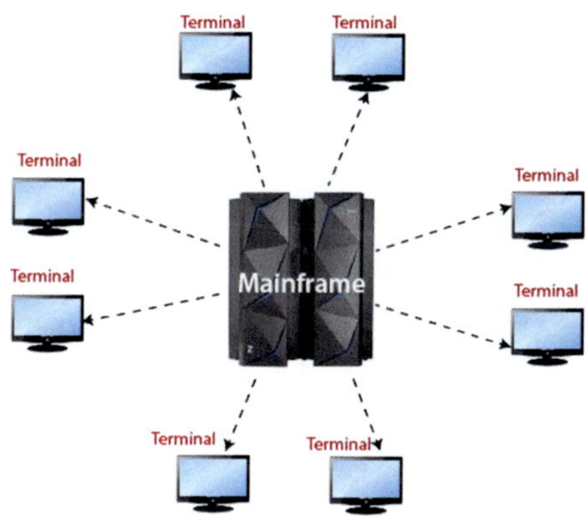

Figure 1.3. The mainframe is a central computer that receives and transmits all data within a network.

Source: https://www.javatpoint.com/mainframe-interview-questions.

Beginnings of mainframe networking: Before the launch of the Internet, staffs in a company considered the network to be terminals which served the organization's day to day transactions. It was a rather predictable workload in regards to the transaction rate and amount of transactions made, besides majority of the work was achievable after hours due to batch processing with help from the mainframe. The major change seen today is with digital transaction processing, this refers to a group of programs which expedite and manage transaction-focused applications, usually for data entry, retrieval transactions and order entry within different industries, such as banking, manufacturing, and airlines (Cowley, 2012).

Without a doubt, the most extensively installed OLTP product, discounting the web servers which front-end majority of OLTP networks, is the IBM Client Information Control System, also known as CICS (spelled "kicks"). Modern-day OLTP applications make use of client/server processors and brokering software which allows for transactions to be done on multiple computer platforms within the network.

Current networks and transactional structures should be equipped to sustain an unpredictable number of concurrent users as well as transaction types. Many transaction programs nowadays must respond in short term intervals—less than a second in a few instances. Case in point, within a bank branch department or over the Internet, clients are making use of digital services when looking up a balance statement or transferring cash balances. As a matter of fact, a digital transaction network has a lot of the features of a standard operating system (OS) (Cowley, 2012).

Why are mainframe networks necessary: In the modern competitive marketplace, responsiveness to client or supplier needs is frequently a decisive factor when it comes to the success of a business. Networks are believed to be among the most crucial resources in a company, both in public and private sectors. The networks are developed to offer a method for satisfying a goal or need. These goals and needs are normally critical, thus the network by itself is also critical.

Take for instance the comparison of a typical transportation network (comprising of roads, rails, highways, and so forth). In case any of these channels were to become abruptly unavailable, then the ability for people to dispense food, clothes or other daily living products can be extremely compromised. Likewise, a computer network gets developed to provide a method for transmitting data, occasionally essential data, from a particular computer to another. In such occasions, the accuracy and overall speed of day-to-day business transactions for big companies are key to their success (Cowley, 2012).

Unplanned disruption in the scheme of things can result in complete failure to handle these daily business processes, which can be costly and possibly disastrous to the business. The prevalent use of networks covers the reach of companies. These remote exchanges with clients, suppliers, and business associates have immensely benefited a lot of companies, and correspondingly positively influenced the general productivity of various countries. The productivity gains, nevertheless, are just as ideal as the network.

Mainframes are commonly used by large corporates as their main transaction processing structures. Transaction processing within this context needs high availability, performance, security, and receptiveness. For instance, clients expect to be in a position to utilize their credit cards any day and throughout the year.

Basically, they need these operations to be safe plus they don't imagine being left stranded at the checkout while waiting for things to happen. By and large, the mainframe is especially developed to be a "top breed" computer that can perform different massive concurrent operations in a variety of transactions each second (Cowley, 2012).

1.5. MICROCOMPUTER COMMUNICATION

A microcomputer makes use of internal communications networks to convey information among its modules. Ports present external connections to allow devices to be linked to a PC. Both ports and cables are required for efficient flow of communication towards and from the input, output, and storage devices.

It is also possible to establish communication lines to other workstations or computer networks, where you require a modem or the NIC (Networking Interface Card.) Modems, buses, and ports are some of the diverse parts of networking and communication. Buses refer to wires which connect the processor's internal modules. These internal mechanisms, such as RAM and CPU chips, relay data on a bus. The narrow buses can transfer around 8 bits of data per time, whereas 16 and 32-bit networking buses are broader and can convey data much faster (Anttalainen and Jaaskelainen, 2014).

Furthermore, slots can present a mechanism for including modules to the inner bus, such that you can expand the computer. The so-called "daughter cards" are designed for plugging into slots found on the "mother-board" plus adding to the modules which one may regard as internal to the structural computer unit. In order for external hardware devices, like a printer or keyboard to interconnect with a computer then it should be able to link up to the processor. This is typically done via a plug known as the port situated at the rear of the computer.

There are various kinds of ports that allow for diverse forms of external implements or peripherals to be linked to the computer. Generally, modems permit one processor to interlink with another that's not connected to it through established cables and ports. The modem translates virtual information (like that stored on a Disk) to sound (analog data), and transfer it through the phone network (Anttalainen and Jaaskelainen, 2014).

The modem that receives the data converts the analog data back into digital format before sending it over to the computer. External modems are boxes that plug into the processor via a port (normally the serial port), plus into a smartphone jack. On the contrary, an internal modem is available in form of expansion cards, and easily fit into the slot within the computer's casing. Most fax modems can send and receive data to and from any normal fax machine, including modem-to-modem networking. The tempo at which modems transfer data is counted in bits a second, commonly known as bps. Much slower modems transfer information at 2400-bps or lower, whereas faster modems are able to transfer speeds of up to 28,800 bps.

1.5.1. Microcomputer-to-Internet

It was only recently that words such as intranet, internet, and extranet applied in just a few specialized settings. Nowadays, they form part and parcel of our everyday vocabulary. The extensive use of Internet has inspired the use of proxies, firewalls, routers, VPNs (Virtual Private Networks), plus now cloud systems and virtualization. Upcoming technologies that have progressed in the past few years have further led to the invention of new business phrases like B2C, M2M and B2B.

The internet is under continuous evolution from one year to another as the ever-growing changes in industry determine variations to course content. Presently, stakeholders in internet processes are required to have the necessary competencies and skills for administering networks and providing effectual technical support to operators while planning for future network development in a business–wide environment. Computer operators must acquire competencies and skills to install, modulate, and maintain workstation, microcomputers, and network operations systems, such as LINUX and Window. Their services also include the installation and administration of networks and extranet/internet solutions, such as Electronic Mail and Web servers, plus understanding and practicing the models of virtualization and cloud computing (White, 2015).

1.5.2. Education Programs for Microprocessor Networking

Upon entering the job market, computer students often find themselves surrounded by other colleagues with greater experience than them, some even becoming their official mentors. Similarly, as you advance in your career path, you will possibly become a mentor to novice tech workers entering their first job.

Nowadays, computer colleges are developing teaching techniques and course program which allows learners to understand the "real world." Basically, you will start with the basic session, and then either proceed on with a similar format into other higher learning modules, or join existing training groups in another successive session based on the semester that you enrolled in (Robertazzi, 2017).

This might mean that at some stage in the program, you may assume the role of a junior computer specialist, surrounded by other more experienced students who will act as mentors. In future, you'll become a mentor who helps out new apprentices entering your class. The computer program may follow any of these semester arrangements: ABC, CAB, CBA or BCA. Every of these session is self-contained.

The course starts by introducing learners to basic micro-computer firmware and software applications. A general review of micro-computer hardware would be presented for the reason of using a processor effectively. Learners also gain a solid foundation in processes such as Microsoft (MS) Windows 7 desktop operations system (Robertazzi, 2017).

Some of the study topics include file management, printing, navigation, configuration, and modification of Windows. Students may also be familiarized with Linux Ubuntu OS. The program introduces scholars to the workings of microcomputer systems. Some of the topics of consideration include microprocessors, bus structures, chipsets, memory arrangement, BIOS, power supplies, input/output devices, troubleshooting firmware, and software issues.

Scholars will assemble micro-computers from different parts, install different OS and facilities, perform tests and even troubleshoot issues. Additionally, they will be taught how to install, organize, and troubleshoot issues with peripheral appliances. Some topics of interest are; SCSI devices, sound cards, disk drives, CD-ROM drives, scanners, network cards, memory, printers, and video cards.

Furthermore, students may be taught how to put up a fully operational microcomputer system, while also using MS Windows device instruments to diagnose or troubleshoot structural faults. Additionally, computer students shall be exposed to theories of operating network modules, network topologies, bridges, routers, networking cards, connection media and gateways among other networking components (Robertazzi, 2017).

1.6. LAN TO LAN COMMUNICATIONS

A LAN-to-LAN system is also known as a Bridge Network. It links up two otherwise different computer networks to allow easy communication between and other systems to work together as one holistic network. Normally, Bridges are used together with LAN in order to expand their reach and cover wider physical spaces which a single LAN may otherwise not achieve.

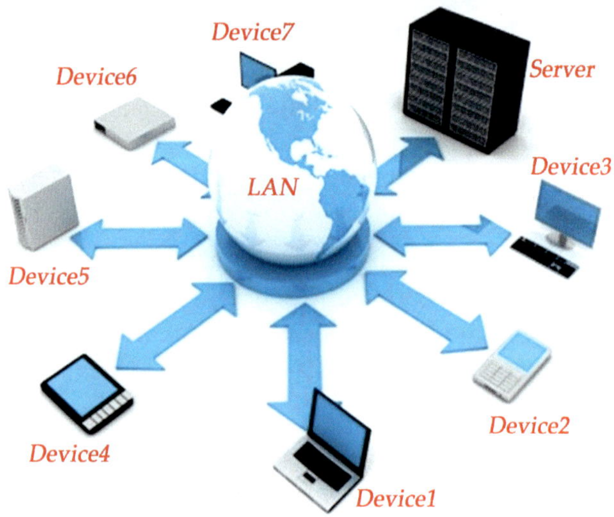

Figure 1.4. A LAN network connects different devices from a local server.

Source*:* https://am7s.com/local-area-network-work/.

This is different from LAN to WAN which is simply a Gateway Network. In gateway systems, hardware appliances normally serve as "gates" between a pair of networks. This might be a firewall, router, server, or any other appliance that allows traffic to move in and out from the system.

1.6.1. Ways to Transfer Data from a LAN Computer to Another

When switching over to a new PC with fresh hardware, you should transfer your individual files from the old PC. There are various commonly used techniques to transfer the files from one computer to another. One is using an External Hard Disk, which also provides data backup of the information in case data is lost.

It's largely a manual procedure which could take much longer. Consider plugging your external hard-disc into the old PC, then copy your documents onto the drive before plug it into the fresh computer and transfer the documents in any of your computer's local hard discs, repeat the procedure for all the folders you intend to transfer to the fresh PC (White, 2015).

Alternatively, you may use a transfer cable. It's possible to transmit data between your LAN computers through a typical transfer cable. This normally comes with a pair of USB3.0 male attachments. When the PC's are linked, the featured software shall assist you to transfer your data easily.

You can also consider using the LAN network to access the web. LANs are available in two main forms: wireless and wired. For the wired option, a cable passes from each workstation to the central box, while a wireless network utilizes radio signals instead of wires. In both ways, you require a central box to effectively connect your LAN to the internet. In case all your workstations are in a single-room and you don't intend to transfer them, then a wired network would be a great option for you. Additionally, wireless is much easier to install, even though the resultant network operates much slower. Combo connections are also probable; most wireless kits have some few jacks for cables to join to the computers which are adjacent enough to operate cables (White, 2015).

1.7. NETWORK ARCHITECTURE MODELS

1.7.1. The OSI Model

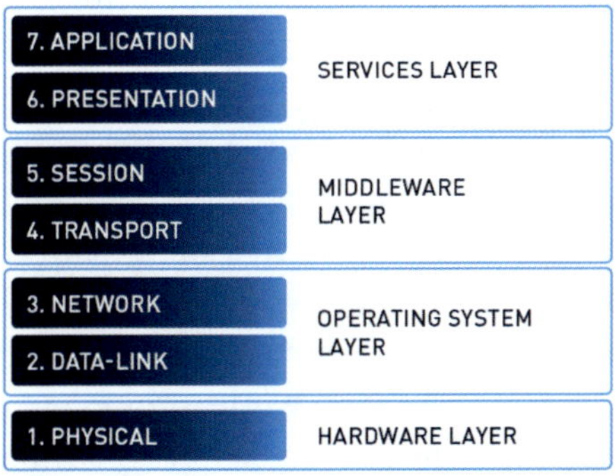

Figure 1.5. OSI forms the basic structural model of most networking systems.

Source: https://blog.paessler.com/is-it-possible-to-monitor-osi-model-layer-8.

The term OSI stands for Open Systems Interconnection. It is a reference model describing how data from the software application found in one computer travels through a physical channel to the software program in another computer. OSI comprises of a total of seven layers, where each layer does a particular networking role.

The OSI model was formed by the International Standardization Organization (ISO) in 1984, plus is now regarded as an architectural structure for the inter-processor communications. OSI architecture subdivides the entire process into seven smaller and manageable roles. Each layer is allotted a particular task. Every level is self-contained, such that tasks allocated to each specific layer may be done independently (White, 2015).

1.7.2. Roles of OSI Layers

In total, OSI layers are seven in number and include the following:

Physical layer: The primary function of the physical level is to transfer the separate bits from a particular node to another. It's the lowest level of OSI system which establishes, preserves, and neutralizes the physical link. It defines the mechanical, power-driven, and procedural system interface specifications. This physical layer describes the way in which two or more appliances can be linked physically. It also outlines the transmission module whether it's simplex, half or whole-duplex module between the paired devices on the network. The level further defines how network appliances are arranged, apart from determining the kind of signal applied for transferring the information.

Data-Link Layer: This layer is ideal for error-free exchange of data frames. It further describes the data format on the computer network. It also delivers a consistent and resourceful communication between multiple devices. The data link is also liable for the exclusive identification of every device that's hosted on a regional network. The data link comprises of two sub-layers. The first one is Logical Link Control (LLC) Level that's responsible for transmitting the data packs to a Network layer covering the receiver that's obtaining it. This system further defines the network level protocol's address from the header while providing flow control to the network. In terms of function, this layer is responsible for framing. This is where the data-link layer interprets the physical's fresh bit stream into modules known as Frames. Data link level adds the header as well as trailer onto the frame. Physical addressing is also possible; this is where the Data link level adds a header onto the frame which consists of a final destination address. Usually, the frame is transferred to the final destination address covered in the header (White, 2015).Furthermore, flow control works as the primary operation of the Data-link level. It's the procedure through which a constant data ratio is preserved on both the sections, so that no information gets corrupted. This ensures that the transferring station like the server with advanced processing speed doesn't surpass the reception station, with reduced processing speed.

In addition, error-control can be reached by including a calculated rate CRC, or (Cyclic Redundancy Check) which is placed onto the Datalink level's trailer that's included to the messaging frame before it's relayed to the physical level. In case any error looks like happening, then it means that the receiver directs the re-transfusion acknowledgment for the damaged frames. Datalink layer further allows for Access Control. Whenever two or several devices are attached to the same networking channel, it means the data link level protocols are applied to determine which appliance controls the link at any particular time (White, 2015).

Network Layer: This layer is responsible for managing device addressing, and tracking the position of devices found within the network. The layer decides which path is ideal for data to pass through from its source to the final location, depending on existing network conditions, service priority and various other attributes.

The main function of this layer is internetworking, which involves securing a logical link between multiple devices. Another role is addressing, whereby a network layer includes the source and final terminus address to the frame's header. Typically, addressing is applied to detect the device connected on the web.

As for Routing, it's a major element of the networking layer as well, where it defines the most ideal path away from the various paths available from the source to final destination. The system is also involved in Packetizing, where a Network Layer obtains packets from the top layer and changes them into distinct packets. The procedure is called Packetizing and is attained through the internet-protocol (IP).

Transport Layer: It's a four-layered protocol that ensures messages are easily transferred in the sequence that they're dispatched and there's no replication of data. The key role of this transport protocol is transferring the data entirely. It obtains the information from the upper section and changes them into lesser units called segments. This layer may be referred to as terminal-to-terminal layer since it offers a point-to-point contact between the source and final destination to convey the information reliably.

There are two main protocols applied in this layer which are I) Transmission Control Protocol. This is a typical protocol which allows the networking structures to easily communicate over the web. It creates and preserves a solid connection between hosts. Once data is dispatched over the TCP network, it means the TCP system subdivides the information into much smaller bits called segments.

Every one of these segments moves over the web system using different routes, ultimately arriving in distinct orders at the final spot. It's the work of transfusion control protocol to re-order the packets, so that they can follow the accurate order at the receiver side. The main role of Transport Layer is service-point addressing. Processors run different programs concurrently because of this reason, the transfusion of information from the source to destination doesn't just cover one computer to the other, but also from a particular activity to another (Robertazzi, 2017).

The transportation level adds the header which comprises of the address called a port address or service-point address. Ultimately, the role of the network level is transmitting the network data from one workstation to another, besides the role of the transport level is also to transfer the message over to the appropriate process.

Once the transport layer gets the message obtained from the upper level, it subdivides the message into several segments, where each section is apportioned a sequence number which distinctly classifies each segment. Once the message has reached its destination, consequently the transport level reassembles it depending on their specific sequence digits.

In addition, connection control is another function of the Transport-Layer. It provides dual services which are connectionless and Connection-based service. The connectionless package considers every section as a private packet, beside they all move in different paths to reach the final terminus. Connection-oriented solutions further connect to the transport module at the destination mechanism before conveying the packets. For connection-based service, the packets move in a single direction (Robertazzi, 2017).

Session Layer: This layer is applied to setup, maintain, and harmonize the communication between connected devices. One of the main functions of the session layer is dialog control. It serves as a dialog regulator which generates dialog between two procedures, or it can be said that it permits for easy communication between different processes which might be either half or whole-duplex. It further allows for synchronization. Basically, the session layer provides some checkpoints when transferring the data sequentially. In case an error happens during the process of data transmission, it means that the transfusion will happen once more from the checkpoint. The procedure is called Synchronization and recovery.

Presentation Layer; The presentation level is mostly concerned with syntax and semantics aspects of the data transmitted between different systems. This serves as an information translator for the network. Additionally, the layer is connected to the OS which converts the information from one presentation style to another. In some cases, the presentation level is also referred to as syntax layer. One of its key roles is translation. Here,

The network in two systems transfer the information as character strings, digits, and so forth. Different processors use different encoding techniques; the presentation layer manages interoperability functions between various encoding techniques. It adapts the information from sender-reliant format into a regular format and mutates the regular format into a receiver-dependent setup at the receiving side.

Similarly, encryption is required to maintain high levels of privacy. This refers to the process of adapting the sender-transmitted data into another structure, and sending the subsequent message through the network.

As for data compression, this is a method of compacting the data, that is., reducing the overall number of bits that are to be transferred. Information compression is very essential in multimedia programs like text, video, and audio (Robertazzi, 2017).

Application Layer: This layer acts as a window whereby users and application procedures can access network protocols. It also handles issues like resource allocation and network transparency. The application layer isn't really an application; however, it performs some of the application level functions. Apart from providing network services to final-users, it's also responsible for file transfer, accessibility, and management.

The application layer permits users to access their documents in a remote workstation, to salvage the files directly from the computer and managing the files within a remote processor.

It also provides mail services, or the facility needed for email forwarding as well as storage. The system offers a distributed database resource and is commonly used to dispense that universal information concerning various objects (Robertazzi, 2017).

1.8. WHAT IS THE TCP/IP MODEL?

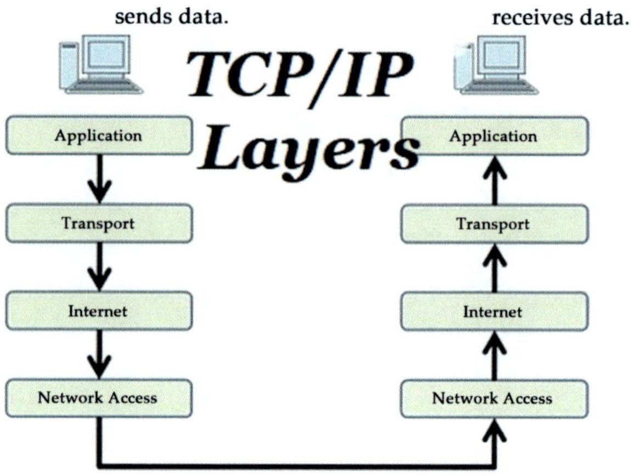

Figure 1.6. TCP/IP has four layers to send and receive data.

Source: https://www.pinterest.com/pin/725712927436639175/.

TCP/IP allows computer users to decide how a particular computer ought to be linked to the web, including how information should be transferred between them. This helps users to form a digital network when several CS are linked together. The word TCP/IP is short for Transit Control Protocol and Internet Protocol. It was particularly developed as a system for providing highly dependable and terminal-to-terminal byte stream through an unpredictable internetwork.

1.8.1. KEY CHARACTERISTICS

- Provides for a dynamic architecture;
- TCP is a connection-based protocol;
- TCP provides reliability and ensures information which comes out of sequence is placed back into order;
- It makes it easier to add extra programs to the network;
- For TCP/IP systems, normally the network stays intact up to the source, provided the destination machines are functioning well; and
- TCP permits you to execute flow control, such that the sender can never overwhelm the receiver with information.

1.8.2. Types of TCP/IP Network Layers

The TCP/IP structure is subdivided into four layers, where each layer consists of specific protocols. For instance, TCP/IP can be seen as a multipart server architecture unit, in which every layer is recognized based on the particular function being performed. These four layers function mutually to transmit the information from a particular layer to another. They are as follows:

Application Layer: This layer interacts directly with application programs, found at the highest phase of OSI model. It is also known as the OSI layer since application level is nearest to the final-user. This simply means that the OSI application level allows operators to easily interrelate with other software programs.

The application layer further communicates with software applications in order to implement a networking component. The reading of data through the application program usually is done outside the OSI scope model. An example of this application level is the application of programs like email, remote login and file exchange. This application-layer allows users to detect communication partners, check resource availability, and harmonize communication, not to mention allowing users to easily log onto the distant host. Furthermore, through various email solutions, this program provides distributed database resources, as well as access for universal data about different objects and services (Cowley, 2012).

Transport Layer: It builds upon the network layer so as to avail data transport straight from the system on a source structure machine to a protocol on the destination system. Transport layer is hosted through single or several networks, plus preserves the overall quality or grade of service functions. Not only that, but the system also determines the amount of data which is to be sent, where it should be sent and the rate as well.

It decides the amount of data to be sent, its destination and speed at which the data will be sent. The layer is based on the message obtained from the application level. It helps ensure that information units are error-free. Furthermore, this layer allows users to manage the reliability of links through error control, flow control, segmentation, and de-segmentation. The transport layer further provides standard acknowledgment of the effective data transmission, apart from sending the succeeding data if no errors are detected (Cowley, 2012).

Currently, TCP is the most renowned example of a transport-layer. It works by partitioning the message obtained from the session level into sections and numbers them in order to form a sequence. Generally, transport layer ensures that the network message is conveyed to the appropriate process on the ultimate destination machine. Furthermore, it ensures that the whole message reaches its recipients without unnecessary errors.

Internet Layer: The internet layer refers to a 2nd level of TCP/IP model. It is also referred to as the network layer. Its main role is to dispatch the packets from whichever network or computer, so as to reach the final destination regardless of the journey they take. The Web layer provides the functional and structural means of transmitting variable length data structures from a given node to another, plus with the assistance of diverse networks. Furthermore, message delivery within the internet layer does provide sufficient guarantee for reliability of data transfer.

Network Interface Layer: Network Interface Layer constitutes the fourth and final level of the 4-layered TCP/IP model. This level is also known as network access layer and helps a lot in defining the finer details of ways that data must be sent through the network. Equally, it measures how bits need to be optically signalled through hardware devices that instantly interfaces with the network medium, such as optical, coaxial, coaxial, twisted-pair, and fiber cables.

The network layer comprises of a blend of the information line. It also defines how the information ought to be sent manually through the network. Besides, it's also necessary for the transfusion of information between a pair of devices connected on a similar network.

1.8.3. Commonly Used TCP/IP Protocols

Telnet: This is a terminal simulation protocol used to gain access to the resources found in a remote host. The host, known as the telnet server, operates a telnet server system (or daemon using the Unix terminology) which receives the link from a distant host known as Telnet client. The connection is availed to the telnet server's OS as if it is a terminal link connected directly through the keyboard and mouse. It is generally a text-based link and generally offers access to the command-line module of the host. Furthermore, it is important to note that the application utilized by the client often is called telnet in many OSs. You must not obscure the telnet system with telnet protocol, which are totally different networking products.

Domain Name Service (DNS): Each host in the network consists of a rational address known as the IP address. The addresses are basically a list of numbers. Upon visiting a website, you are usually directed to a host that bears the IP address. Here, DNS assists in mapping out website names to the host's IP address, where the website resides. It certainly makes it simpler to locate resources on the network. Upon typing in the website's address into your browser, it will first dispatch a DNS request to the DNS server in order to resolve the IP address's name. When the name is finally resolved, then a HTTP session would be established along with the Internet Protocol Address.

Dynamic Host Configuration-Protocol (DHCP): As you may realize, nearly every host needs some logical address like an IP address for communication within the network. Normally the host receives this logical address through physical configuration, or a DHCP protocol. Through DHCP, a host may be given an IP address mechanically. To comprehend the significance of DHCP, consider having to manage about 5000 hosts in the network and allocating IP addresses manually.

In addition to the IP address, hosts need various other information like the DNS server address in order to communicate and resolve gateways, subnet masks and names among other factors. Furthermore, DHCP may be applied to make all this information accessible alongside the IP address.

Hypertext Transfer Protocol (HTTP): HTTP forms the basis of the internet. The program is used to transmit Webpages and other digital resources directly from the HTTP server or Web Server onto the HTTP or Web Client. When using a web browser, such as Firefox or Internet Explorer, you are using the web client. This program makes use of HTTP system to transmit web pages which you directly request from the distant servers.

File Transfer Protocol (FTP): FTP is a network protocol commonly applied to transfer files between a pair of hosts. Similar to HTTP and telnet, one host operates the FTP server system (or daemon) where it is known as FTP server and the FTP client operates the FTP client system. A client linking to the FTP system may be called upon to authenticate, prior to being given any entry to the file configuration. Upon authentication, the client may watch directory listings, receive, and send files, as well as perform different other file-related roles. Same as telnet, FTP client application found in most OSs is known as FTP. Therefore, the protocol and application should are .

Simple Mail Transfer-Protocol (SMTP): STMP is commonly used to dispatch e-mails. STMP is an email client you can configure in order to send e-mails. The mail client serves as SMTP client in this situation. Furthermore, SMTP would be used between a pair of mails servers in order to send and obtain emails. But the end client actually receives emails through POP3 protocol.

Trivial File Transfer-Protocol (TFTP): TFTP is a simplified version of FTP. While FTP permits the user to check a directory for directory-based functions, TFTP allows sending and receiving files. It is a tiny yet fast protocol/ However, it doesn't support validation. Due to this integral security risk, TFTP is not broadly used.

1.9. STANDARD PROTOCOL FOR TRANSFERRING FILES FROM ONE COMPUTER TO ANOTHER

The Internet Protocol (IP) suite is a conceptual model as well as a group of communications protocols that are applied in the Web and similar computing networks. It is commonly referred to as TCP/IP since the foundational protocols found in the suite consist of the (IP) Internet Protocol and (TCP) Transmission Control Protocol. Different versions of the internet protocol were developed, which were called the Department of Defense (DoD) prototype since the formation of the networking process was funded by U.S. DoD in conjunction with DARPA.

Its application is similar to a protocol stack. Generally, the Internet Protocol (IP) suite provides terminal-to-terminal data communication that specifies how data needs to be packetized, addressed, transferred, routed, and received. The functionality is structured into 4 abstraction layers, which categorize all related protocols depending on the range of networking involved (Anttalainen and Jaaskelainen, 2014).

Right from the lowest to highest point, the layers form the link chains, containing communication systems for data which stays within one network segment or (link). The web layer, offering internetworking between autonomous networks consists of the transport layer, which handles host-to-host communication, and the application layer, which offers process-to-process information exchange for applications.

Generally, the technical standards that form basis for the Internet protocol (IP) suite and its fundamental protocols are preserved by the Internet Engineering Taskforce (IETF). This Internet protocol suite precedes the OSI system, which is a more detailed reference framework for common networking systems (Cowley, 2012).

1.10. BASIC ARCHITECTURAL PRINCIPLES

Conceptual data flow refers to a basic network topology with two hosts (point A and point B), which are joined by some link that connects their individual routers. Moreover, the application found on each host is designed to implement read and write functions, as if the procedures were directly linked to each other through some form of data channel.

Following the creation of this pipe, majority of the details that make up the communication would be hidden from every successive process, since the underlying tenets of communication are applied mostly in the low protocol layers. At the transport level the communication shows up as a mere host-to-host, without prior understanding of the application information structures or the connecting routers, whereas at the internetworking level, personal network boundaries are navigated at each router (White, 2015).

The end-to-end transmission procedure has evolved with time. Its foremost expression placed the preservation of state and general intelligence at the side, and presumed the Web that linked the edges reserved no state and focused more on speed and ease of use. Real-life need for firewalls, web content caches and network address translators have additionally inspired changes around this particular principle.

According to the robustness networking principle, implementation should be conservative in terms of its sending behavior and plus liberal in terms of its receiving behavior. Meaning, the network designer should be careful to send only well-developed datagrams and accept any datagram which it can easily interpret.

Another aspect to consider is that the software found on other hosts might have deficiencies. As a result, this software might end up being exploited by legal but vague protocol features. Moreover, encapsulation is commonly used to offer abstraction around the protocols and services used. Encapsulation is typically aligned together with the protocol suite division into levels of broad functionalities (White, 2015).

Typically, an application (which forms the highest degree of the model) applies a group of protocols for sending its information down through the layers. This data is additionally compressed at every level. One early structural document, RFC 1122, stresses architectural modalities over layering. The RFC 1122, named Host Requirements, additionally is organized into paragraphs that refer to it layers, though the document itself refers to various other architectural

The UDP is a standard transport layer protocol, offering a basic connectionless datagram solution. The Transfusion Control Protocol offers flow-control, connection setup, and dependable data transmission. The web layer transfers datagrams across different network boundaries. It also offers a standard networking interface which conceals the real topology or (layout) of the fundamental network connections.

It's thus also the layer which forms the basis for internetworking. Certainly, it describes and lays the basis for the Internet. Also, this layer outlines the addressing as well as routing structures applied for TCP/IP protocol suites. The main protocol in this range is the (IP) Internet Protocol, which describes IP addresses. The system's key role in routing involves transportation of datagrams onto the subsequent host, working in form of an IP router, which has connection to a network that's nearer to the ultimate data location (Robertazzi, 2017).

The link layer describes the networking techniques within the range of the native network link, where hosts communicate without any intervening routers. The layer comprises of protocols used to define the local structural topology, including the interface that's required to implement the transfusion of Web layer data-grams to the nearest hosts.

1.11. LOGICAL AND PHYSICAL CONNECTIONS

A logical network chart typically shows network appliances such as firewalls, routers, and sound gateways. It displays VLAN IDs, subnets, IP addresses and subnet masks. It further shows traffic flows, routing protocols, network segments and routing domains. The data resembles that of the (L3) Network Layer from the OSI Model. Note that L2 appliances (example, switches) aren't normally found in a logical chart. Instead, it is only defined with regards to a (rail) line.

Similarly, logical network diagrams are used for managing the IP address domain within the business. Additionally, they can submit network-based proposals to management because they conceal majority of the physical components. They are ideal for making alterations or extensions to the network. Furthermore, vendors can use logical network charts to provide suggestions for the clients' consideration (Robertazzi, 2017).

Furthermore, a physical network chart displays how the network appliances are physically tied together because all ports found on all appliances on the network become represented here. It includes patch panels, fiber, and interfaces among other physical modules. This network also shows the topology precisely as it appears with physical links in-between the devices. A physical diagram displays port assignments including how the ports become attached to the other instrument's port.

In most cases, the physical network chart is mostly utilized by the IT personnel to clearly record the physical links on the network. It's crucial to remember that these particular diagrams are useful for diagnosing network problems, detecting potential security as well as other risks and weak spots, plus planning network variations and expansion.

The physical network diagram showcases the interconnectedness of the components in the network, consisting of wires and cables. Contrarily, the logical network chart displays how they network with one another through physical connectivity. Typically, the physical network chart is utilized when one wants to envisage the physical network configuration of any business, while the logical network chart would be utilized only to recognize protocols for the information transmission within a network (Robertazzi, 2017).

1.11.1. LAN PHYSICAL NETWORKS

Physical Network are designed to define Layer 1 locally: specifically, how the wires are physically run. While there have been various popular forms of physical topologies throughout the years; a few, like the ring and bus structures, have gradually faded out as star topology grows more dominant.

Generally, Network buses are brittle: in the event that the network cable breaks at any point along the bus; it means that the whole bus can go down. For instance, if the line between Nodes A and B break down, then the whole bus shall get destroyed, including the link between Terminal B and C. one defective NIC may also impact a whole bus.

1.11.1.1. Types of Physical Networks

- Tree: The tree is also known as hierarchical network: meaning it is a network lacking a root node, or branch nodes which are triple levels deep at least (dual levels would instead make it a star). All tree topologies have a root node which directs all tree traffic. Additionally, the tree works as a legacy framework system; where the root node acts as the mainframe.
- Ring: A physical ring structure joins together network nodes found in a ring: in case you track the cable from one node to another, you'll ultimately finish where you started.
- Star: The Star topology is a dominant physical networking structure for LANs. It was first popularized through the assistance of ARCNET, then later approved by Ethernet. Every node is linked

directly to a core device like a switch or hub. Stars have greater fault tolerance: besides any particular local cable disruption or NIC failure just affects one node. Considering that each node is cabled back to the central point, a bit more wiring is needed as opposed to the bus (whereby a single cable run joins nodes to one another). This value disadvantage is typically offset by the error tolerance advantages that star networks provide.

- Mesh: The mesh system interlinks network nodes with each other. It can either be fully connected, having a total of four web servers interconnected, or partially connected whereby each node features multiple connections attached to the mesh, though individual nodes may not directly join to each other.

Most meshes have superior convenience and are typically used for highly accessible (HA) server clusters. Every one of the Web servers found in a mesh system is capable of sharing the bulk of Web traffic, while preserving state information passing between each structure. In case a web-server within the mesh is disrupted, the others will continue staying up in order to sustain the traffic load.

1.11.1.2. How Logical and Physical Networks Are Connected

The logical structure relies both on network and physical hardware. While the concept of a digital domain supported by the physical realm is actually a simple one to understand, a few of the secondary sequence effects of connections between these two realms might not be as noticeable or immediately obvious.

When checking the physical setup infrastructure upon which such structures are maintained, there are two basic issues to contemplate in cyber operations: ensuring the individual systems and infrastructure remain intact and operational, also while rendering the opposite systems and frameworks unable to perform so.

Furthermore, logical systems may also be applied to make certain modifications in the physical realm. In complex objects of physical hardware, it means that software generally manages the way that firmware functions. Modifications done to the software are capable of affecting whatever the firmware connects with, such as networks, other structures, and even people.

1.11.1.3. Logical Networks Operate on Physical Hardware

The logical infrastructure operates through different network infrastructure, automation devices and computer systems. Whenever such a complex structure loses contact with the different utilities which are crucial to its functionality, such as power and communications medium, it becomes significantly less useful, usually to the stage of being considered a rather costly paperweight.

When running operations within a conflict-based cyber system, whether defensive or offensive, ensuring that the physical hardware keeps running to support such activity may be tasking. Even in traditional corporate competitions, an element of modern technology has started to enter the mix in form of multiple computer structures and network-connected appliances, besides the intelligence availed by this technology can offer critical information from which to lay the basis on cyber, as, and conventional, operations (White, 2015).

In military operations, especially those in remote locations with minimal existing infrastructure that you can speak of. Working in such harsh settings is often less than ideal for the sustained functionality of computing apparatus. The overall cost of environmentally hardening equipment is typically more than changing off the shelf computers. Additionally, such devices may potentially pose a risk for opposing factions to attack, either on a logical or physical level. For such cases, ruggedized appliances are often needed so as to have some expectations for the appliances to continue operating over a duration of time.

Furthermore, at an advanced level, the infrastructure must be kept functioning for such devices to utilize. This kind of infrastructural technology is normally found in data centers, including other areas which host crucial computing equipment, even though it is not typically hardened to endure the standards of attack which are normally experienced in cyber conflicts.

Through using redundant infrastructures, systems, utilities, and different other necessities, it can be quite difficult to pull systems down because of high resiliency levels. Contrarily, since the technologies which allow for robust systems and setups are normally available, you may find them also implemented by the opponents (White, 2015).

Conversely, the issue of trying to render the apparatus and infrastructure found on the opposite side unworkable from a physical standpoint may come up. Especially when physical processes are being done on foreign soil, the network operators under attack might have a special "home court" advantage.

In other cases, computer operators may face well-structured data centers with hardened and adequate backup resources for providing power and easy networking in emergency cases. These might prove to be rather hard to take offline. Mostly, it's a blend of legacy apparatus with some modern technology (such as, encrypted phones) together with using nonconventional networking processes like web-based drop boxes.

Considering the ease of developing backup structures on different infrastructures, it is completely possible that several systems may have to be brought down to eliminate the cyber abilities of the opponent. With modern technology, Web access can be delivered through microwave, phone lines and radio signal plus different other solutions, apart from being shared via mesh networking to allow for greater connection levels. Through today's advanced technologies, it is possible to make a computer system operate at a lower level from the laptop or a smartphone's data connection. For such cases, a blend of logical and physical attacks might be needed to fully take the system offline (White, 2015).

In case a device is detached from the network, then a backup communications strategy could possibly be applied to restore back communications to the appliance, or an expert may be needed to physically move to the appliance and reconfigure it. This kind of attack might be simple and eventually also easy to fix, though using it to interrupt network infrastructure across the enterprise may bring a whole organization to an abrupt halt within short notice, apart from being rather time consuming to repair.

Attacks on physical structures may also have outcomes of a more severe nature which may go far beyond simply frustrating network and system managers. For instance, cyber-attacks targeting implanted medical instruments, like pacemakers and pumps used for distributing medication, have grown to become quite common in recent time, to the extent of research being performed to develop firewalls for such instruments (Robertazzi, 2017).

1.11.2. Logical Computer Connections

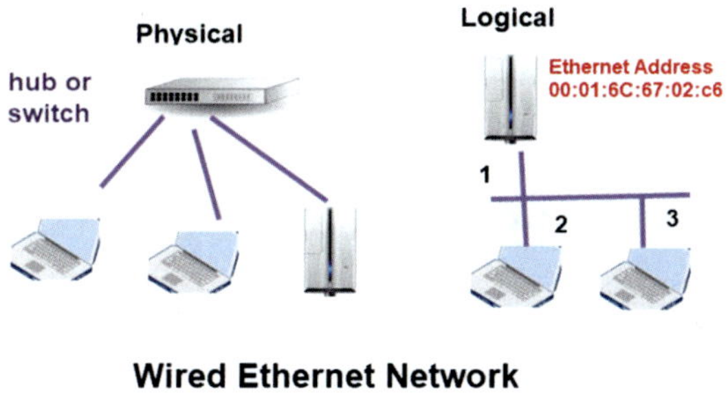

Figure 1.7. Logical network provides the shortest route for data to reach its destination.

Source*:* https://stevessmarthomeguide.com/basic-networking-course/.

In everyday life, transportation networks consist of physical items which you can physically hold or touch using your hand, like subway rails and railroad ties. The logical network components don't have these similar physical properties like the physical networks. Same as virtual reality (VR) in video games which present the illusion of activities like driving a real vehicle or firing up a weapon, logical frameworks are based on components that you can't actually see or hold, though they are still existent (Anttalainen and Jaaskelainen, 2014).

A network consists of multiple pieces and sections that link up the source and terminus. These pieces and components are divided into two groups: physical components which has been mentioned above and logical components. Together, these two components constitute the infrastructure and final-user aspects of a network, allowing you to interconnect with others on the network easily.

As an example, image that you are boarding the train from New York to Buffalo. The physical route of your journey may move you through another intermediate city before reaching Buffalo. However, in your mind, the trip looks as if it is going straight from NYC to Buffalo without passing through any intersecting city. This is because you are not actually staying over while in the middle city, but merely changing trains there.

In this illustration, the physical element are the rails between the 3 cities. The logical element is the beginning and ending points of the two cities since you are only concerned about where you begin your journey and where the trip stops (Anttalainen and Jaaskelainen, 2014). The same logical and physical concepts shown in this description apply to networking structures.

1.11.2.1. Network Physical Modules

The physical modules of a network consist of network hardware devices, like the switch and cabling. Generally, this collection of cables and devices, transport the data directly from its source to the destination, constituting the overall physical network. Some of the common components include:

Switches: In case there isn't any straight path from one town to the next in the example shown, then either train passengers will have to alight from one train to board another, specifically at the demarcation spot (train station), or alternatively the trains themselves will need to adjust their routes at rail change-point stations along the route. Network switches function in a similar way by linking network paths together, offering a path for the frame going from source point to the destination.

Cabling: To connect two or several points on a computer network, there should be some kind of medium for carrying the data from one terminal to the other, such as the railroad paths between train stations. Generally, a medium is described as the physical module through which another thing is transferred or carried. Different kinds of media are applied today for networking communication, like, fiber-optic lines or copper cable.

Typically, copper cabling transports electrical signals, like those produced by computer modems or phone handsets. On the other hand, fiber-optic cabling transmits light signals that are transferred as light pulses. Visualize turning a normal flashlight on/off in the Morse code. A fiber-optic transmission system works in more or less a similar way as the Morse code, though is much quicker and runs using a different code.

CHAPTER

2

Computer Networking and Communication: Fundamentals of Data and Signals

CONTENTS

2.1. INTRODUCTION

The transmission of data, which is also referred to as data communications, is the process of transferring data from point to another, or from one point to multiple points through channels of communication. These channels include optical fibers, copper wires, computer buses, storage media, and wireless communication channels. This data is transmitted as signals that are electromagnetic, these include microwave, electrical voltage, infrared signal, or radio-wave.

Analog transmission refers to the ability to convey information in any element, including image, data, voice, video or signal, by the use of a continuous signal which has variations in its phase, amplitude, or a different element that is in proportion to a certain variable. These messages either undergo representation by certain sequences of a pulse through a line code which is referred to as baseband transmission, or through a limited set of waveforms that continuously vary which is referred to as passband transmission, all done with the use of a digital modulation method.

Figure 2.1. The transmission of data is the process during which data is transferred amongst two or more digital devices. This data undergoes transmission from a device to a different one in a format that is either a digital or analog. In general, the transmission of data enables components within the devices to communicate.

Source: https://www.networkworld.com/article/3429610/a-data-transmission-revolution-is-underway.amp.html.

Modem equipment is what helps with the passband modulation as well as the demodulation that corresponds. It is also referred to as detection. In accordance with what the main definition of digital signals is, both passband and baseband signals are able to represent bitstreams and can both therefore be considered as digital transmission. A definition that is alternative only makes a consideration of the baseband signal as a digital transmission, while passband transmission of data that is digital is considered as a type of digital to analog conversion.The transmitted data may be messages that are digital coming from a certain source of data such as a keyboard or even just the computer. The signal may also be analog, for example, a video signal or a phone call that has been digitized into a bitstream, such as the use of analog to digital conversion together with compression of data or even the use of pulse-code modulation schemes. Codec equipment helps in carrying outsource coding as well as decoding (White, 2015).The transmission of data is a section of electrical engineering and telecommunications. It is also possible to cover the basic principles of the transmission of data within the data communications topic of either computer engineering or computer science, which is also inclusive of networking protocols as well as computer networking applications, such as inter-process communication, routing, and switching.Despite the fact that the Transmission Control Protocol deals with transmission, the Transmission Control Protocol together with other transport layer protocols are studied in computer networking, however, they are not mentioned in any course or textbook to do with the transmission of data.

Tele-transmission is a term that involves both digital and analog communication. Most definitions refer to analog transmission as the ability to transmit a message signal that is analog without it being digitized through an analog signal, either as a baseband signal that is not modulated, or as a passband signal through the use of an analog modulation method such including FM or AM.

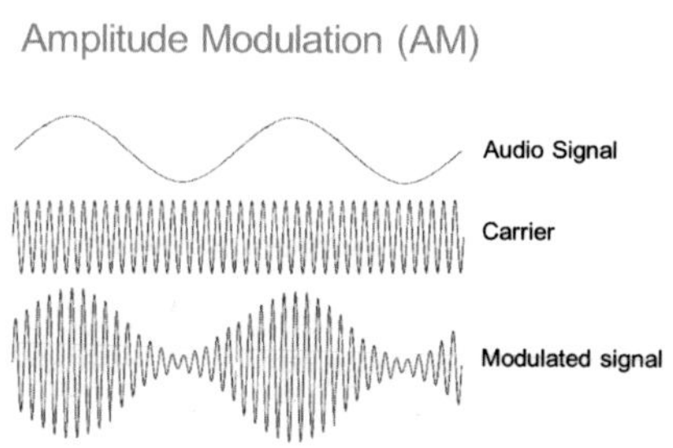

Figure 2.2. The dissimilarity between FM and AM is due to alteration of the carrier. If radios use AM, amplitude is varied to ensure incorporation of the sound information. If radios use FM, the frequency is varied

Source: https://slideplayer.com/amp/1423275/.

There may also be inclusion of analog-over-analog pulse modulated baseband signals, for example, the pulse-width modulation. There are other definitions that refer to analog transmission as a passband transmission of bitstreams with the use of methods of digital modulation such as frequency-shift keying, amplitude-shift keying, and phase-shift keying. All these can be found in data transmission or digital transmission textbooks. The coding theory and the information theory are what cover the aspects of data transmission that are theoretical.

2.2. DATA AND SIGNALS

Physical layers are meant to ensure the movement of data which are signals that are in the electromagnetic form across a medium for transmission. We deal with the transmission of data across various network connections regardless of whether the data being transmitted is sending pictures that are animated from a certain work station, numerical statistics from a certain computer, or making a bell ring from a control center that is distant.

Data can either be digital or analog. Analog data is a term used to refer to data that is continuous, while digital data is used to refer to data that is in a discrete state. This can be described using a clock as the example. Analog clocks have the minutes, the hour, and the second hand which helps in giving information in a form that is continuous because the hands move in a continuous manner. A digital clock, however, is able to provide the minutes and hours in a sudden manner as time can change from 9:04 to 9:05 without showing the continuous movement.

Digital and analog signals are utilized for the transmission of information, normally through signals that are electrical. These technologies work by transforming information (video or audio), into signals that are electric. There is one major difference between the digital and analog technology. In the analog technology, information undergoes translation into electric pulses that have amplitudes that vary. In the digital technologies, the information is translated into a format that is binary (one or zero), where a single but represents two amplitudes that are distinct (Emilio, 2013).

Analog signals have many different levels of intensity over a certain time period. As waves move from one point to another, they pass through and are inclusive of many different values within the path. Digital signals however, only have defined values that are limited in number, and despite the fact that each value is able to acquire any number, it simply used one and zero.

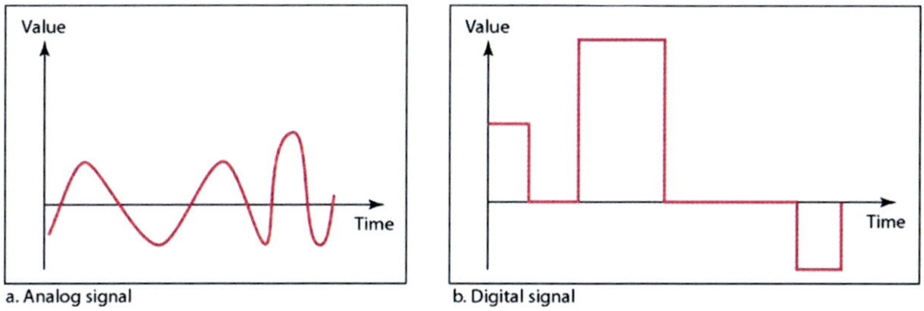

Figure 2.3. Above is an illustration of a digital and analog signal. Analog signal is a continuous line while digital signal shows sudden jumps

Source: http://www.myreadingroom.co.in/images/stories/docs/dcn/Fundamentals%20of%20Data%20and%20Signals_Digital%20and%20Analog%20Signals.JPG.

There are many differences between analog and digital signals. Here are a few:

- The analog signal has a signal that is continuous and helps in making representations of measurements that are physical, while digital signals are time signals that are discrete and these can be generated through digital modulation.
- Analog signals undergo denoting by sine waves, and digital signals by square waves.
- The analog signals use values that are of a continuous range for the representation of information, while the digital signals use values that are either discrete or discontinuous for the representation of information.
- Analog signals can be deteriorated by noise while they are being transmitted and also during the read/write cycle. Digital signals are immune to noise and they avoid deterioration during transmission and the read/write cycle.
- Analog hardware has no flexibility, while digital hardware can be implemented in a flexible manner.
- Analog signals can only be used in analog devices and they are mostly used for the transmission of videos and audios, while digital signals are mainly used on digital and computing electronics.

- Processing of analog signals are normally done in real-time, and they also lead to the consumption lower quantities of bandwidth. For digital signals, it is not guaranteed that the processing if the signal can be done in real time, and it also leads to the consumption of much more bandwidth for the processing of the same amount of information.
- Analog signals are stored in the form of waves, while digital signals are stored in binary bit forms.
- Analog signals are more affordable and they are also portable, while digital signals are more expensive and they are not easily portable.
- Instruments that deal with analog signals normally have a cramped scale at the lower ends and they also provide a couple of errors that are observational, while those that deal with digital signals lack observational errors such as approximation and parallax errors.

Digital and analog signals are available in two forms: non-periodic and periodic. Periodic signals are able to finish a certain pattern within a time frame that is measurable which is referred to as a period, and it also leads to the repetition of that pattern over periods that are subsequently identical. When one full pattern is completed, it is referred to as a cycle. Non-periodic signals are able to change without having to exhibit a cycle or pattern that can be repeated over a certain period of time.

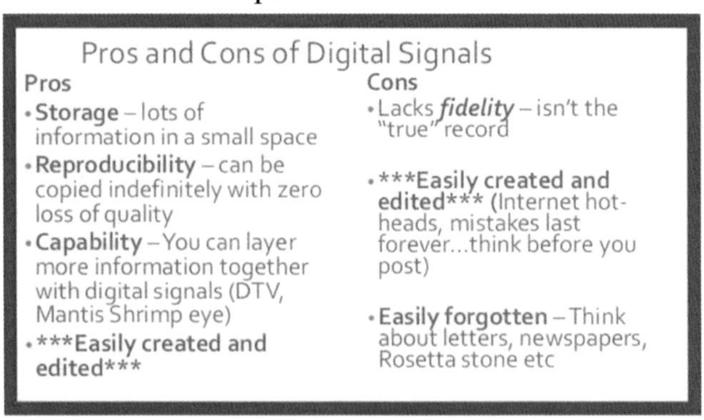

Figure 2.4. Above are some of the advantages and disadvantages of digital signals, which allow information to be layered together

Source: https://alpine.instructure.com/courses/15677/pages/analog-vs-digital-data-transfer.

There are also periodic analog signals, and these can be either composite or simple. The simple periodic analog signal is also referred to as a sine wave, and these cannot undergo decomposition into signals that are simpler. The composite periodic analog signals, however, have many different sine waves.

2.2.1. Advantages of Digital Signaling Over Analog Signaling

Firstly, the major benefit of digital signals over analog signals is considered to be that the digital signal has an exact signal level, and this is not vital. Therefore, the imperfections of actual electronic systems do not damage the digital signals. The electronic systems normally destroy analog signals. This means that digital compact discs are way more robust in comparison to the analog Long play.

Secondly, codes are normally used for transmitting information. The codes are meant to be utilized to either ensure that certain information is kept secret, or as a way to break down the information into much more manageable pieces so as to ensure that the technology used can ensure transmission of the code. For example, any numbers and letters that are being sent using Morse code are done so using dashes and dots.

Thirdly, digital signals are able to ensure that information is conveyed without being destroyed by noise, due to the fact that each component of information is determined by either the presence of or lack of a data bit. Analog signals have continuous variations and any level of noise can affect their value.

Fourthly, signals that are digital can undergo processing with the use of circuit components that are digital, and these are normally more affordable and they can undergo production in many different constituents on one chip. In addition, digital techniques can help in minimizing the propagation of noise through the demodulation system.

Fifthly, it is not possible for digital signals to undergo corruption by noise and other elements.

This is because they are able to represent the desirable signals of the series of numbers being sent. Sixthly, digital signals tend to use a lower amount of bandwidth, allowing for storage of more information in the same space. Seventhly, digital signals can undergo encryption so as to make sure that only the person receiving the data can decode it. Other advantages include:

- Digital signals allow for signals to be transmitted over longer distances;
- Digital signals are transmitted at a rate that is higher and also with a broadband width that is wider;
- Digital signals are much more secure;
- With digital signals, it is much easier to perform the translation of human video and audio signals in addition to other messages to a machine language;
- Digital technology has less electromagnetic interference; and
- Digital signals allow for signals to be transmitted to many different directions in a simultaneous manner.

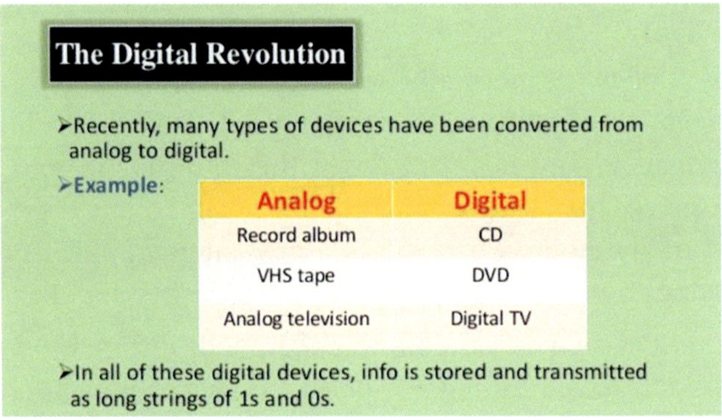

Figure 2.5. There are many devices that have been converted from the analog to the digital form. These include record albums, VHS tapes and analog TVs that have been turned into Compact Discs, DVDs, and Digital TV

Source*:* https://www.slideshare.net/RojoniAkter/analog-vs-digital-67431315.

2.3. COMPONENTS OF A SIGNAL

The three main components of a signal are frequency, amplitude, and phase. These three components represent the sine wave.

Peak Amplitude – this refers to the absolute value of the signal's highest intensity in proportion to the energy that it is able to carry. For signals that are electric, the peak amplitude generally undergoes measurement in volts. In telecommunications or measurements of an audio system, the peak amplitude is used. If we are using zero as a reference, it is referred to as the maximum value that is absolute of a certain signal.

Frequency – The amount of time a signal needs to finish one cycle is referred to as a period. The number of periods that are found in one second are referred to as the frequency. Waves that are longer and slower such as those of an ocean are normally defined using the period instead of frequency. Those that are fast and short, such as the radio or an audio file are normally defined using frequency rather than period.

Phase – this refers to the specific point in time on a wave-form cycle. A full cycle is referred to as 360° of phase. It can also be referred to as the ability to express relative displacement among or between waves that are of the same frequency.

2.4. BANDWIDTH

This is the capacity of network communication links, that can either be wireless or wired, to perform the transmission of the maximum quantity of data from one section to the other over an internet connection or a computer network in a certain time period – normally one second. Bandwidth helps in describing the rate of data transfer. One of the most common misconceptions of bandwidth is that it is a measure of the speed of a network (White, 2015).

A data connection that has more bandwidth is able to receive and send more data at a time. It is possible to compare bandwidth to the amount of water that is able to flow through a pipe. The larger the size of the pipe, the higher the quantity of water that can flow through it at a time. This means that if the capacity level of the link of communication is high, it allows for more data to flow through it each second. The users are able to pay for the amount of capacity their connections to networks are. The higher the level of capacity, the more money one has to pay for it.

2.4.1. Bandwidth and Speed

It is important to understand the connection between the bandwidth and speed. At times they are used interchangeably but not in a correct manner. The speed is used to refer to the data sending rate, while bandwidth is used to refer to the speed capacity. When using the initial example of the water pipes, speed is used to refer to the pace at which the water flows through the pipe, while bandwidth is used to refer to the pipe's diameter.

Figure 2.6. Above shows an illustration of low and high bandwidth. When the internet has a large bandwidth, it is able to transfer data set faster

Source: https://www.lifewire.com/what-is-bandwidth-2625809.

2.4.2. Importance of Bandwidth

There are bandwidth limits at every single deployment location, for example, a business. This means that the capacity is limited. Due to this, it is required for many devices in a certain space to perform while sharing bandwidth. Different devices use different levels of bandwidth. Television sets tend to use a lot of bandwidth while devices such as tablets tend to use much less. So as to maintain a speed that can be tolerated on more than one device, one needs a higher level of bandwidth.

2.4.3. Measuring Bandwidth

Traditionally, bandwidth is normally described in bits per second. However, network links in this modern time have a capacity that is much higher, and this is normally described in a measure of megabits per second or gigabits per second.

Bandwidth connections can either be asymmetrical or symmetrical. When the connection is symmetrical, the capacity of data is similar in the download data, as well as the directions for uploading it. When the connection is asymmetrical, the upload capacity as well as the download is not similar. In connections that are asymmetrical, the download capacity is larger than the upload capacity.

2.4.4. Calculating Bandwidth

Bandwidth calculations have become much more complicated due to the advances in technology, and these can all be dependent on specific type of link that will be used. For example, when there are different forms of time division multiplexing as well as different forms of light waves in an optical fiber, it is possible to have the transmission of more data through a certain connection at a time. This leads to an increase in the bandwidth. In networks that are wireless, bandwidth refers to the spectra of frequencies that are licensed by operators from the National Telecommunications and Information Administration and the Federal Communications Commission for using in the US.

It is possible to use a bandwidth test to measure the effective bandwidth, which refers to the highest rate of transmission that a link can reliably provide, in which the capacity of the link undergoes determination by measuring the required time for a certain file to leave an initial point and download at its destination successfully, over, and over again (Ibe, 2017).

Organizations are required to make calculations on how much bandwidth they require for running the different applications on their networks, all in addition to testing. So as know the amount of capacity they require, they are expected to make calculations of the number of people who might be using it at a time and thereafter perform a multiplication of that number with the capacity of the bandwidth that is needed by each application.

So as to make a calculation on the bandwidth that is required for the cloud, it is necessary to be aware of the capacity that is required for sending and receiving traffic from clouds that are public. It is possible for congestion, on the connections that are being used for reaching the providers of the public cloud, to affect the bandwidth capacity, especially if the data is moving through the internet (Ibe, 2017).

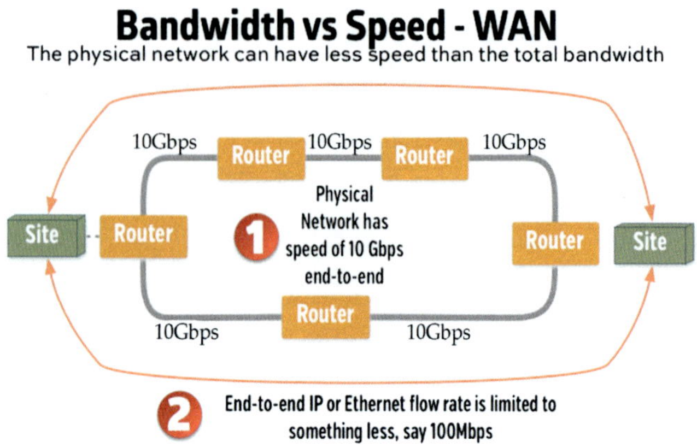

Figure 2.7. The speed refers to the bit rate of a certain circuit. Bandwidth refers to the speed amount that can be utilized. A physical network can have a lower speed than bandwidth

Source: https://etherealmind. com/basics-difference-bandwidth-speed/.

There are two main steps that can be used to calculate the bandwidth requirements when a certain organization is looking the amount of bandwidth they require for each application. These are:

- • Determining the amount of network bandwidth that is available, all in bytes per second; and
- • Determining the average use that is needed by the specific application, also in bytes per second.

After one is able to determine the bandwidth of the network, it is important to find out the amount of bandwidth being used by each application. It is possible to know the number of bytes per second that an application is sending through a network by using bandwidth testing.

2.4.5. Factors Affecting Bandwidth Performance

There are some factors that affect the performance of the bandwidth. The full capacity of a certain network connection is just one aspect that has an effect on the performance of a network. The network throughput can be degraded by latency, jitter, and packet loss, and all these can also make a link that has a high capacity perform just like one that does not have enough bandwidth.

A network path that is end-to-end normally has many different network links, and each one of them has a bandwidth capacity that is different. Due to this, the link that has the least amount of bandwidth is normally referred to as the bottleneck. This is due to the fact that the least amount of bandwidth connection can lead to a limitation of the whole capacity of data in all the connections.

2.4.6. Bandwidth on Demand

There is normally a set price by the month for the maximum available bandwidth for communication links that are dedicated. The bandwidth in demand, however, is an option that allows the user to add onto the quantity of bandwidth that is available for certain used or even for a certain time. This is a technique that helps in providing more capacity on a link for communication for the accommodation of bursts in case of a need for more bandwidth due to data traffic.

Instead of over-provisioning the network with dedicated links that are expensive, this technique has been able to ensure that the bandwidth capacity is increased as required for certain events or a point in time during the day, in wide area networks (WAN). It can help in increasing the bandwidth of telecommunications networks that are shared, and thus can all be achieved by asking the users to pay for the increases in bandwidth (Ibe, 2017).

This technique can be provided by may providers if these services, due to the fact that the network links that are provided to the customers have a bandwidth that is added through these providers, however, the users are only required pay for the capacity they require. In some occasions, the provider of this service is able to provide a higher bandwidth without additional fees.

2.4.7. SD-WAN makes the Bandwidth Requirements Easier

This is the software defined WAN technology which can provide the users with an additional capacity, due to the fact that it is able to make bandwidth from many different connections available to the users, instead of just one. This is normally inclusive of different bandwidth links including the Multi-Protocol Label Switching connection, in addition to a cellular connection.

2.4.8. Bandwidth Throttling

This is the ability of network administrators to make adjustments, either up or down, based on the speed that data is moving through a certain network.

There are certain reasons why this would happen, such as network congestion that is limiting, especially on networks that allow public access. It can also be used to limit its use by certain users or a specific group of users. It can also be used for the evening out of usage amongst the network users.

It is possible to check for bandwidth throttling by using an online speed test. The speed test measurs the speed between the test server and a device by using the internet connection of the device. One needs to perform multiple tests in one day to ensure accuracy of the results because there are many factors that can affect them (Ibe, 2017).

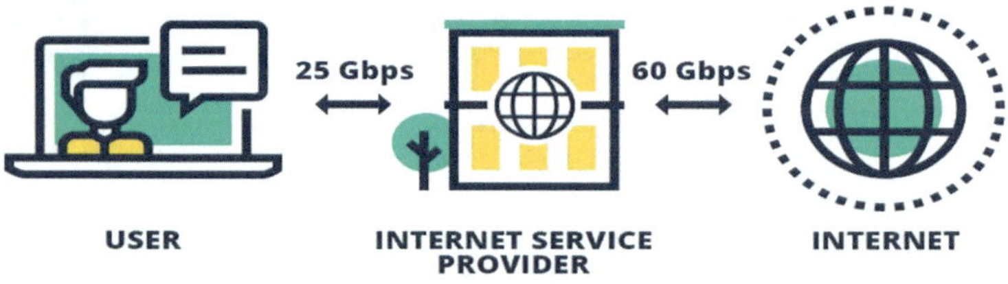

Figure 2.8. ISP throttling involves the intentional reduction of the internet speed. It helps regulate traffic within the network and prevents congestion

Source: https://pixelprivacy.com/resources/stop-isp-throttling/.

2.4.9. Data Transfer Throttling

This involves intentionally restricting the amount of digital, especially to prevent the transmission of bulk or spam mail through a network server. This technique can reduce the spread of worms, viruses, and other different types of malware that can be acquired through the internet.

2.5. ATTENUATION

In general, attenuation refers to losing the signal strength that is required for transmission. It is measured using decibels. An increase in attenuation leads to a transmission that becomes unintelligible and distorted, for example, and email one is trying to send. So as to get rid of the distortion, the networks work by sending many different repetitive signals so as to make sure that at least one will reach the destination successfully. This then leads to the reduction in the general speed that is present due to the sending of extra signals (White, 2015).

There are a couple of things that can cause attenuation. These include:

- ● Noise: excessive noise on a certain network such as electrical currents, wire leakage, and radio frequencies may lead to an interference with the signal thus causing attenuation. The higher the level of noise, the higher the level of attenuation.
- ● The physical surrounding: the physical elements in the surrounding such as wall barriers, wires that have not been properly installed, and wall barriers may lead to the distortion of the transmission therefore causing attenuation.
- ● The travel distance – when the distance that a transmission has to travel from its initial position, such as at the workplace or at home, to where the provider of the connection is, is long, it tends to experience much more noise as it travels.

There are different rates of attenuation in copper and fiber. All the different signal types can have attenuation, whether it is fiber, satellite, copper, etc. Fiber, however, outshines both copper and fiber. Fiber signals are able to use high-frequency wavelengths of light that have undergone insulation in glass tubes to travel. Due to the fact that light has a resistance to certain noise sources such as radio frequencies and electricity, fiber connections tend to have an attenuation rate that is very low.

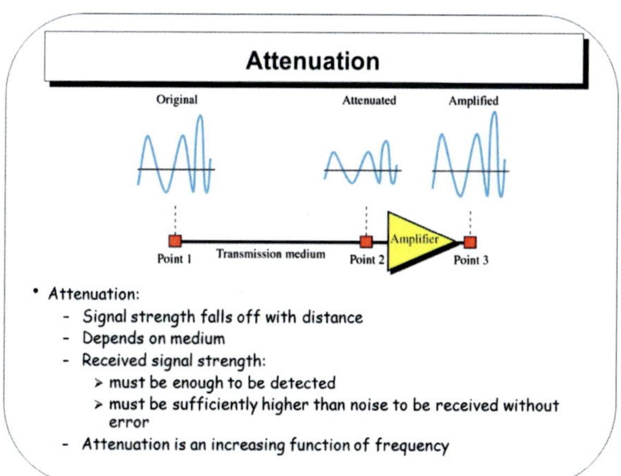

Figure 2.9. Attenuation works by lowering the signal strength. It can happen with any form of signal, both analog and digital. It can also be referred to as loss when signals are transmitted over long distances

Source: https://slideplayer.com/amp/5172608/.

Due to the fact that copper signals are equipped with frequencies that are electrical which are noise susceptible, they tend to be affected more by the physical elements of the surrounding in comparison to fiber. These elements include improper installation or even temperature, and they may have a negative effect on the copper line therefore leading to an increase in the rate of attenuation. In general, the lower the level of attenuation decibels of a certain connection, the better the connection.

The level of attenuation one experiences as well as the level at which is causes an impact on its strength is all dependent on the distance between the service providers and your internet. The longer the distance that is has to travel, the less the speed of connection will be.

2.6. CONVERTING DATA INTO SIGNALS

2.6.1. Transmitting Digital Data with Digital Signals: Digital Encoding Schemes

Encoding refers to the process of being able to convert data or a certain set of characters such as alphabets, symbols, etc. into a format that has been specified, for there to be data transmission that is secure. Decoding can be referred to as the reverse of encoding which involves extracting the data from the format that has been converted.

Data encoding involves the use of many different voltage patterns or levels that are current for representing 0s and 1s of the signals that are digital on the link of transmission. There are four main types of line encoding: bipolar, unipolar, polar, and Manchester.

There are a couple of ways one can ensure the mapping of digital data to digital signals. These include:Non-Return to Zero: These codes have a 0 to refer to a level of low voltage, and 1 is a level of high voltage. Non-Return to Zero codes behaves in a manner that allows them to stay constant in the bit interval. There will be no indication of the start or end of a bit and it will be able to achieve maintenance of a similar voltage state, if the previous bit and the present but have a value that is similar. There are two main variations of the non-return to zero code. These include:

- • The NRZ-Level – in this level the polarity of the signal changes only when there is a change in the incoming signal from either 0 to 1 or 1 to 0. It is similar to NRZ, however, there should be a change in polarity in the first bit of the input signal.

- ● NRZ-Inverted – at the incoming signal, if the 1 occurs, then there will be a transitory occurrence at the start of the bit interval. If the incoming signal has a 0 that occurs, then there will be no transitory occurrence at the start of the bit interval. The Non-Return to Zero codes have a major disadvantage, which is that there is a complete disturbance of the synchronization of the receiver clock with the transmitter clock, when a string of 0s and 1s occur. Therefore, there needs to be addition of a separate clock line.

2.6.1.1. Bi-Phase Encoding

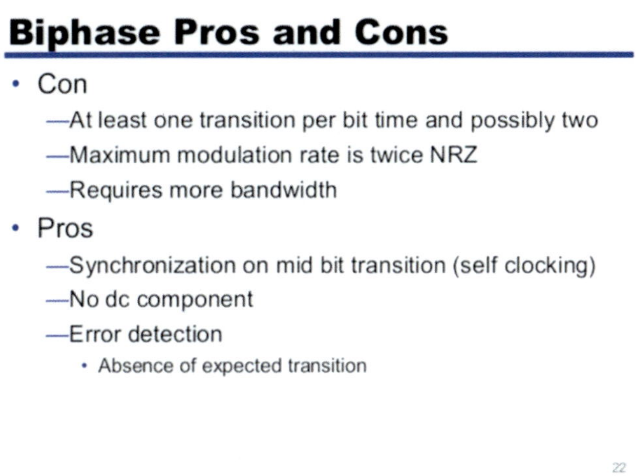

Figure 2.10. Above are some advantages and disadvantages of the bi-phase encoding technique. Its maximum rate of modulation is twice that of nonreturn to zero.

Source*:* https://www.slideshare.net/MdShafiulAlamSagor/l8-signal-encoding-techniques.

The level of the signal is double-checked for each bit time, both at the beginning and also in the middle. This means that the rate of the clock is twice the rate of transferring data, and therefore the rate of modulation is as well doubled. The signal is able to provide the clock. This coding requires a greater amount of bandwidth. There are two main forms of Bi-phase Encoding. These are:

- ● Bi-phase Manchester – in this form of coding, at the middle of the bit interval is where the transition is supposed to be done. The resultant pulse provides a transition which is from high to low, for the input bit 1, in the interval's middle point. At the same time, for the input bit 0, then there is a low to high transition.
- ● Differential Manchester – this form of coding, the middle of the bit interval is where the transition occurs. If at any point the transition occurs at the start, then 0 will be the input bit. If there is no transitory occurrence at the start of the bit interval, then 1 will be the input bit.

2.6.1. 2 Block Coding

There are different forms of block coding, however, 8B/6T encoding and 4B/5B encoding are considered the famous ones. In both if these processes, the bit numbers undergo processing in different ways:

- ● 4B/5B encoding – to send data using Manchester encoding, a double speed clock is necessary instead of the Non Return to Zero coding. According to the name, it involves mapping 4 bits of code with 5 bits, as long as there is no less than 1 bit in the group. One can avoid the clock synchronization problem that occurs in the Non Return to Zero Inverted encoding through the assignment of a word that has 5 bits that is equivalent, to replace every 4 consecutive bits block. In general, this idea of choosing a 5-bit code requires it to have one 0 that is leading and not more than two 0s trailing it. Therefore, the choosing of the words need to be done in a manner that allows for two transactions to happen for every block of bits.
- ● 8B/6T encoding – this uses two levels of voltage for sending one bit over one signal. However, if more than 3 voltage levels are used, it is possible to ensure that more bits per signals are sent. For example, using 6 levels of voltage for representing 8 bits on one signal, then this is referred to as 8B/6T encoding.

All these techniques help in the conversion of digital data into digital signals through the compression or coding of the data so as to ensure that data is transmitted reliably.

2.6.2. Transmission of Digital Data with Analog Signals

Transmitting digital data with analog signals happens when the signal varies continuously from one state to another one in form of waves, similar to what we observe in human voice. Modems are able to ensure the translation of binary data that is digital, and has been made by the computers, into signals that are analog that are needed by circuits for voice transmission. One modem is normally utilized by the transmitter for the production of signals that are analog, and the other by the receiver for the translation of these signals back into signals that are digital (White, 2015).

There are three main characteristics of the sound waves that undergo transmission through the voice circuit. The wave height is the first one, and this is referred to as amplitude. Decibels are used to measure amplitude. Human ears are able to make detections of amplitude through how loud a sound is. Every single wave of sound has two sections, the first one is the half of the wave that is above the zero point of the amplitude and the other half is found below. Both of these normally have a similar in height.

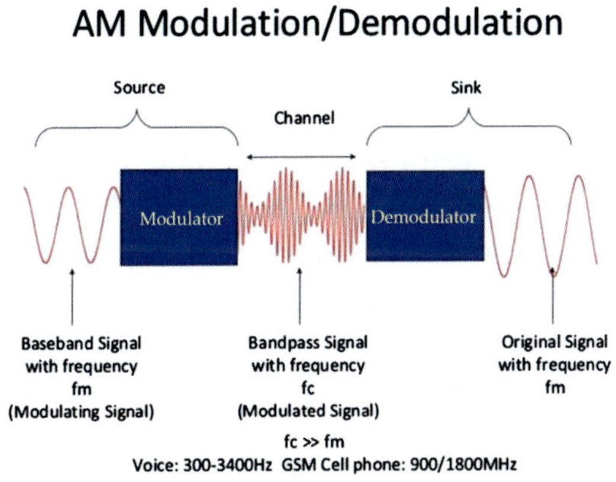

Figure 2.11. Modulators are able to convert low signal frequencies to high signal frequencies

Source: http://www.padakuu.com/article/32-modulation-and-demodulation.

Frequency is the second characteristic and this is the length of the wave. It is normally expressed as the number of waves that occur every second. Hertz are used to measure frequency. The pitch of the sound is the manner in which our ears are able to detect frequency. When the pitch of a sound is high, it means that there are many short waves for each second and when the pitch is low there are longer but fewer waves for each second. Phase is the third characteristic and it refers to the beginning direction of the wave. Degrees are used to measure the phase.

2.6.2.1. Modulation

When simple sounds are transmitted through telephone lines, we are able to represent the different values of the data through the shape of the sound waves that are being transmitted. This is done through the transmission of a carrier wave, which is a simple sound-wave, through the circuit and thereafter ensuring that the shape is changed in a manner that will allow it to represent a 0 or a 1.

The changes in the shape are what are referred to as modulation. There are three important techniques for modulation and these include frequency modulation, amplitude modulation, and phase modulation. It is important to note that the receiver and the sender need to have come to an agreement on the symbols that are supposed to be utilize as well as on the rates of the symbol which includes the number of symbols that will be sent every second (Ibe, 2017).

Amplitude Modulation: In this type of modulation, the height of the wave is what is changed. 0 helps in defining one amplitude and 1 is used in defining the other amplitude. For example, if the tallest wave is representative of the binary 1, and the shortest is representative of the binary 0, when the device that is sending the waves want to ensure transmission of a 1, it will work by sending a wave that has a high amplitude. Amplitude modulation is much more noise susceptible while it is being transmitted in comparison to phase modulation and frequency modulation.

Frequency Modulation: In this form of modulation, the 1 and 0 undergoes representation by a number of waves every second. In this situation, there is no variation in the amplitude. The specific number of waves that are being transmitted every second is what is represented by the 1 and the different number of waves for each second is what is represented by the 0.

Phase Modulation: This is much more difficult to grasp. The term phase is used to refer to the beginning wave direction. The wave can either have a 0° Phase wave which means that they start by moving upwards and to the right, and there is also the phase of 180°, where the waves start by moving downwards and to the right. In this modulation technique, one symbol of the phase is a 0 and the other is a 1.

The three main techniques for modulation can each be refined to allow them to send multiple bits simultaneously. For example, in the amplitude modulation, it is able to send 1 but for every wave by the definition of 2 amplitudes that are different, one for 0 and one for 1. It is, however, possible to ensure sending of 2 bits on one wave through the definition of 4 amplitudes that are different.It is also possible to refine this technique further to enable sending of three bits at a time by making definitions of eight different waves each having different levels of the amplitude, or 4 bits by making definition of 16 symbols, each also with different levels of the amplitude, etc. It, however, becomes difficult at some point to find the differences between the multiple amplitudes. They have such small differences; it is possible for the smallest amount of noise to cause disruption of the signal (Ibe, 2017).

2.6.3. Transmission of Analog Data with Digital Signals

2.6.3.1. Pulse-Code Modulation

This is a technique that is used for the representation of analog signals in a digital manner. It is considered the standard form audios that are digital in compact discs, digital telephony, computers, and other applications for digital audios. In a pulse-code modulation stream, there is regular sampling of the amplitude of the analog signal, and this is done at intervals that are uniform. In addition, each sample undergoes quantization to the value that is nearest in a range of steps that are digital.

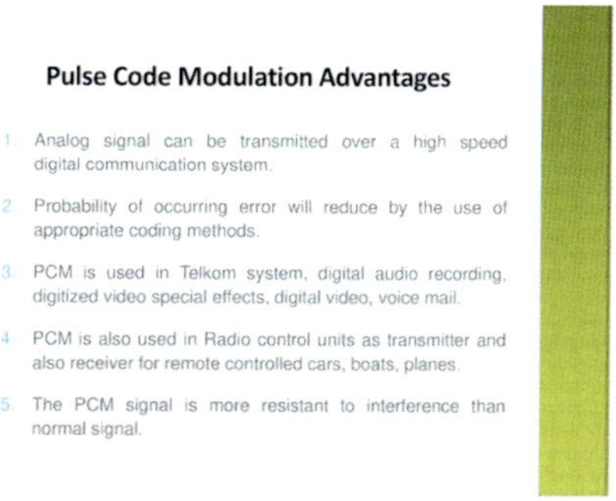

Figure 2.12. Above are some of the advantages of the pulse code modulation method. It enables analog signals to be transmitted quickly through a digital communication system

Source*:* https://slideplayer.com/amp/14445266/.

There is a specific type of pulse-code modulation referred to as the linear pulse-code modulation, in which the levels of quantization are uniform in a linear manner. This is different from the pulse-code modulation encodings where there is a variation in the levels of quantization as an amplitude function. Despite the fact that pulse-code modulation is a term that is more general, it is mostly used for the description of data that has been encoded as linear pulse-code modulation.

A pulse-code modulation stream has two main characteristics that help in determining the fidelity of the stream to the initial analog signal. These are:

- ● The rate of sampling which refers to the number times samples are taken in each second.
- ● The bit depth which determines the number of most likely digital values that can be utilized for the representation of each sample.

Modulation: A sine wave, which has been quantized and sampled for pulse-code modulation, also contains vertical lines to show that the wave has been sampled at regular intervals. One of the values that are available on each sample is chosen. The pulse-code modulation process mostly undergoes implementation on one integrated circuit which is referred to as an analog-to-digital converter. This helps in producing a representation that is fully discrete, of the input signals, and these can easily undergo encoding as digital data for them to be stored or manipulated. A couple of pulse-code streams can also be multiplexed into aggregate data streams that are larger, mainly for transmitting many different streams through one physical link. Time-division multiplexing is a technique that is used widely, especially in the public telephone system.Demodulation: Producing accurate analog signals from discrete data requires electronics which are the same as those that are used for the generation of digital signals. These devices are digital-to-analog converters. They supply the production of a current or voltage that can provide a representation of the values that are presented on their digital inputs. After this, the output can then undergo filtration and amplification for it to be used.For the recovery of the initial signal from the data that has been sampled, it is possible to use a demodulator which use the modulation procedure in a reverse manner. After each period of sampling, the demodulator is able to read the following value and it thereafter makes the output signal transit to the new value. Due to these transitions, the signals are able to attain an amount of high frequency energy that is significant, because of the effects of aliasing. So as to eliminate the frequencies that are not desired, the demodulator is able to pass the signal through a filter for reconstruction that helps in suppressing energy out of the frequency range that is expected.

2.6.3.2. Delta Modulation

This form of modulation refers to analog-to-digital and digital-to-analog conversion of signals that is utilized to transmit voice information where it is not important to have good quality. Delta modulation is the easiest method of differential pulse-code modulation, in which the dissimilarities between samples that are successive undergo encoding into n-but data streams. In this modulation technique, the data that has been transmitted is lowered to 1-bit data stream. Its main characteristics are:

- There is approximation of the analog signal with a set of segments.
- Each section of the signal that has been approximated undergoes comparison to the bits that precede it, and the bits that succeed it undergo determination through their comparison.
- There is only sending of the information that has changed, which means, there is only the sending of a decrease or increase in the amplitude from the initial sample, whereas, a condition of no changes leads to retaining of the signal that has been modulated as the same 1 or 0 state of the initial sample.

So as to attain a high signal to nose ratio, this modulation technique is required to use techniques of oversampling, which means, the sampling rate of the analog signal needs to be several times higher in comparison to the Nyquist rate (Ibe, 2017).

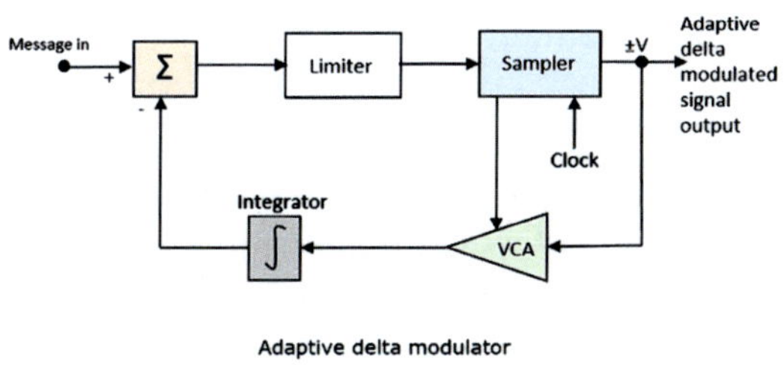

Figure 2.13. Some of the features of delta modulation include: simple design of quantization, good quality, and simple design of a demodulator and a modulator

Source: https://www.tutorialspoint.com/digital_communication/digital_communication_delta_modulation.htm

Forms that have been derived from this modulation technique include delta-sigma modulation, differential modulation, and continuously variable slope delta modulation. A superset of delta modulation is the differential pulse code modulation.

Instead of having the absolute value of the input analog wave form quantized, this modulation technique is able to quantize the dissimilarities between the steps that are current and those that are previous. A quantizer that is able to convert the dissimilarities between the previous steps' average and the input signal helps in making the modulator.

It is possible to use the comparator that is referenced to 0 to realize the quantizer, where the output is either 1 or 0 if there is a negative or positive signal. It can only quantize one bit at a time, thus making it a bit-quantizer. The demodulator can be referred to as an integrator that has a rising or falling output when it receives a 0 or 1. The integrator has a low pass filter.

Due to the fact that a delta modulated system quantizes only two levels as well as 1 bit at a time, it follows a signum function. There are two noise sources in this modulation technique, which are granularity due to a large step size and slope overload due to a small step size that is not able to perform tracking of the initial waveform. A study done in 1971 was able to show that there is less objection ability with the slope overload in comparison to granularity, mostly due to the signal to noise ratio measurements (Emilio, 2013).

One of the ways in which delta modulation is used today is the recreation of legacy synthesizer waveforms. Due to an increase in availability of field-programmable gate arrays and game related application-specific integrated circuits, we can now control the sample rates in an easier way to prevent issues with granularity and slope overload.

2.7. SPREAD SPECTRUM TECHNOLOGY

This is a technique in radio communication and telecommunication responsible for spreading the frequency domain of a generated signal that has a specific bandwidth, which results in a signal with a wider bandwidth. This signal may be acoustic signal, electromagnetic, or electrical.

They are used for many different purposes, such as to establish secure communications, prevent detection, limit the power flux density, or enable multiple access communications.

2.7.1. Spread-Spectrum Telecommunications

This mainly uses a signal structure that is sequentially noise-like for spreading the information signal that is normally narrowband over a band of frequencies that are relatively wide-band. The receiver is then able to make correlations of the signals that have been received for the retrieval of the initial information signal. There are originally two motivations: hiding the fact that there was communication happening, which is at times referred to as the low probability of intercept, or resisting the efforts of the enemy that aim at jamming the communications (Emilio, 2013).

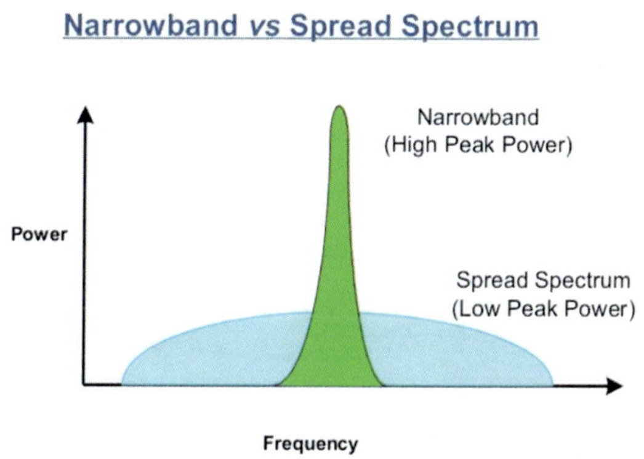

Figure 2.14. Difference between the spread spectrum and the narrowband. The spread spectrum in blue has a low peak power and the narrowband in green has a high peak power

Source: https://www.slideshare.net/gkdelhi8/spread-spectrum-technologies.

Some forms of spread spectrum include: chirp spread spectrum, Frequency-hopping spread spectrum (FHSS), time-hopping spread spectrum, and direct-sequence spread spectrum. The FHSS and direct-sequence spread spectrum have employed pseudorandom sequences, which have been generated using their generators. Some of the advantages of the spread spectrum include:

- There are some methods that have been used since the 1950s in the communication systems in the military that have been able to spread signals from a radio over a wide range of frequency, for several higher magnitudes of frequency from the lowest need. The spread spectrum has a main principle, which is using carrier waves which are noise-like, and as implied by the name, wider bandwidths in comparison to those that are required for easy point to point communication at a similar rate of the data.

- They are resistant to jamming. They have a direct sequence that helps to resist narrowband jamming in continuous time, and also frequency hopping which works better to resist pulse jamming. In direct sequence systems, the detection performance is affected by the narrowband jamming, almost as if the quantity of jamming power has been fully spread all through the bandwidth of the signal, in which, most times it is weaker than the noise in the background. This, however, is different from the narrowband systems which have a low bandwidth for the signal, where the quality of signal that has been received will drop significantly if the jamming power ends up concentrating on the bandwidth of the signal.
- It is resistant to eavesdropping. In direct sequence systems the sequence of spreading or the pattern of frequency hopping is normally not known by any person who is not supposed to receive the signal. In this situation, the system makes the signal obscure and lowers then possibilities of an enemy making sense of it. In addition, for a certain noise power spectral density, the system need an equal amount of energy for every bit, before they can spread as systems that are narrowband. This means that there is an equal amount of power before it is spread. However, due to the fact that power of the signal is spread over a bandwidth that is large, the power spectral density of the signal is much lower. Most of the time, the power spectral density is much lower than the noise power spectral density, so as to ensure that the enemy is not able to make a determination of whether there is existence of a signal. However, for applications that are mission critical, especially those that employ radios that are commercially available, there is no provision of adequate security by the spread-spectrum radios, unless there is use of long non-linear sequences for spreading, in addition to the encryption of messages.
- It is resistant to fading. Spread-spectrum signals that have a bandwidth that is high are able to provide a diversity in frequency, that is, there are very low chances of the signal encountering extreme multi-path fading all through its bandwidth. In systems that use direct sequencing, one can detect the signal through the use of a rake receiver.

- They provide multiple access which is also referred to as code-division multiplexing. It allows for more than one user to transmit at the same time in a frequency band that is similar, provided they utilize spreading sequences that are not the same.

2.7.2. Spread Spectrum Clock Signal Generation

This is used in some of the digital systems that are synchronous, mostly those that have microprocessors, so as to ensure that the spectral density of the generated electromagnetic interference is reduced. A digital system that is synchronous is one that has a clock signal as it's driving power, and due to its nature that is periodic, it has a frequency spectrum that is unavoidably narrow. Actually, a clock signal that is perfect tends to have the concentration of its energy at one main frequency together with its harmonics.

Synchronous digital systems that are practical work by radiating electromagnetic energy on several narrow-bands that have undergone spreading on the frequency of the clock as well as its harmonics, which leads to a frequency spectrum that is able to exceed the limits of regulation for electromagnetic interference, at specific frequencies (Ibe, 2017).

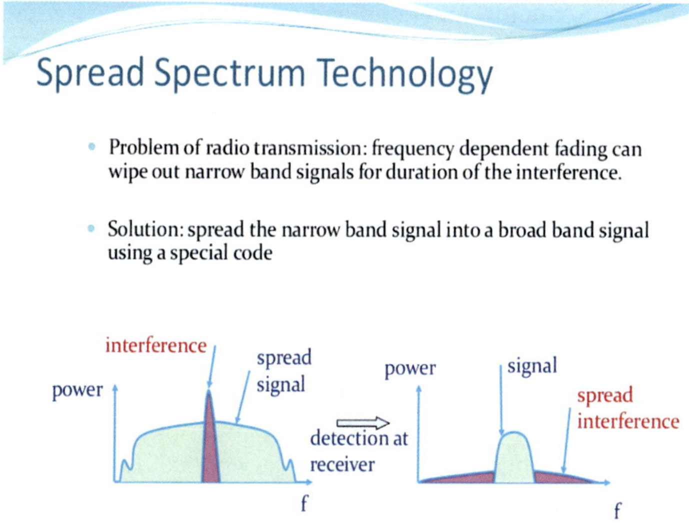

Figure 2.15. One can fix a radio transmission problem by spreading the narrowband signal into a broadband signal

Source: https://www.slideshare.net/nanhen1/performance-of-spread-spectrum-system-17912807.

One is able to avoid this problem by using spread-spectrum clocking which is able to utilize one of the previously described methods for reducing the peak radiated energy. This means that the emitted electromagnetic signals comply with the regulations of electromagnetic compatibility.

Gaining regulatory approval has become a popular technique, due to the fact that it only needs simple modifications of the equipment. It has been found to be much more popular with electronic devices that are portable.

Because these devices are designed to be cheap and light, electronic measures for the reduction of electromagnetic interference, such as metal shielding, cannot be used. In that cases, one has to use active electromagnetic interference reduction techniques, including spread-spectrum clocking (Emilio, 2013).

Spread-spectrum clocking, however, can also end up creating issues for those designing them. One of the main issues is misalignment of the data or clock. Being able to disable the system can be helpful.

It is important to note that this technique does not aid in reducing the total energy that has been radiated and thus the systems may still end up causing interference. Being able to spread energy over a bandwidth that is larger ends up reducing magnetic and electrical readings within narrow bandwidths.

2.8. DATA CODES

2.8.1. EBCDIC

This is the extended binary coded decimal interchange code. It is a binary code with 8-bits that works with alphanumeric and numeric characters. It was created by IBM. It is used to present numbers, letters, and symbols in binary language. It is widely used in mainframe and IBM midrange computers. It was initially created between 1963 and 1964 to enhance the capabilities of the decimal code that was binary coded. It is normally used in OS/390 operating systems (OSs) of IBM and text files of S/390.

It is different from the ASCII character set that is normally utilized by many different computers. EBCDIC is also not compatible with the ASCII character set. EBCDIC consists of 256 different characters. On the other hand, ASCII is the standard for personal computers (PCs). When one needs to move texts from or to a computer from or to a mainframe, there is a file conversion utility that can be used for the conversion between ASCII and EBCDIC (Emilio, 2013).

This code was gotten from the character codes that were utilized in the punched card machines that were pre-electronic and were created by IBM. This was not fully compatible for the modern computers. One of the main inconveniences it caused was having to use codes that were non-contiguous for the alphabetic characters, as well as the lack of a number of characters that were meant for punctuation and used a lot in modern software, such as the square brackets.

Since it's time, 6 or more versions of EBCDIC that are not compatible have been developed. The latest development is inclusive of the characters in the ASCII code, however, it also has certain characters that cannot be supported in ASCII (Emilio, 2013).

2.8.2. ASCII

This is the American Standard Code for Information Interchange. This is an encoding standard for characters so as to enable electronic communication. They help in representing texts in telecommunication equipment, computers, as well as other devices. Most of the schemes for encoding characters that are used today are based on this code, however, they are able to support many more characters.

This code was initially generated from the telegraph code. It was used commercially for the first time as a 7-bit teleprinter code, which Bell data services promoted. On the 6th of October, 1960, they started working on the standard of the ASCII, together with the American Standards Association. It is the first version was published in 1963, and after it was revised, it was released again in 1967, and again in 1986 after further updating. In comparison to the previous telegraph code, the ASCII that had been proposed as well as the Bell code had been ordered for sorting that was more convenient, that is, alphabetization of features that had been added as well as lists for different devices instead of the teleprinter (Ibe, 2017).

CHAPTER

3

The Media: Conducted and Wireless

CONTENTS

3.1. TRANSMISSION MEDIA

A transmission media also known as communication channel is defined as the path or that facilitates the transfer of information from the sender to the receiver. Usually, data to be transmitted is inform of an electrical signal-electromagnetic signal therefore the communication channel makes use of electromagnetic energy to facilitate the transmission. There are different types of communication media classified according to the pathway used when transferring information. They are classified as either physical or conducted media (Janyani et al, 2019).

Usually the conducted media makes use of cables to facilitate the transmission of the signals. Some of the conducted media include the twisted pair wire, fiber-optical cable and the coaxial cable. For the conducted media they depend on a physically seen and tangible medium for the transmission of the signals. They are said to have a physical existence and are usually limited by the physical geography. The different examples of the conducted media are distinguished by their characteristics which include the physical appearance and the transmission speed among others.

The physical media is also known as the wireless media. This form of media makes use of the electromagnetic waves such as the radio waves in the transmission of the signals and therefore are an unbound from of data transmission. They are different from the conduct media as they are not limited by physical geography. They include the radiated/wireless media. The wireless media is further classified into seven groups consisting of the terrestrial microwave transmission, cellular radio transmission, infrared transmission, satellite transmission, personal communication systems, pagers, and the multichannel multipoint distribution service (White, 2015).

3.2. CONDUCTED MEDIA

They are the tangible medium used in data transmission. They are made up of the twisted pair cables, two wire open lines cables, coaxial cables and the optic fiber cables. The two wire open line cables are not commonly used today.

3.3. THE TWISTED PAIR CABLES

In this type of cabling, the two pairs of the conductors of a single circuit are wound around each other (twisted) in a double helix manner. This is done for the purpose of creating a more electromagnetic compatibility this means that when twisted in this manner, there will be a reduction in the development of electromagnetic field around the two wires as data is transmitted. It also reduces crosstalk with other pairs of conductors. Crosstalk refers to the mixing of signals that were to be sent by a given pair such that by the end of the transmission, some of the signals were sent by another pair.

There are different ideologies and principles used in the making of the twisted pair cables. For one it has to be in a balanced circuitry. The ideology behind the balanced circuitry is so that effects such as noise currents are reduced. For an ideal twisted pair cable, the currents flowing within the wires are nearly equal. It is also ensured that the two wires have almost the same distance from the source of the interference and both wires are equally affected by it. There are two types of the twisted pair cables. They include the unshielded twisted pair (UTP) and the shielded twisted pair.

3.4. UNSHIELDED TWISTED PAIR

Unshielded Twisted Pair does not have a shield that protects it from the electromagnetic interference or the electric noise from the environment. This has led to the tendency where such cables are used in environments that are not electrically noisy. The cables consist of copper wires and an insulator such as polythene. The insulators most at times are usually colored. The copper wires and the insulators are then covered in a polythene jacket. For most of these cables the colors: white/blue, white/orange, orange/white and blue/white are subject to it. These types of cables are majorly used in the Ethernet networks as well as telephone systems. In telephone systems, they are used in indoor telephone applications.

Figure 3.1. An unshielded twisted pair cable.

Source: https://www.fiberoptics4sale.com/blogs/archive-posts/95046918-what-is-unshielded-twisted-pair-utp-cable.

The UTP used in outdoor telephone cables consists of bundles of pairs of cables that may have different or the same twist rates. It is chosen according to its ability and its experience with crosstalk. In recent trends, the UTP are used for short and medium length network connections. There are factors that come into play when it is used against other types. For instance, its bandwidth has increased over the years enabling it to transmit larger amounts of signals. It is also cheaper to use compared to other conducted media.

3.5. SHIELDED TWISTED PAIR

These pair have a braided shield wound on the wires. This is done to protect the wires from the environmental noise. The braided shielding creates an electrically conductive barrier which attenuates the electromagnetic waves produced towards the shield. In simple terms it provides a channel through which induced currents are circulated and returned to the source. This is made possible through the ground reference connection. The shielding used may not be entirely braided as there are other construction materials used in shielding the wires.

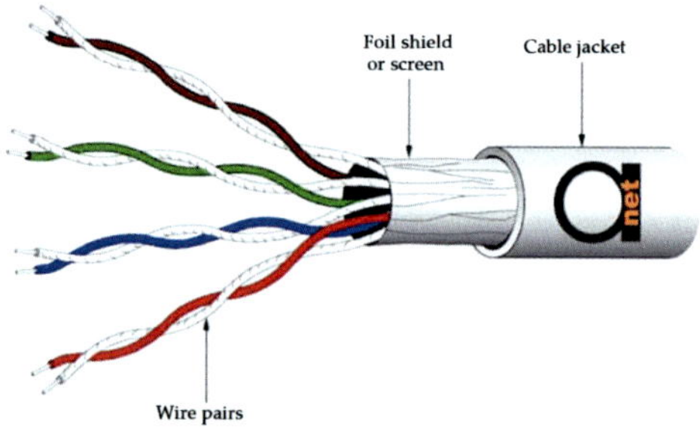

Figure 3.2. A shielded twisted pair cable.

Source: https://www. ad-net.com.tw/intro-screened-twisted-pair-sctp-screened-shielded-twisted-pair-sstp-sftp/.

3.5.1. Individual Shielding

In this type of construction, the cables are shielded using aluminum foil. The shielding is done for each twisted pair. The advantage of this type of shielding is that it protects the pair and the neighboring pair from crosstalk. It also protects the pair from external electromagnetic interference that may be entering or exiting the cable.

3.5.2. Overall Shielding

This construction makes use of the braided shielding across the twisted pairs. This is done within 100 ohms of the twisted pair. Over the individual shielding is an outer foil referred to as braided shielding. They are used to prevent the electromagnetic interference from entering or exiting the cable.

3.5.3. Individual and Overall Shielding

This is a combination of the individual shielding and the overall shielding. Between the twisted pair is the individual shielding that involves the use of foil. The braided shielding is used on the outer surface. They include the screen foiled twisted pair among others. They protect the cables from external electromagnetic interference entering or exiting the cable. They also reduce chances of crosstalk with neighboring cables.

There are different categories of the twisted pair cables according to the type of signal it is suitable to transmit (voice or data) and also the processing speed.

3.5.4. Advantages of the Twisted Pair Cable

It is readily available in the market: The cables are sold in the markets or electronic shops, making it easy for an individual to access the cable. They are sold in different lengths and sizes according to the user's preference

It is the cheapest: Compared to other forms of cabling, the twisted pair cable is the cheapest in terms of use in the networking field. This may be attributed to the fact that it is readily available in the market. Also, it can carry a higher bandwidth of signals compared to the other conducting media. It is considered to be cheap as it allows mass production for telephone use.

It is easy to handle and install: This is attributed to the fact that the installation equipment is cheap. This was the personnel who conducts the installation will have all the tools required. The installation equipment is also readily available in the market.

Facilitates linking: As it is the backbone of telephone networks, the twisted pair cables allow the easy linking for the telephone signals to distant sites.

Transmission is less interrupted: Due to its twisting nature, the electromagnetic interference getting in and out of the cable is hindered from causing any disturbance during the transmission process. This is attributed to the shielding done on the cables.

Crosstalk is minimized: As the wires have been shielded, when they are placed closer to other wires the chances of the crosstalk are at a minimal.

3.5.5. Disadvantages of the Twisted Pair Cables

Low data transmission rates: As the wires are twisted, they are twisted according to their transmission rates and most of the times the transmission rates should strike a balance. Therefore, a majority of them have low transmission rates. This is the reason why a majority of these cables are used to transmit the signals over a short or medium distance from the source. The shorter the cable the higher the transmission rate. The low transmission rates can also be attributed to the type of signal being carried. For instance, transmitting audio will be faster and easier than transmitting the video.

Sensitivity to electromagnetic interference and eavesdropping: These cables are highly sensitive to the electromagnetic interference. This is why most of the cables are placed in regions of low electromagnetic interference. The eavesdropping in this case refers to the crosstalk. The susceptibility of the wire in an electromagnetic interference depends on the schemes used in twisting the wires. Therefore, the installation process is a key factor as it will determine how long the cable will last in the given field.

Imbalance: Though the cables are created on a basis of creating balance, the difference between the two wires can cause a difference in the cables leading to an imbalance where by chances are that the current in the cables may not be the same.

3.6. COAXIAL CABLES

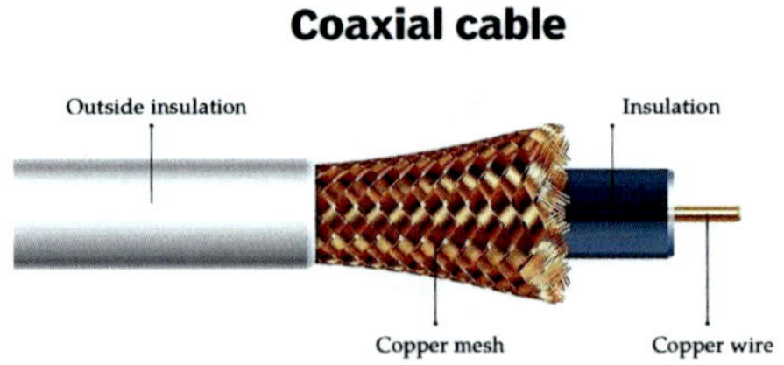

Figure 3.3. A coaxial cable.

Source: https://searchnetworking.techtarget.com/definition/coaxial-cable-illustrated.

A coaxial cable is an electric cable made up of an inner conductor which is surrounded by a tubular layer of an insulator (dielectric insulator). The insulator is then surrounded with a tubular conducting shield which in most cases is made up of woven copper. For some they have an outer insulating sheath which is referred to as a plastic jacket. Due to the fact that the outer shielding and the inner conductor share a geometrical axis, the cable got its name coaxial. The coaxial cables resemble those used in the TV connections. The center core is surrounded by a dielectric insulator to reduce electromagnetic field interference on the cable.

The cable conducts the signals using the inner conductor made up of either copper plated steel wire or solid copper. The stranded copper is used as it has good flexibility characteristics. A silver-plated conductor is used when the high frequency transmission is required. The dielectric used may be made of plastic or air spaced depending on the inner conductor. The dielectric used can therefore be a great source of information on the electric properties of the given cable. The cable can be categorized into two depending on the number of the dielectric insulators:

- Thin coaxial cable: This type of cable contains only one dielectric insulator. It is also referred to as thinnet.
- Thick coaxial cable: They are also known as thicknet. This cable has two dielectric insulators around the core. Another characteristic of this is that the core is usually thicker compared to the thinnet.

For lower cases of losses in the transmission signals, polythene is used as the insulator in this cable. The shield is made up of woven metal material which may vary from one to four depending on the type of the metallic material used. It is set to ground potential.

3.6.1. Characteristics of Coaxial Cables

Transmission: The coaxial cables have good transmission rates. This is attributed to the good shielding of the cables. Transmission varies depending on the type of signal that is being transmitted.

In the analog signals, the coaxial cable amplifies the signal in every few kilometers. It can also transmit signals to a maximum of 500 MHZ and the transmission is closer if the signal is moving at a higher frequency.

In digital signals the coaxial cables have repeaters at an interval of 1 Km. The transmission is done at a closer range to allow the high data transmission rates. Therefore, the coaxial cable can transmit both analog and digital signals. The cables are also less susceptible to electromagnetic interference or crosstalk.

It makes use of the light emitting diode during transmission. This is because it has a relatively wide operating temperature range. It is also long lasting and cheaper to use. However, the injection laser diode is used in most cases because it is more effective and it allows greater data rate during transmission.

Bandwidth: The coaxial cables have a higher bandwidth that ranges from 400 to 600 MHZ. A typical bandwidth travels at a speed of 10 Mbps.

Susceptibility: The coaxial cables are less susceptible to electromagnetic interference or Radio Frequency Interference. This makes it less prone to data loss. It also experiences minimal cases of crosstalk between cables that are closely placed. Therefore, it is safe from electronic eaves dropping.

Attenuation: Most of the inner cores are a made up of thin wires. Due to this property most of the cables experience high attenuation rates. This is why they require repeaters at a given interval to reduce the cases of attenuation.

Impendence: The impendence of the cable is usually determined by the type of the dielectric constant. The dielectric constant is determined by the nature of the dielectric used.

In the coaxial cable the impendence is established using the dielectric constant of the inner insulator as well as its radius. The same is done for the outer dielectric. This because the cable has two insulators; an inner insulator and an outer insulator.

Cabling: In the coaxial cables, the cabling is uniform and the length of the cable is comparable to the wavelength of the signals. It also is dependent on the impendence so that the cable used has a uniform characteristic that will minimize the signal losses.

3.6.2. APPLICATIONS

As the coaxial cables are used in transmission lines, one of their applications involve them being used in the radio where their role is to connect the receiver to the radio transmitter.

They are also used in computer networks (CS) where they are used in Ethernet connections. Some the cables are used in the television transmission signals.

3.6.3. Types of Coaxial Cables

Hard line: This cable is used in the broadcasting as well as radio communication. It consists of copper, silver, and gold tubing. The shielding is made up of all the three metals stated above but it depends on the quality of the hardline as some of the cables have shields made up of aluminum.

The hardline cables are usually thick with some ranging to half an inch to 13mm.

Radiating cable: It is also known as the leaky cable. This cable is similar to the hardline the difference being that it is made up of tuned slots that cut into the shield. The slots are usually tuned to a specific radio frequency.

Triaxial cable: It is also known as traix. It is made up of three-layer shielding, sheathing, and an insulation. The outer shield plays the role of protecting the cable from environmental interference.

There are other examples of the coaxial cables which include the twin-axial cables, semi-rigid cables, rigid line cables and the RG-6.

3.6.4. Advantages of Coaxial Cables

It can be used in high frequency applications: This is attributed to the skin effect. The skin effect is an outcome of high frequency signals that are propagating on the outer surface of the conductor. This is if the conductor at the center of the cable is made up of copper cladding materials. It is beneficial in the long run as it improves it tensile strength. It also causes a reduction in the weight of the cable.

They are cheap: The cost of coaxial cables is relatively cheaper. This may be attributed to the fact that the coaxial cables are readily available in the market. Their installation is also cheap. Its usage in a long-term duration is also cheap as they are made of many layers which will reduce the wear and tear effect.

Control attenuation: For the coaxial cables, it is easy to improve the attenuation. This is made possible through the use of the outer conductor which brings about the shielding effectiveness. The coaxial cable also has an outer jacket which can protect it from the interference from the environment. The plastic property of the jacket makes it resistant/retardant to fire.

Less susceptibility: For the coaxial cables, they are less susceptible to radio interference and the noise interference this is in comparison to the twisted pair cable.

Larger bandwidth: The coaxial cables have a higher bandwidth transmission signal compared to the twisted pair.High flexibility: It is easy to bend the coaxial cable. There is also an ease in wiring and expanding the cable.Has a high stability under high loads: This means that it has the ability to transfer high rates of data. It also has a high rate of transferring the signal. This ability is due to the fact that it has good shielding materials.It can carry different types of signals: In the transmission of signals, the coaxial is able to transmit voice, data or even video signals on the pathway. It is also useful as it transmits the signals simultaneously.

3.6.5. Disadvantages of Coaxial Cables

It is bulky: Most of the cables are thick and therefore have more weight making it a hassle to move it from one point to another.

Installation over long distances is expensive: Due to the nature of the coaxial cable, its thickness and stiffness, it may be expensive to install the cable over long distances. For cables such as thinnet, this attribute contributes to the fact that it is difficult to bend the wire.Difficulty in solving trouble shooting problems: As the cables used are long and a single cable is used during the transmission, if there is a breakdown at any point of the wire, the entire network will shut down. The fact that it's a single cable, it may be difficult to identify which part of the cable has been damaged.

3.7. FIBER OPTIC CABLE

This is a cable made up several optic fibers used in carrying light.

Figure 3.4. A fiber optic cable.

Source: https://www.indiamart.com/proddetail/fiber-optic-cable-20267243462.html.

They consist of the optical fibers being covered with plastics layers and the plastic layers are then covered by a tube (protective tubing) to protect the wires from environmental interference. These types of cables make use of light in its transmission from one point to another on the given network. The transmitter, in this case, is the LED which converts the electric signals into light. On the receiving end, the light has to be transformed to electric signals before they are passed to the final device. This makes need for the photosensitive devices at the reception stage. The devices convert the light received into electric signals.

A fiber optic cable is made up of different parts which include:

- The core – this is the central part of the cable. It is made up of a hollow transparent glass. The glass part is what makes to users of such cables to be careful when handling them;
- Cladding – this is the layer above the core. It is mostly a single protective layer. This layer contains light bending properties. This is used in the scenario where by light is traveling outside the core. The layer will bend the light and make it move it back to the core;
- Buffer – this is the layer surrounding the cladding. Its function is to strengthen the cable; and
- Jacket – this is the outer most layer and its function is to cover the cable.

3.7.1. Types of Fiber Optic Cables

There are two main types which include these two components:

Single mode fiber: This type of cable has a narrow center core. It is used in light transmission over long distances. It has an extremely high bandwidth and tends to have a low attenuation. However, the attenuation depends on factors which include the:

- Wavelength of the light being used;
- The diameter of the optic cable; and
- Distance to be covered by the optic cable.

The disadvantage of this cable is that it is expensive to purchase and install. It also requires one to be extremely careful when handling such a cable.Multimode fiber: These cables have a thicker center core compared to the single mode fiber. They allow multiple light inputs into the cable at given angles though this facilitates modal dispersion. Modal dispersion refers to the distortion of the light from the pathway they were to follow.

The disadvantage of using this cable is that they have a high attenuation rate. They can also be used in light transmission over short distances.

It is important to know that the light rays in the core travel through total internal refraction.

3.7.2. Characteristics of Fiber Optic Cable

- Bandwidth: The fiber optic cables have a bandwidth of 100 Mbps to 1 Gbps meaning that it carries large amounts of data.
- Segment length: These cables carry data over fairy large distances of 2–100Km
- Interference: These cables are not susceptible to electromagnetic interference. This is attributed to the fact that there are minimal to zero electric signals entering the cable. This ensures the safety of the data being transmitted. This is why these cables are mostly used in areas that are prone to noise interference.
- Attenuation: The fiber cables are less likely to be prone to attenuation. Therefore, the repeaters are kept at larger kilometer intervals.
- Nodes: In most cases the cables have two nodes.
- Connectors: The most common connectors used are the ST and SC.
- Size and weight: The fiber optic cables have small diameters and tend to be light weight.
- Transmission: They transmit signals over longer distances compared to the copper core cable. It transmits data in the rates 100Mbps to 2Gbps.
- Installation: The installation of the fiber cable is expensive. This is due to the fact that it is difficult to install the fiber cable if one is not well experienced. It is also a tiring process as one has to carefully handle the cable to ensure that the internal glass does not break.

3.7.3. Advantages of Fiber Optic Cable

Greater bandwidth: The fiber optic cables offer a lager bandwidth for data transmission compared to the copper cables though they both may be having the same diameter. The single mode fiber offers a larger bandwidth compared to the multimode fiber.

Faster speeds: The fiber optic cables carry the light signals at speeds slightly slower than that of the speed of light. This is because the cables have a core that uses light in the transmission process. There also fewer losses during the transmission of the signals.

Longer distances; The fiber optical cables are able to transmit the signals over long distances but this is dependent on the type of cable used. It also depends on the network as well as the wavelength.

They are sturdier: The cables are lighter in weight and also thinner. These properties make it more durable as they can withstand pressure pull and is less likely to get damaged.

Better flexibility: The fiber optic cables have many applications, for instance they can be used in Ethernet connections.

Low attenuation: The fiber optic cables have a low attenuation and this allows the repeaters to be placed at relatively large distances.

Usability: The fiber optic cables can be used in dangerous places. This is because they do not create electrical signals.

3.7.4. Disadvantages of Fiber Optic Cables

Restricted application: These cables are mostly restricted to the ground and therefore cannot be used in mobile communication.

Limited power supply: The surfaces on the optical surfaces are limited to using low power. Extra costs will be added if higher power emitters are incorporated.

Delicate: The optical fibers are very fragile. This is due to the glass layer in them. This therefore means that these cables cannot be twisted or bent.

Expensive installation: The installation of the fiber optic cables tends to be expensive. This is because the installation process tends to be difficult and carefully handled.

3.7.5. Difference between the Fiber Optic Cable, Coaxial Cables and the Twisted Cable

Transmission signal: In the twisted cable transmission takes place using electric signals over a metallic conducting wire the coaxial cable transmits over inner conductor in an electric form while the optical fiber it takes place over glass fibers and light is used during the transmission.

Interference: The twisted cable is greatly affected by interference from a magnetic field while the coaxial is less affected compared to the twisted cable. Fiber optical cables are seldom affected by the electromagnetic interference hence the least interference.

Components: The twisted cable is made up of two insulated copper wires while the coaxial cables have four parts consisting of the conductor wire, layer of insulation, ground conductor and an outer shield known as a jacket. The optical fiber wires are made up of optical fibers made of glass or plastic.

Cost: The cost of the twisted wire is much cheaper compared to all other conducted media. This is because of the performance whereby the fiber optic cables have the highest performance followed by the coaxial cable and finally the twisted pair cable.

Noise rejection: The twisted pair cables are the poorest in effective noise rejection and the fiber optical cables are the best in noise rejection and are not affected by the electrical noise.

Attenuation: The twisted pair cable experiences the highest attenuation compared to the other conducted media while the fiber optic cables have the least attenuation among the rest.

3.8. WIRELESS MEDIA

Wireless media are the media that carry electromagnetic signals using radio waves and microwaves signals. In wireless media, there are no cables or wires that are involved for wiring but the electromagnetic signals are transmitted using the radio waves and microwaves. The wireless media are in different types which are discussed and they include Terrestrial microwave transmission, Satellite microwave transmission, Mobile telephones, Cellular digital packet data, Pagers, Infrared transmissions, Bluetooth, Wireless application protocol, Broadband wireless systems. They are discussed and their advantages and disadvantages stated and discussed for better understanding of the wireless media and what goes on around the wireless media.

3.8.1. Terrestrial Microwave Transmission

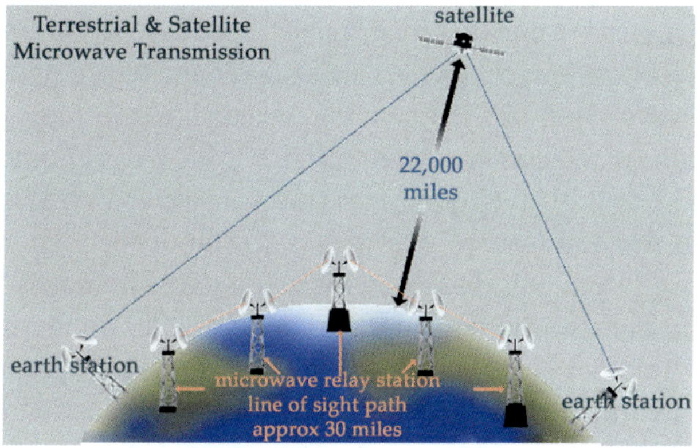

Figure 3.5. Terrestrial and satellite microwave transmission.

Source: https://scis.athabascau.ca/html/courses/comp200/fo/comp200/grphc060.html.

Terrestrial microwave transmission is the transmission of data by using the microwaves to transmit them. Repeaters are made and designed in such a way that they are 30 miles apart because of the design of the earth surface is curved. Terrestrial microwave transmission is majorly used by the manufactures of the televisions and the radios as the signal that is used in these devices come from a huge parabolic dish that is normally positioned in a very high position so that it can take all the signals that are found. Microwaves like all other waves are a type of electromagnetic radiations that is radiations that came about because of both electric and magnetic waves being interlocked. The microwaves are electromagnetic waves which have wavelengths that have a range of one meter up to one millimeter and its frequencies normally have a range between 300 MHZ and 300 GHZ such that the 300 MHZ is for the one-meter while 300 GHz is for the one millimeter. Though these are the commonly known ranges for the microwaves different sources have given different microwave frequency ranges including both UHF and EHF bands. The microwaves are also defined by the radio frequency engineering as having a frequency range of between 1 and 100 GHz which means that the wavelengths, therefore, range between 0.3 meters and three millimeters. The nature of how microwaves travel is defined as the microwaves travel by line of sight which is they travel in a line where they have sight of which is different when compared to other waves that possess lower frequencies like the radio waves which may diffract when they encounter obstacles like mountains but the microwaves do not diffract if they encounter obstacles but they follow the surface of the earth as ground waves. They can also reflect which is the bouncing back of the wave from the ionosphere. Visual horizon may be a limit to communication using a microwave to more than sixty kilometers that are forty miles. The microwaves communication is also absorbed by gasses that are present in the atmosphere that makes it a limit to the communication using the microwave for distances close to one kilometer. Microwaves are a common technology that is incorporated in the modern technology. Microwaves are most commonly used in microwave radio relay, networks, in the cancer treatment, in the medical sector, communication links like the television and the radios, the sensor of the remote, the internal parts of a radio and many more, therefore, it makes them more advantageous in the use of the modern technology as it is incorporated in it and use in the modern technologies that are being invented in the era today (White, 2015).

3.8.2. Advantages of Terrestrial Microwaves Transmission

Terrestrial microwaves transmission can deliver a large amount of data: Terrestrial microwaves can deliver a lot of information from one place to another and therefore it is advantageous. The ability to transmit a lot of data and information is because the terrestrial microwaves transmission are known as having high frequencies and by high frequencies, it is directly linked to transmission of a huge amount of data and information. The microwave repeaters and the high frequencies also enable the transmission of data and information using the terrestrial microwaves transmission to transmit over a long distance and therefore a lot of people who are very far can receive the information. For example, an individual in Africa can easily receive information about what is happening in America or other continents through the radio or television because of the terrestrial microwave transmission. It, therefore, can link many countries and continents together. The process that is involved in the repeater receives the signal through its antennae and it has the duty of converting the signal that it received into an electrical signal which is a form that can be transmitted using the radar as a microwave signal which is fully strengthened. These signals can move through the atmosphere of the earth since they are terrestrial meaning the earth's atmosphere. The signals are then taken to the receivers which were positioned on the top of buildings and towers at a very high position. This advantage of the terrestrial microwaves transmitters enables the transmission of a lot of data and information between long distances and therefore they don't have to have cables and wiring for this process to take place.

Terrestrial microwaves transmission is easily affordable: By being affordable it means that it is cheap and therefore it does not have to be founded on a very large budget that may not be afforded by some individuals and therefore the prices are fair. Terrestrial microwaves transmission of information and data is cheap since the cost that is encountered when construction of the system is low when it is related to other forms of transmitting data such as the wired forms. This is because the terrestrial microwaves transmission does not require any cables and wires for the cabling or wiring as it is a wireless form, therefore, it does not need any attenuation equipment that may be very expensive and unaffordable.

3.8.3. The Disadvantages of Terrestrial Microwaves Transmission

Terrestrial microwaves are hindered by solid obstacles: Terrestrial microwaves transmission is easily hindered with solid objects and other obstacles and therefore they cannot maneuver through hills, mountains, tall buildings and other solid obstacles that may be present in their way. This is disadvantageous because, in the current world, a lot of tall buildings are being put up especially in the cities and also in the more developed rural areas. It is therefore very hard to send a message or information from one city to another due to the presence of these buildings that hinder the progress of the transitional microwaves transmission. The only solution to this problem is putting up the repeaters between two towers in case they experience an obstacle along the way. this will solve the problem at hand since the terrestrial microwaves signals will can be bounced off of solid objects and therefore communication will be enabled and this problem will be easily avoided and solved appropriately.

Terrestrial microwaves transmission is subjected to being hindered by electromagnetic and other interference: Terrestrial microwaves transmission can be hindered by electromagnetic interference and they will make the terrestrial microwaves transmission not to perform as it is expected. This is because they are also electromagnetic waves and when electromagnetic waves meet an electromagnetic interference, destruction may occur eventually and the performance is degraded. The electromagnetic interference includes the motors that operate on electricity, transmission lines that give out electricity, wind turbines and many others. This electromagnetic interference can give out electromagnetic interference that finds a way to make the communication with terrestrial microwaves close to being impossible as it brings about destruction. A good example of this is how when they are wind turbines close by then the television signals are usually distracted and therefore you cannot watch a movie continuously without any disturbance. Another thing that can cause a disturbance in the terrestrial microwave transmission is the presence of moisture in the air, rain or fog. It is seen when one uses the television and there comes rain meaning it starts raining it seen that the television signals begin getting distracted. Research is being carried out on how to solve this problem in the most applicable way possible.

Terrestrial microwaves transmission requires a lot of employees: Terrestrial microwaves transmission also require very many employers and therefore this possess as a disadvantage because the more the employers the higher the amount of money required for maintenance is since the employees need to be paid for the work they are performing. The role of the employees is they regulate the frequency band since they need to be regulated all the time. There are very many terrestrial microwaves transmitters all over the world to ensure that the information is transmitted all over the world and therefore this only leads to their being the need of very many employees that will work on regulating each terrestrial microwave transistor that is present in the world. This only leads to an increase in the amount of money spent on paying the employees and the managers of these employees and therefore it becomes quite expensive. This goes against the advantage that was stated earlier on that this means is a cheap means of delivering information.

3.9. SATELLITE MICROWAVE TRANSMISSION

A satellite microwave transmission is easily seen as a microwave repeater in the galaxy. The satellite microwave transmission is made with transponders. These transponders listen to some portion of the electromagnetic spectrum when an incoming signal occurs, the transponders make them louder and then they rechanneled it to other frequencies. Some satellites known as the geostationary satellites are most commonly put in an orbit that is usually on the top of the equator. They are normally positioned high enough and its speed makes them to have maintenance of a position above a precise place on the surface of the earth. The signals are received by the antennae that are normally placed in an exact point (Janyani et al, 2019).

3.9.1. Advantages of a Satellite Microwave Transmission

Satellite microwave transmissions have the following advantages:

- They can be used by wireless devices for passing information at all times;
- They have wide coverage and therefore only a single satellite is necessary in a whole country;
- The installation of a satellite microwave transmission is easy and therefore it does not require a lot of management;
- They are cheap and easily affordable compared with VSAT site;
- Service is easily obtained from a particular provider which makes it easy for use;
- They are also used for many applications. For instance, they are used to predict the weather by many countries around the world.

3.9.2. Disadvantages of Satellite Microwave Transmission

- Reliable yet costly – the satellite microwave transmission is reliable because of its precise design. However, it is costly because the materials, which are used for its design, are scarce and expensive.
- It requires constant monitoring even after it begins its operation. This needs to be done so that it performs effectively and maintains its place in the orbit.
- It has a short life span: Satellite microwave transmission can last only up to 16 years. After that, it loses its operational value and cannot be used anymore.
- The installation process is also costly because it requires several processes that may incur charges along the way.
- It requires high skilled personnel to carry out its manufacturing and all the process that revolve around.

3.10. MOBILE PHONES

Mobile phones are technological devices to communicate and pass information all over the world. They are forms of wireless communication since they do not require any wiring to pass the information, unlike the wireless telephones that they evolved from. Mobile phones can be used for communication by persons who are far away from each other and therefore they are most commonly used. Mobile phones deliver information using radio waves at a given frequency. Therefore, they can deliver information to any individual provided that they have access to network. The following paragraphs describe the functions that a mobile phone can perform.

Mobile phones are used as a means of communication. Communication refers to passing of information from one individual to another such that the information received is the one that was intended. A mobile phone is used for communication since it can send a message via SMS or one can make a telephone call and pass the message. It is very effective and fast (White, 2015).

Mobile phones software has evolved and new software gave rise to new applications, such as the social media platforms, that can be installed and used for communication and entertainment. The social media platforms have connected very many people as people can share their daily life experiences and they can use the internet to spread information to many other people. Social media platforms include WhatsApp, Instagram, Facebook, and Twitter that people normally use to pass information. The advantage of social media platforms is that they connect people all over the world more cheaply than making calls and sending messages.

Mobile phones are also used as a means of entertainment since mobile phones have the ability to download games, music, and videos that one can watch when they are bored. This prevents many people from being idle and they find a means to pass their time when they have nothing to do and when they are bored. The use of mobile phones for entertainment can also be when an individual live stream a movie and watches them during their free time and every time that they are bored (White, 2015).

Mobile phones are also used for businesses and as a source of income for many unemployed individuals. The use of mobile phones for income is applicable in platforms like the online business where people invite people from their contacts to their page and with this, they get a certain percentage of money. Other people also advertise their goods to the people in their contacts and with this they are able to get possible customers and this can enable them to increase their sales by a certain percentage hence the businesses that adopt the use of the mobile phones are able to attract a lot of customers.

Lastly, the mobile phones can be used to make bookings and reserves such as when an individual wants to visit a specific area and spend some time in a specific place that is far from their homes they can easily make reserves using their phones and they can be able to know the quality of hotels that they are going to spend their time in since they normally have ratings accompanying them and hence the individuals traveling can reserves good hotels that may have the capability of reaching their level and are affordable to them (White, 2015).

The advantages of the mobile phones as a source of wireless media include:

They are cheap and easily affordable: Mobile phones are not that costly as they were before. Mobile phones are easily available as they go for prices as low as five hundred Kenyan shillings. Another advantage of the mobile phone that makes them cheap and easily affordable is that communication using the mobile phones is very cheap such that one does not need a lot of money so that they can send a message to another individual and hence it becomes easily affordable by most people.

Mobile phones are very fast: When using a mobile phone to communicate, information is delivered to the other party very fast and there is no limit on how far the message can travel. Using mobile phones therefore enable the passing of information fast and the feedback is sent almost immediately back to the person that sent the message. In the case of an emergency, it can easily be solved because individuals will communicate the emergency to the individuals concerned and they will be able to solve it way faster than if a messenger was sent with the information concerning the emergency.

Disadvantages concerned with mobile phones include the following:

Mobile phones are very addictive: Mobile phones are addictive in the case many people spend the better part of their day using their mobile phones such that they fail to perform their duties. Using mobile phones excessively may cause a rise in the number of individuals that are addicted to their phones and this is disadvantageous because it has led to an increase in the number of people who die due to accidents as many people texts while they are driving and through this they cause a lot of accidents and may end up hitting other people that could lead to their death.

Mobile phones cause illnesses and diseases: By using mobile devices, they easily expose the individual to many health risk and diseases such as, when a person uses a mobile phone too much, they can damage their eyes due to the high intensity of light that the mobile phones emit. Using mobile phones will therefore make very many people to end up having to wear glasses whenever they are awake. Also, mobile devices emit radiations that can cause hazardous diseases like the cancers, therefore one should avoid getting addicted to their mobile devices.

3.11. CELLULAR DIGITAL PACKET DATA

Cellular digital data packet is a wireless service that enables people to have the access to mobile internet. The cellular digital packet data is used to access the internet and therefore, the data is used by internet providers. These cellular digital packet data are provided by service providers, such as Safaricom or Telcom.

3.11.1. Advantages of Cellular Digital Packet Data

- They are used for online and scientific research.
- They are used for entertainment for example, the online games, live streaming movies and videos, watching news and documentaries through platforms such as the YouTube because one cannot access these services if they lack cellular digital packet data
- They are used for communication through social platforms like Instagram ad WhatsApp that people can send messages to their loved ones no matter the proximity and space that separates them.
- They are cheap and easily affordable by many people and therefore this makes them advantageous.

3.11.2. Disadvantages of Cellular Digital Packet Data

- It is addictive as it causes many people to spend their time in their internet and they fail to perform their duties and this becomes an addiction when it reaches the point where they cannot be separated from their technological devices
- It may corrupt morals and therefore lead to immorality as people may visit sites that promote the corruption of their morals.

3.12. BLUETOOTH

Bluetooth is a wireless service that is used to transfer information from one device to another device. Bluetooth involve the sharing of information by sending and receiving information from one device that sends to the other device that receives the information. It does not require any wring so that one can send the data and information but one connects directly through radio transmission the massage and information intended is sent. Many people use Bluetooth devices as a means to share folders and applications or they connect to their mobile phones and use the Bluetooth device it listens to music and entertain themselves

The advantages of Bluetooth include:

They are fast: Sharing of anything using the Bluetooth is very fast and therefore a certain information can be sent very fast within minutes. This is advantageous because one can end up transferring a large sum of information from one individual to the other without having to wait and in a short span of time. Transferring information using the Bluetooth has enabled many individuals therefore to prefer this method of sharing information and of connecting devices since it enables them not to waste their time having to wait.

They are very easy to use: Another advantage of using Bluetooth devices is that they are not complicated and therefore they are very easy to use. The use of Bluetooth technology does not need personal training being carried out but they only require the individual to follow the rules that are set aside and they will be able to connect and utilize.

They are cheap and afforded: Bluetooth devices are very cheap and therefore they can be afforded easily. Since they are wireless devices, they do not require any wiring that may cause them to end up being expensive and unaffordable.

The disadvantages of the Bluetooth include the following:

They are limited to a certain distance: Most Bluetooth devices are only applicable to devices that are close to each other for them to be able to connect. In case the devices go far away from each other than the Bluetooth connection is lost and this therefore proves disadvantageous since people who are far away cannot send a piece of information to another party unless they come close together and they connect. Most Bluetooth devices have a space limit of about 5 meters which can therefore be disadvantageous to many.

They are easily disrupted: Another disadvantage of Bluetooth device is that they can easily get disrupted when they are in the process of sharing some information. Just like other electromagnetic materials, Bluetooth devices are affected by several factors that can disrupt their progress such as magnetic and electric factors and other environmental factors. This is very disadvantageous since one can be sending useful information to a certain individual and just when the information is almost sent a disruption occurs and they will have to start from the initial point of sending the information again and this may be hectic and tiresome.

3.13. PAGERS

A pager is a wireless simple radio that can only listen to one ratio. It is designed in a way that it is tuned into one frequency and it can only receive the signals that are sent by the radio transmitter to them. Pagers exist for a particular network that are tuned in to the same frequency from the transmitter and therefore they have a built-in receiver that receives the same frequency broadcast from the transmitter as long as the pager is switched on at the moment.

3.13.1. Advantages of the Pager

They deliver the right message to the right person: By delivering the right message to the right person it means that when an individual is using a pager to receive information they are assured that the message they receive is the correct message that was meant for them since the pagers only listen to one frequency and therefore only the message that is set by the transmitter that is designed to send messages to this receiver can reach the person.

This advantage applies more commonly in hospitals when the ill person ay wants to send a message to the doctors to come and assist him

They are also cheap hence easily affordable

3.13.2. Disadvantages of the Pager

A pager does not notify the sender that the receiver has received the message that they sent and therefore the receiver may receive the message and they fail to act and it will be taken as if they did not receive the message from the start.They are also limited in the sending capacity as they cannot send pictures to the receiveThey run on replicable batteries which may add up as a cost to the owner.

3.14. INFRARED TRANSMISSION

Infrared transmissions are the energy that are present in the places where there is electromagnetic spectrum at wavelengths longer than visible light and shorter than radio waves and wavelengths higher than radio waves and lower than visible light. They are also higher to the microwave's frequency but smaller than the frequencies of the visible light. The infrared transmission is used in omen wireless devices that include

The remote-control boxes, local area networks (LANs), the cordless modems, motion detectors, fire sensors, night vision systems and medical equipment's that are used for diagnosis. They are therefore useful and advantageous to wireless media.

3.15. WIRELESS APPLICATION PROTOCOL

The wireless application protocol is a communication protocol that functions as a protocol that is used in passing of information through the wireless networks that involve the mobile phones. Its role is to assist the mobile phones to have access and connectivity to the internet ad therefore they play a major role in the mobile phones.

3.15.1. Advantages of the Wireless Application Protocol

They have ease of use. This means that they are designed I ways that are not complicated and therefore they can be understood easily and can be used easily with different individuals with a lot of ease.

They are cheap hence easily affordable. The wireless application protocol is very cheap and therefore they are easy to use when they are used, they do not incur a lot of costs. Costs are avoided easily due to the fact that they are wireless and therefore they do not require any wiring and cabling hat make manufacturing expensive.

The design is quite simple and therefore the manufacturing tools are cheap and easily available. The elimination of cost enables many wireless application protocol technologies to be invented from time to time and this possess as a very advantageous tool.

3.16. BROADBAND WIRELESS SYSTEMS

The broadband wireless systems work in the same way as the wired broadband by enabling connection to the internet. They are wireless because they do not need any wires to perform their functions. Broadband wireless systems operate using wireless fidelity radio waves. Every technological device, that has the access to the internet, normally has a wireless adapter whose function is to change the data into a radio signal in a language that the signal can understand. A wireless router receives the signal, decodes it, and then sends it to the Internet through a wired Ethernet connection.

3.16.1. Advantages of Broadband Wireless Systems

- They are wireless and therefore they do not have to consume a lot of space in the apartment and home;
- They are relatively cheap;
- They are easy to use;

3.16.2. Media Selection Criteria

Cost: The cost of setting up media, purchasing and installing the cable are important aspects to consider. Though there are some media that are costly, they can also be preferred because of high quality of transmission they offer.

Speed: The speed of the medium determines the rate at which the data signals will be transmitted. Therefore, according to the required speed of the transmission, the media will be chosen and in most cases those with high transmission speeds are chosen.

Distance and expandability: The distance is in relation to the length of the area to be covered. In most cases, if the transmission has to occur over relatively large distances, then the wireless transmission will be more suitable for the transmission. Expandability is also a factor. This accounts for the ability of the media to be expanded in terms of the transmission media.

Environment: Depending on the environment, the media to be used will be selected. In a very noisy environment we prefer to use cables rather than fiber optic cables.

Security: When selecting the medium, we need to account for the safety of the data being transmitted. This means that the media should have minimum cross-talking and attenuation.

CHAPTER

4

Making Connections

CONTENTS

4.1. INTRODUCTION

A computer network consists of a chain of computers, which communicate through the transmission of data, exchange information, and share resources. For computer networks (CS) to be complete, one needs to combine the hardware aspect like routers, modems, wire cables and the software aspect of technology like operating systems (OSs) and applications. CSs are also defined by the location, where the network is located. For instance, we have a local area network (LAN), which is used to connect computers that are found within the same physical space like an office or a home or a wide area network (WAN) which has the capability of connecting computers all over the world. CS plays a critical role in ensuring smooth flow of business, entertainment, and research transactions.

4.2. MODEMS

4.2.1. Basic Modem Operating Principles

A modem, also known as modulator-demodulator, is a head hardware device that basically converts data into a format that can be transmittable in order to transfer the data from one computer device to another computer. Binary signals are converted from the computer into analog form. The converted data is then transmitted through the telephone line. A modem has the ability to transfer data among several computers through telephone lines. Carrier-wave signals are modulated by the modem in order to encode digital information for transmission. It can be one or more carrier wave signals. After transmission, the modem then demodulates the signals to decode the transmitted information. The modem tries to achieve a system where signals being produced are able to be transmitted with ease and decoded accordingly to reproduce the original digital data. Radio and light emitting diodes are among the means of transmitting analog signals that can be used by modems. Digital data of a computer is converted into a modulated electrical signal in order for it to be transmitted over a telephone line and then the transmitted electrical signal is demodulated by another modem at the receiver's end to convalesce the digital data. This type of modem is the one that is commonly used. During the classification of modems, the maximum amount of data the modem can send in a given unit of time is usually considered. The unit of measuring is expressed as bits per second (bits/s). The symbol rate is also used to classify modems and it is measured in baud. This is the number of times a new signal is transmitted per second like one bit per symbol (White, 2015).

4.2.2. Data Transmission Rate

Modem speed is the measure of how much data can be transferred in a given amount of time. Typically, modem speeds are measured in bits per second. Because of the technology being used in telephone services for dial-up modems, the quickest speed available is 56 kilobits per second. This is the same as 1000 bits per second. Data which is in digital form, be it sound, video or data files, are converted into computer language consisting of ones and zeros so that it can be comprehended and transcribed the computer. Digital data is converted into analog signals by the modem so as to enable its transmission through telephone lines and from analog signals to digital data from the other computer or phone network. This is the process of modulating and demodulating data. Over time, there has been the advancement of data transmissions. X2 and KFlex were originally being used for non-standard technologies which was developed by manufacturers of modems. For industry standards, V.90 was developed and it advanced to V.92 which is the standard being used by industries in order to ensure there is compatibility (Meadow, 2002).

Electrical current is important when one needs to send and receive signals via phone networks. In the world of data communication, the more the data, the more the current that will be needed (that is bits per second). Although electrical current is vital when sending and receiving signals through phone networks, it is also important to regulate the amount of current being inputted. This is because when you apply too much current, there is a huge risk of the phone network developing challenges. An example of such a challenge is crosstalk. This is the unintended licking of signals from one phone line to another. A good example of such a challenge is the time where you can be on a phone talking to someone and you hear a conversation from a different telephone network. Due to this problem, the amount of speed available for analog modems was limited by the Federal Communications Commission as they decided to reduce the range of current being transmitted by phone company equipments.

The Federal Communications Commission decided to reduce the amount of data being transmitted per second from 56 bits per second to 53 bits per second in order to prevent crosstalk from occurring. Data speed has a huge significance when transferring data. Faster modem speeds increase the feasibility in transmission of complicated forms of data such as audio and video. Over the recent times, the development of a fast modem in terms of data transmission has enabled the development of detailed websites and the sophistication of business and gaming operations. Also, fast modem speeds have enabled users to do a wide range of activities, ranging from video sharing, online gaming to video conferencing (Meadow, 2002).

Different modems have the ability to transfer data information at different rates. As earlier stated, dial-up modems have the capability of reaching download speeds of 56 kilobits per second while DSL modems are capable of downloading at speeds of 10 megabits per second. Due to the sharing of bandwidth by other users, the actual speed of cable modems has been slightly reduced but in theory, download speeds of cable modems are 30 megabits per second.

Generally, the rate of uploading is slower than the rate of downloading for normal models. Modems have different features that indicate its functionality. Normally modem have lights that indicate if the modem has been switched on or off. One is also able to check the current modem speed by going online and logging in the specified websites.

4.2.3. Standard Telephone Operations

The telephone is one of the most important inventions in the world. It created a two-way conversation by simply dialing numbers. Telephone networks have the capability of extending worldwide and therefore one is able to communicate with another person in different parts of the world. This is in contrast with almost a century ago where for one to deliver a message to a different person in a different part of the world, it would have taken several weeks. Telephone connection has not changed since its invention. It is simple to use and one can connect it to a wall jack in a house. A home telephone contains three parts: the speaker, the microphone and the hook switch. The function of the hook is to connect and disconnect the telephone from the main network. Normally, the phone connects to the network when the handset is lifted.

The speaker is composed of a small 50-cent, 8 ohms' speaker and the microphone is made of carbon granules which have been compressed between two thin metal plates. When someone speaks through the microphone, the sound waves compress and decompress the carbon granules, thus altering the resistance of the granules and modulating the current flow in the microphone. Pulse dialing is used to dial a number.

This is done when you rapidly tap the switch hook five times and the phone company will be able to identify that you have dialed the number 5 (Dhotre and Bagad, 2008).

The only disadvantage with using pulse dialing telephone is that one is able to hear the echo of their voice through the speaker when talking. This became very irritating and over time companies introduced a duplex coil to block the echo of your own voice. Major advancements were made and now a modern telephone contains a bell in order for it to ring, a touch-tone keypad, and a frequency generator. A modern phone still looks like this.

The modern phone is simple in nature but minor adjustments made it more reliable and conducive. Unlike the previous telephone, the modern phone constitutes of an electronic microphone and amplifier and a circuit. The carbon granules and loading coil in the old phone was replaced by a circuit. The ringing tone was also modified to make it more appealing as the mechanical bell was replaced by a speaker and a circuit.

Wires and cables: Wiring the network takes place in your house. Copper wires, which are paired, are pulled from a box on the roadside to a box at your house. The box at your house is normally known as the entrance bridge. Wires of different colors, such as red and green, are connected to each phone jack in your house. In the event that your house contains two phone lines, then two separate pairs of copper wires are pulled from the road to your house. The other pair is also colored differently for distinction. Yellow and black is the preferred color. A digital concentrator is placed along the roadsides and inside the digital concentrator. There are thick cables packed with more than 100 copper pairs, which will run directly to the phone company's switch in your area. The digital concentrator usually looks like a small-sized refrigerator (Dhotre and Bagad, 2008).

The main function of the digital concentrator is to digitize your voice at 8000 samples per second and 8-bit resolution. Voices from other telephone networks are all combined in the digital concentrator and all of them are sent down a single wire to the telephone company. The medium of transferring the voices is usually a fiber-optic cable or a coax cable. Every telephone network in an individual's house is connected to a line card which enables one to hear the dial tone when you pick up the phone. In the case where you are calling someone connected to the same office, a loop is created between your phone and other phone using a switch. This is different when a long-distance call is being made because your voice is digitized and combined with other voices from different networks. The receiving party will be able to listen to your voice and get connected to you using a fiber-optic line which transmits the voice. Not only the fiber optic cable is used to transmit the voice but we can also use satellite and microwave towers. The process of creating your own telephone network is simple because you only need two telephones, a 9-volt battery, and a 300-ohm resistor and these are things that can be found at your local store. Your telephone is then connected to the phone company using two copper wires usually red and green. The red wire is used to supply your phone with 6 to 12 volts of direct current at about 30 mill amperes and the red wire is the common. This takes us back to the old telephone where they utilized carbon granules in modulating the current that is, letting more or less current through depending on how sound waves compress and relax the granules. On the other end of the receiving call, the speaker then places the modulated signal.

The electronic switch in the modern phone system replaced the operator and this works by sensing the completion of a loop which in turn plays a dial tone when you pick up the phone. This will let you know that the switch and your phone are functioning properly. A combination of 350 Hz tone and a 440 Hz tone is the mechanic that is used in the creation of the dial tone sound. In the case that the number is busy, you hear a busy signal that is composed of 480 Hertz and a 620 Hertz with a cycle of one and a half second on and one and a half second off. Phone companies usually limit is there frequencies to a bandwidth of about 3000 Hertz so as to allow more long-distance calls to be transmitted. Because of the limitation of the frequencies, frequencies below 400 Hz and frequencies above 3400 Hz in your voice get eliminated. This can be elaborated when using a computer, call up someone and play a 1000 hertz sound file. You will notice that the person will be able to hear your tone clearly however, the person will have challenges hearing a 4000 Hz tone and as the frequency progresses to about 6000 hertz, no voice will be heard at all (Meadow, 2002).

4.2.4. Connection Negotiations

Remember that a modem simply works by converting digital binary codes into an analog code for transmission over a telephone network. This is the basic function of a modem though, there is much more to what a modem does than this. During the procedure, there are voices of a modem dialing a telephone line, another modem answering and the two modems negotiating to determine at what rate to communicate. The modems are automated to enable communication at the highest rate that can be supported by both modems. Below is a simplified state machine that describes how a modem initiate the call.

- A ring input leads to a conversion to the ringing condition whereas a busy condition leads to a conversion back to the idle condition. This process occurs in the dialing condition. You will find that in modems that have a better design, a timer will be set and a modem will attempt to dial again after some time has passed.
- When there is a modem connected at the end of the other telephone line, the reply tone is perceived and the state machine transforms to the modem perceived condition. A timer is usually set after every 15 seconds which will cause the modem to transition back to the idle condition in the case where there is no modem on the other end of the line.
- When the telephone is in a modem perceived condition, it radiates a signal that recognizes the highest possible connection rate for example, 55 kilobits per second. In the case that the other modem has the capability of operating at the same rate as the other modem, it will respond with a signal that is seen by the modem as an id1 response input.
- In the case that the other modem does not have the capability of operating at the same connection rate as the other modem, which in our case is 55 kilobits per second, then the timer will expire and the modem will radiate a different signal that will recognize a lower rate in order to create a connection.
- When the far end modem accepts and answers to the other modem id signal, then the near end modem radiates a training sequence which is a pre-agreed signal that allows the modem at the far end to compute the disability on the telephone channel and set up adaptive filters to compensate for these disabilities. The far end modem also does the same thing by transmitting a training sequence which enables the near end modem to configure itself in order to get the required adaptive filters.
- A connected state is then accomplished when both the modems have configured themselves to their filters. More sophisticated modems also include a timer. If convergence does not happen, the modem will try to reconnect at a different rate.

4.2.5. Compression and Error Connections

By nature, modems are often faced with errors. There are errors that are hard to be noticed such as noise on the telephone lines which is a very common happening as it easily imitates the sound used by the modems to transfer information. There is a minimal amount of error that can be allowed as it causes little challenges when reading and writing simple text. But in other modem functions, such as transfer of files even the slightest error can lead to the destruction of the whole file. In the event that modems increase in the rate of transmitting data, up to more than the required or regulated bandwidth there is a high probability that random noises will be present and this will cause occurrence of mistakes. Bandwidth of above 2400 bits per second can lead to the occurrence of such noises. There have been the introduction and implementation of file transfer protocols which has helped in dealing with this challenge. The file transfer protocol operates by breaking down a file into a series of frames or packets which contain a number of bytes from the original file. In order to identify if a file had a particular error while it was being received, an additional data commonly a checksum or a CRC, is incorporated to every packet. When the additional data is added to the frames, the packets are then transferred to a remote system which calculates the checksum or CRC of the data and compares it to the received check checksum to check if it was received well. When they packet have been checked and it has been confirmed that the data was well received, an acknowledgment letter (ACK) is sent back and this is used to prompt the sender to transmit the next frame (Meadow, 2002).

In the case that the data was not properly received, the receiver transmits a not acknowledged (NAK) message back to the sender prompting the sender that the data frame is damaged. An overhead is introduced when this procedure takes place that is, the introduction of extra checksum or CRC utilizes up time in the route that could otherwise be used to transmit more information. This is deemed to be a minor problem unless the frames are very small. A more challenging problem is the time that is used by the receiver to inspect the frame, compare it to the CRC and then transmit an acknowledgment message back to the sender. The delay brought about by this process grows relatively with the increase in the speed of the modem. A newer protocol system known as the sliding Windows enables the sender to begin transmitting the next packet even before the receiver is able to send back a message notifying the sender if the package is corrupted or not. Only if the ACK does not reach for some time will it resend the package (Meadow, 2002).

4.2.6. Security

Because of the interconnection that is created by modem between your computer and the outside world, there has been numerous security concerns regarding the usage of modems. Modems can be used in institutions to extract information that is confidential. Models have also been used by outsiders to gain access to your computer without authorization. Computer scientists have the ability to reprogram a modem or subvert a modem so as to reveal your passcode. Hackers also have the ability to eavesdrop communication on a modem. Modems are still being used to gain access into corporations and businesses despite the fact that there is rise in the internet usage. This is because corporations spend most of their resources in safeguarding their internet connections and they leave modems unaudited and unguarded. It is costly to run remote access software in computers when installing modems. This challenge can be tackled by providing modems to organizations and administering them in a secure manner. The administration of modems in a secure manner can be done by physically placing the modems in an area where it cannot be easily accessed by people who might alter or rewire its program. A manager can be hired to keep an eye on the configuration switches of the modem to ensure that they remain unchanged. There are features in modems such as the ability to allow remote configuration and testing that can enable personnel's to abuse your modem. During the administering of modem, they should ensure that such features have been disabled. Your modem's telephone number should be as private as your personal passwords so as to limit the access of people to the telephone number as publicizing the telephone number increases the chances that somebody might try to use them to break into your system. When troubleshooting the modem system, one should ensure that the modems have been unplugged from the phone line. This will ensure that social engineering attacks are less feasible. One cannot completely hide a modems phone number because it will be needed during calling and therefore other measures need to be put in place to ensure that security is being enhanced. Such measures can be regularly changing the modem phone number let us say on a yearly basis (Meadow, 2002).

4.2.7. Banners

When a modem is called, the message that is displayed by the modem or by the computer which has been connected with the modem is known as a banner. Most modems display the banner messages only after the person has successfully authenticated the connection but some banners are displayed by the answering system before the color types anything. Banners have the significance of enabling callers to know that they have reach to the correct system. Banners also include notices and any document that has legal restrictions. Although banners are significant in the usage of modems, they are also prone to attacks as they provide useful information that can help hackers to break into a system like disclosing the OS version being used by the organization. In the 1980s, the messages 'welcome' was contained in the banner and it was rumored that it gave permission for computer intrusion by attackers and it's therefore suppressed evidence because the system banner did not inform them that the keystrokes were being recorded (Carne, 2004). After the controversy, there were recommendations that were made on what should be put in a banner

- The banner should clearly state that unauthorized use of the system is prohibited and legal action can be taken against any person found guilty;
- State that any user of the modem will be monitored;
- Inform the user that he or she has agreed to be monitored as a condition of using the computer system; and
- If the computer is connected or related to the Federal Government, there are additional penalties for breaking into such systems.

Some of the recommended messages that should not be included in the banner include;

- Do not use the word 'welcome';
- The name of your organization should not be identified;
- Contact information and telephone numbers should not be included; and
- The name of the computer's OS should not be listed down.

A caller ID and an automatic identification number should be purchased. This can be done by properly programming your computer in order to provide such information to the host computer when the information is received over the telephone lines.

Another way of securing your modem is by using separate modems for inbound and outbound traffic.

To prevent eavesdropping of modem networks a company can put the following measures into play. Visually inspect your telephone line, have your telephone line electronically swept and use cryptography. Some of the places where telephone conversations over a modem can be tapped include your premises, outside your window, on the wire between your premises and the central office, at the phone's company central office, along a wireless transmission link, at the destination industrial spies and through law enforcement.

Finally, security can be enhanced by managing unauthorized modems with telephone scanning and telephone firewalls. A telephone scanner program can be installed in order to locate unknown and unauthorized modems. There are computer Consulting firms which are able to perform telephone scanning as a part of security audit. In the events that the risk of penetration by modem is high and telephone scanning is not applicable, setting up telephone firewalls is important in order to mediate telephone calls between your organization and the outside world. A telephone of firewall is a device that is placed between your telephone system and an outside communications circuit. Multiple ports of digital T1 telephone lines are contained in a telephone firewall. The PBX is then plugged into the telephone firewall and the firewall is plugged into the exterior T1s. The telephone firewall then analyzes every information that is contained in the conversation and in the event that the firewall recognizes a certain data that is not authorized to operate in the modem, the firewall then terminates the call and the event is logged out (Carne, 2004).

4.2.8. Self-Testing (loop back)

Self-testing using the loopback test is a form of testing whereby signals from a communication device are transmitted and the same signal is sent back to the same device that sent it in order to check if the device is working properly or to check for the node that has failed in a network. The wrap plug is a specialized type of plug that is used in performing the loop-back test. It is normally inserted in a pot on a communication device. The function of the wrap plug is to cause a loop-back effect whereby the signal that was transmitted is returned as received data therefore simulating a complete communication circuit by the use of a computer. A loop back is therefore defined as a signal that was sent as part of the loop-back test. When a look back test has been completed, the information on your personal computer (PC). should match the original data. There are three types of loopback tests namely; local analog loopback test (V.54 loop 3) which allows you to verify that the modem transmitter and receiver circuits are properly functioning, remote digital loopback test (V.54 loop 2)which allows you to verify that the local computer or terminal, the two modems and the transmission line between them are properly functioning and the local digital loopback test (V.54 loop 2)which allows you to verify that the remote computer or terminal, the remote modem, the serial ports, the telephone line and the local modem are functioning properly (Carne, 2004).

4.2.9. Internal Versus External Modems

If a computer needs to have an internet access, it should contain a modem. There are two types of modems: internal and external.

Internal modem: As the name suggests an internal modem is a modem that comes pre-installed inside a computer. Basically, an internal modem is an external modem and a serial port mounted upon a PC bus card. An internal modem can be powered by a computer using its own power supply.

External modem: An external modem is a network device that is in a self-contained enclosure different to a computer. External modems are portable and can be moved from one computer to another although they require a universal serial bus (USB) to function. In the case that a computer is not able to fit an internal modem in its system, an external modem can be used. It is powered by an external source.

Advantages of the internal modem.

- Internal modems are relatively cheaper compared to external modems.
- Once an internal modem has been installed, there is little or no upkeep in order to maintain it. Things such as dusting and regular cleaning is not required.

Disadvantages of the internal modem

- One huge advantage of internal modems is the user of the modem is unable to directly supervise and check the status of the modem. In the event that internet access has been compromised, one is unable to identify.

Advantages of the external modem:

- One is able to view the status of an external modem because it has features that identify if there is a problem. Such a feature includes light and other sensors.
- Because the external modem has its own power supply source, it does not lead to a fast drainage of a computer's power-supply which means that a computer lasts longer and it is more productive because less heat is generated inside the computer.

Disadvantages of the external modem

- External modems require regular dusting and vacuuming in order to maintain it.
- External modems are relatively expensive than internal modems.

When purchasing a modem, it is important to consider that when you want to spend less money in maintenance, an internal modem is the best option. This is because you won't have to worry about dusting and cleaning or taking up a plug on your surge protector. If you want to beef up security of your documents and reduce the amount of heat being generated inside the computer. an external modem is the best option. It is also important to note that broadband modems cannot be purchased in form of an internal modem.

4.2.10. Modem for Laptops

One is able to access internet using an internal laptop modem. A laptop modem comes as a standard part of your laptop integrated right into the main circuit board that is, the motherboard. A standard telephone code can be used to connect your laptop modem to your phone system by plugging one end into a phone jack and the other into your laptop. A modem is measured by its speed of transmitting files. All dial-up modems since 1990 have the same rate of transmitting files and that is 56 kilobits per second. Currently, such a speed of transmitting files is considered to be relatively slow. A phone call plugs into a hole that is contained on the modem. Laptops contain two modem jacks and one of the holes is used to connect the laptop to the phone Jack which is also called the line jack. The second hole can be used to connect a phone and that's the phone Jack. One is not able to connect a phone to the internet while the computer is also online. The same mechanism that a phone is used by humans to make a phone call is the same mechanism a computer uses that is, dialing a number then making melodic tones at the other computer which also screeches back the melodic tone. The cost of making a call on phones applies to computers as well and hotel surcharges also apply. In the case that one is traveling overseas, the charges change because you are in a different country and different rates apply. Most of the times an extra charge is given to modem made phone calls. In the event that your laptop does not contain a modem, one can readily install a modem PC card which will act as a modem (Carne, 2004).

4.3. 56K DIGITAL MODEM

Before the introduction of the 56k digital modems, there was the use of the 28.8k and 33.6k modem. The use of these previous modems was such a good invention that people thought that there will be no more advancements. Although these models were good in usage, they had some limitations. That is, there were numerous disturbances of the analog telephone lines during communication. Also, in order for one to operate the modems using high internet rates, you will need different types of modems which was not available in usage over the standard phone lines. The introduction of the 56k digital modem solved all these difficulties that were being faced because one is able to access faster internet connection using your standard phone lines. The 56k modem come with technology that depends on a half digital connection to achieve its higher speeds. Although the 56k modem solved the issue of disturbance of the analog telephone lines, due to the large number of digital lines, this disturbance still exists but at a lower level and this has made it possible to transmit data with a maximum speed of 56 km per second.

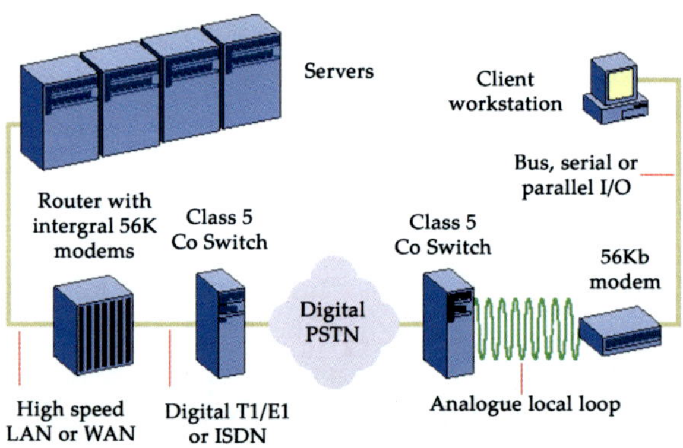

Figure 4.1. 56K digital modem connection.

Source:-https://www.pctechguide.com/serial-communications/56kbps-modems.

4.3.1. Evolution of the 56k Digital Modem

A proposal was submitted by 3com which is a telecommunications company to the UTI calling for the 56k recommendation in September 1996. In April 1997, the ITU officially set up a rapporteur's group with the objective of finding out about the 56k standard technology. A meeting in Orlando in December 5th 1997, the working party agreed to a compromise on the two remaining technical issues virtually assuring a standard determination at the meeting in 1990 January. Eventually the standard specifications of the 56k was determined in Geneva, Switzerland, and it was officially given its series number that is the V. 90. The technicalities of the 56k standard modem was therefore determined but there was room for editing. The ITU finally completed the formalities at which time they determined 56K recommendation becomes a decision which is also referred to as ratification. This happened in September 1998.

4.3.2. Technology behind the Design of 56k Modem

In order to comprehend how the technology behind the design of 56k came about, it is important to see how the traditional analog modem worked. Normally, data inside a computer is in digital format that means data is stored in a computer language which consists of ones and zeros (1s and 0s). Telephone lines are analog in nature meaning they transfer information in a series of peaks and valleys. Because of this transition in digital and analog format, the modem modulates outgoing data from a digital format to an analog format and once the data is received on the other end, the modem from the other end demodulates the analog data into a digital format. Due to the limiting factor in the rate of data transmission in analog phone lines, there was the inherent noise which was being caused by the Shannon's limit. The connection system between the internet service provider (ISP) and the phone company he has become increasingly digital. Even though there has been an increase in digitization, the Shannon's limit is still a limiting factor though it has been greatly reduced and therefore there is less noise during communication. Because of the increased digitization companies have taken opportunity of this system to achieve higher speeds that were originally achievable using the analog pathway. The use of this technique utilizes a large portion of the digital network that just happens to have an analog portion. In order to rely on the half digital connection, your ISP must be able to provide digital phone lines to the public switched telephone network. (PSTN). If your ISP have the 56k technology, then they already have digital lines. The 56k modem technology has been optimized in performance and can be used in processors such as TI, Intel, ADI, ARM, and other vendors. The 56k modem has a stand-alone license although it can be customized to meet specific requirements (Carne, 2004).

4.3.3. Features of the 56k Digital Modem

- It is compatible for a multitasking environment;
- It is compliant with draught upgrades as recommendations are approved;
- Supports modem MIB (RFC 1696); and
- Outlines 22 modulation rates in a range of 28,000 bits per second to 56,000 bits per second in increments of 1/3 to 1 kilobytes per second.

4.3.4. Advantages of the 56k Technology

- Normal telephone lines can still be utilized;
- Updates are available just like the other existing modems;
- The maximum download speed is 56 kilobits bits per second; and
- The maximum upload speed is 33.6 kilobits per second.

4.3.5. Disadvantages of the 56k Technology

- The still exist challenges of interference; and
- Telephone charges still apply.

4.4. ALTERNATIVES TO TRADITIONAL MODEMS

4.4.1. Channel Service Unit/ Data Service Unit (CSU/DSU)

This is a digital communication device that mingles the functions of both data service unit and channel service unit. At the demarcation point, that is where the device lies between the telephone company and network and the customer network. The CSU/DSU acts as a local interference between the data terminal equipment (DTE) at the customer's premises and the telecommunication digital communication line like the T1 line.

How the channel service unit/data service unit operates: The CSU/DSU is the counterpart to analog modems as it possesses the same functionality. They have the same similarity as external modems. The CSU/DSU comes in different sizes that can be installed in rack. Because the signals from both ends of the CSU/DSU is digital, there is no need of converting the signals from a digital form to analog form then converting it back to a digital form but it converts the digital data into a format that is suitable for a specific digital transmission line being serviced. The digital signals are then buffered and an acceptable rate is adapted to and from the telephone company network. The CSU/DSU provides a barrier that protects a customer premise equipment from electrical disturbances. It also enables data frames to be properly formulated and timed for the telephone company network (Quirke, 2000).

CSU/DSU: Once the digital lines have arrived at the customer premises, they are terminated with four wire connections having various connector types which include; RJ-45, four-sided terminal blocks and M-Block connectors which is specifically used for V.35 interfaces. Using the CSU/DSU, the four wire connections are properly directed to the appropriate connector by appropriately adjusting itself to the line speed of the digital data service line (DDS). The autosensing feature is the one that helps in the adjustments. From the customer's premise, the CSU/DSU is then connected directly to the router and afterwards the connection is then extended to the customer's network. A similar CSU/DSU is found at the central office at the end of the CVD line which is used to feed into the carrier backbone network. The name CSU/DSU was made to become a generic expression that shows the device that connects the device responsible for managing the interface with the DTA in the telecommunication network.

4.4.2. Cable Modems

This is a peripheral device that is used in the connection of a computer to the internet. It functions on coax line cables which provide high rates in internet access. Cable modem have been branded as broadband devices due to the fact that they provide a continuous connection to the internet and a high-speed data transmission rate. Dial-up modems which were initially being used during the first inventions of modem was used to provide data transmission rates of 56 kilobits per second but cable modems and DSLs were invented and they replaced dial-up modems because they provided fast internet access. The first cable modems to be invented provided download and upload speeds of up to 3 megabits per second. This was 60 times faster than the speed being provided by the dial-up modems. Currently, the standard modem is being manufactured have the capability of transmitting data up to 50 megabits per second. Other companies such as Comcast provide modems with speeds of up to 505 megabits per second. Cable modems ethernet ports are connected to the computer or routers using the standard RJ45 Port. Due to the current technological advancements, cable modems are directly connected to a home router which enables multiple devices to access the internet at the same time. Other cable modems come with an already installed wireless router and this implies there is no need of a second device. Cable modems work differently compared to the traditional models which was being used to modulate and demodulate signals (Quirke, 2000). This is because cable modems deal with digital data and it works by sending and receiving data digitally. Below is an example of a Motorola cable modem.

4.4.3. ISDN Modem

The integrated services digital network (ISDN) is a digital telephone network connection that has the capability of transmitting information, voice, and video through a normal telephone line. When the ISDN was created, it was meant to tackle the challenge of transmitting information by providing a faster way of transferring information. Although phone companies beat the modem manufacturers in their own game and designed devices that transmit information quickly, the ISDN lost its functionality. Businesses that are involved in high traffic data transmission still use the ISDN to simultaneously send information and make calls.

Benefits of ISDN: Businesses should consider carefully what type of ISDN modem to purchase. This is because they might get expensive due to their capabilities of transmitting data at fast rates and at the same time making phone calls. But due to its superiority, most businesses don't mind making use of the ISDN.

- The ISDN has a quicker dial up rate compared to analog phones as it can take a maximum of 3 seconds to connect with another computer.
- Because of its digital nature, it has the ability of consistently providing data at a rate of 64 kilobits per second.
- It is multi-modal in nature meaning that one route has the ability of transmitting data, voice, and video at the same time.

Because there are many models of ISDN in the market, businesses find it challenging to determine the best type of modem to be used in their businesses but generally, all businesses agree that the usage of ISDN in businesses is an advantage rather than a disadvantage when it comes to costs.

There are numerous features that businesses need to look for when selecting the best kind of ISDN model to purchase. The first factor is the speed of data transmission. Most ISDN use hi/fn compression in data transmission, however, a modem that have the ability of using Microsoft (MS) compression have the capability of transferring more data per second making it a preferable choice for businesses. Another factor to consider is the number of ports being provided. The larger the modem, the higher number of ports. Higher number of ports lead to lower data transmission. Hence if a business does not require many ports, it is advisable to purchase a modem with fewer ports in order to maintain fast data transmission. If a business has a modem with unnecessarily high speed, it is worth trying a larger modem with more ports. A smaller modem might contain one digital port and two analog ports (Quirke, 2000).

The third factor to consider is the amount of processes that the modem can handle at the same time. For instance, if a printer and a phone call are being used at the same time when another call comes in, the modem can be able to accommodate all the functions. Once the printer and the phone call have been completed, the speed of data transmission will increase. However, some modern do not have the automatic switch feature. Lastly, businesses should consider the type of warranty attached to the ISDN modem. The duration of warranty in most modems is up to 4 years.

4.4.4. DSL Modems

The digital subscriber line (DSL) is a digital device to connect a PC or a router to a phone line. The digital modem provides a digital subscriber line service. The digital subscriber line modem usually operates by connecting a computers PCl slot to a single computer via an Ethernet and USB port or it can be installed. A common digital subscriber line that is being used is used to combine the operations of a digital subscriber line modem and a router enabling multiple computers to be connected to the internet through an ethernet port or an integral wireless access point. The wireless access point is also known as residential gateway. It manages the connection and sharing of the digital subscriber line.

4.5. HIGH-SPEED INTERFACE PROTOCOLS

An interface is defined as a common boundary between two objects. It is a differential emitter-couples logic (ECL) used in WAN router connections. The standard form of this interface is designed by Cisco Systems and T3plus networking. Due to the fact that consumers have a familiarity with how elements act, it is important that predictability and consistency is maintained when designing interfaces. There are four components of interface standards. They include:

- Input controls, such as list boxes, drop down menus, toggles, buttons, and radio buttons.
- Navigational components, such as slider, tags, icons, and search fields.
- Informative components, such as tool tips, notifications, and progress bar.
- Containers, such as accordion.

The EIA-232F interface standard has been in existence for many years. Although, due to technological advancements, its features have been complex to design and difficult to support. in 1962, it was designed with the aim of standardizing the interface between DTE and data communication equipment. It was commonly used by Industries as it was a low-cost serial interface between DTE and peripherals. The EIA-232 standard ensured there was compatible voltage and signal levels, common pin-writing configurations and minimum amount of control information between the DTE and DC. It Incorporated the following features;

- Electrical and signal features – in terms of signal voltage levels, rates of change and impedance, transmitted data had electrical and signal characteristics.
- Mechanical interface features – houses both female and male connection pins.
- Handshake information – a fully interlocked handshake exchange of data between equipment at opposite ends of the communication channel was enabled at the interchange circuit.

4.5.1. Fire Wire

Fire wire also known as IEEE 1E94, is a method used to transfer data between digital devices. Equipment used to transfer audio and video, utilize this method. It is a fast method of transmitting data as speeds reach up to 800 megabits per second. FireWire has the ability of connecting up to 63 devices and it is presumed that in the future speeds of up to 3.2 gigabits per second will be attainable. Windows OS and Mac OS support fire wire. Due to the fast speed of data transfer used in FireWire, it has enabled many multimedia functions such as non-linear video presentation and editing, document imaging desktop and commercial publishing and home multimedia such as personal computing. FireWire has low overhead costs. It has it has the ability to combine asynchronous data and real-time data in one connection and finally, it has the ability of mixing high-speed and low-speed devices on the same network. This provides a strong universal connection among computers and consumers worldwide (Dhotre and Bagad, 2008).

4.5.2. Universal Serial Bus

Universal serial bus (USB) is a plug-and-play interface that enables the computer to communicate with peripheral devices. There is a broad range of devices that can be connected with the computer using a USB. Such devices include a keyboard, mouse, flash disks and memory cards. In 1996 the first version of the USB was commercially released to the market. All current computers contain a USB Port. Laptops, desktops, tablets, and smartphones are examples of the devices that contain a USB. USB comes in varying shapes and sizes. The common types of USB include mini-USB, MICRO-USB, and USB Type-C. The mini-USB has been greatly replaced by the USB type-c and the micro USB. The USB 1. X has the capability of transferring data at rate of 12 megabits per second and can support 127 peripheral devices. The USB 2.0 has the capability of transferring data at rates of 480 megabits per second or 60 megabytes per second. The USB 3.0 also known as super speed USB, has an improved performance when compared to the earlier versions as it has an improved bandwidth capability and power management. It supports data transfer rates of 5 gigabits per second. The USB 3.1 is capable of transferring data at rates of 10 gigabits-per-second.

USB has the ability to support versions below or above its current number that is, it is capable of Supporting forward and backward compatibility. Although, older versions only transfer data at their specified rates whereas advanced versions transfer data at their specified transfer rates. The maximum length of high-speed devices is 5 m and 3 m for low-speed devices. Longer cable lengths can lead to data loss and therefore the regulated data lengths enable preferred transfer timing. However, USB lengths can effectively be different extended by using USB hubs. One is able to get different USB cables in the market for different USB speeds (Dhotre and Bagad, 2008).

4.6. DATA LINK CONNECTIONS

4.6.1. Asynchronous Connections

Asynchronous connection uses hardware flow control or software flow control to control the data being transmitted. Asynchronous connection is formed over private and public telephone networks or null modem links to issue temporary connection between two deadlines. Charges incurred in connection is related to the distance between the deadlines and the duration of the phone call. Transient network traffic is suitably used when using asynchronous connection.

You will find that asynchronous connection is used when communicating through mobile, teleworking, and when accessing internet services temporarily. In order to create an asynchronous creation, an installation of an asynchronous serial interface in the host machine and a modem which represents the interface between the host machine and the analog telephone network is established.

The modems situated at every deadline communicates to establish a phone call during the connection stage. More modems can be installed in the asynchronous connection through the modification of the database file in the modems. This can be done provided that the modems have software that support the installation (Carne, 2004).

4.6.2. Synchronous Connections

Synchronous connection uses independent clocking signals to synchronize the data transmission. During establishment, they use dedicated leased line. Unlike asynchronous connection, synchronous connection provides a permanent connection between the deadlines. Charges depend on the duration to which you leased the connection.

This means that the quantity of data transmitted is an independent variable to the cost incurred. Organizations prefer synchronous connections when it comes to bulk transfers of information as it enables for continuous data traffic through the use of LAN to LAN interconnectivity. Synchronous connection is established through the synchronous serial interface installed in the Host machine.

Because asynchronous connection is formed when solstice PPP is started, there is no independence in terms of connection during the connection stage.

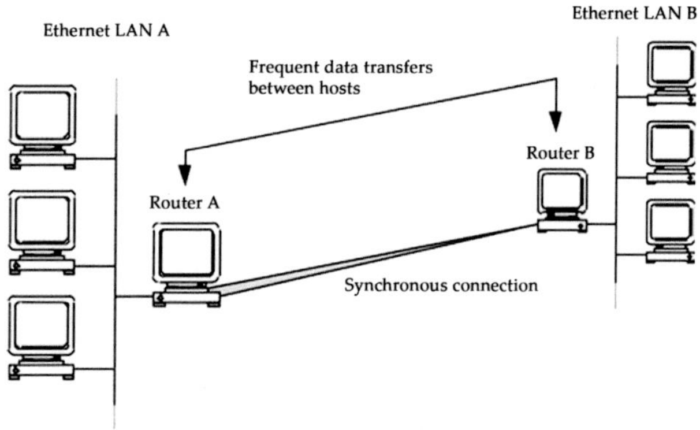

Figure 4.2. Synchronous connection between LANs.

Source: https://docs.oracle.com/cd/E19096–01/sol.ppp301/805–4018/pppintro-4/index.html.

4.6.3. Half Duplex, Full-duplex, and Simplex Connections

These are the three modes of transmission referring to the direction in which a signal flows between two connected devices.

Regarding the direction of communication, the simplex mode is unidirectional, the half-duplex mode is two-directional mode where processes happen one at a time, and full-duplex mode is simultaneous (Dhotre and Bagad, 2008).

When sending or receiving data, in simplex mode the sender can only send data but cannot receive data back. In half-duplex mode the sender can send data and receive data through multiple separate processes. In full-duplex mode the sender can send and receive data simultaneously.

In terms of performance, the simplex mode is the worst performing mode, the half-duplex is slightly better than the simplex mode and the full-duplex mode has the best performance during transmission when compared to the others (Carne, 2004).

An example of a device that uses a simplex transmission mode is a keyboard. A walkie-talkie uses the half-duplex transmission mode and a smartphone uses the full-duplex transmission mode.

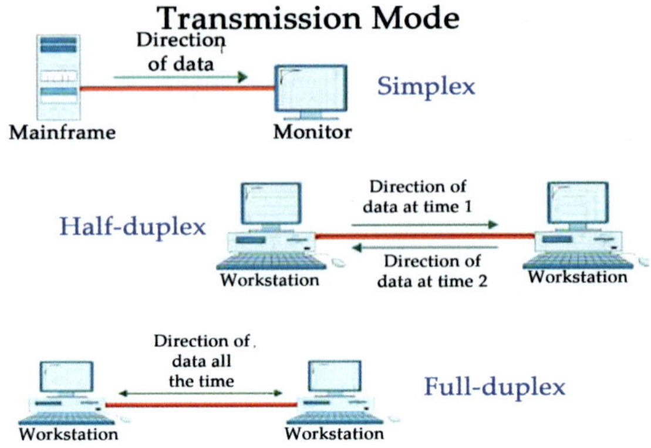

Figure 4.3. Simple, half-duplex and full-duplex transmission mode.

Source: http://hafizahabdullah.blogspot.com/2013/08/fp303-cn-simplex-half-duplex-and-full.html.

Terminal-to-mainframe computer connections enables a direct and shared connection between the terminal and the mainframe computer. This makes it a superior form of connection compared to other forms of connection. Multiple terminals are able to share the same connection with only one mainframe computer. The mainframe is the primary device whereas terminals are secondary devices. Polling by the mainframe needs to occur in order to allow the transmission of data by the terminal to the mainframe. Hub polling and roll call polling are the two fundamental modes of polling. When using the roll-call polling, the mainframe polls each terminal in a round-robin (RR) fashion. For instance, if there are terminals X, Y, and Z which are sharing the same connection, polling begins at terminal X and if X has some data, it will transmit it to terminal Y. After transmission, terminal X stops becoming the primary and the primary is transferred to Y. If terminal Y has nothing to transmit, it will communicate to the primary and it will poll the primary to terminal Z. Once terminals Z has completed transmitting data, the cycle begins at terminal X to proceed with the polling process. When using hub polling, the mainframe polls the first terminal and this terminal passes the poll onto the next terminal. For instance, when terminal X has completed transmitting data, it stops being the primary and terminal Y is polled and once terminal Y has completed transmitting data, it stops becoming the primary and terminal Z is polled and this process is continuous.

CHAPTER

5

Multiplexing

CONTENTS

5.1. INTRODUCTION

The need for sharing information with each other is greatly increasing. It has been propelled by many communication and social media platforms. As more information needs to be distributed, the more the demand of having a more efficient and fast way of sharing it. Multiplexing has been invented to provide a fast way of passing information from source to destination. It mainly deals with transmission of multiple data signals by combining them together into a single data signal. Multiplexing divides a single large medium into several small medium channels through which each single data signal among the multiple is to be transmitted from source to destination. At the destination, the combined data signals are separated into individual data signals.

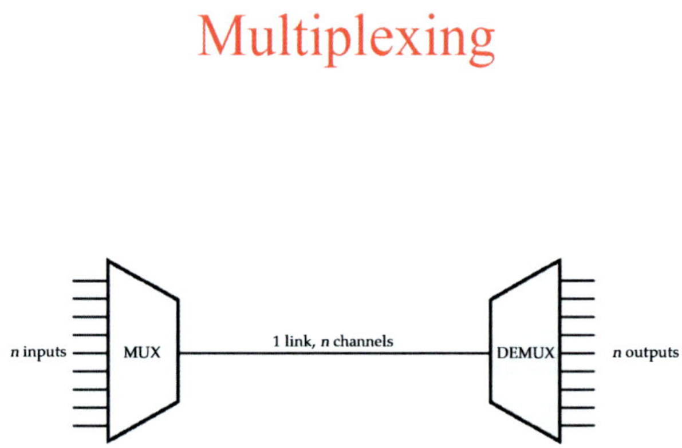

Figure 5.1. Illustration of the multiplexing process.

Source: https://slideplayer.com/slide/8689145/.

5.2. INVENTION OF MULTIPLEXING

Multiplexing was invented for the purposes of telephone communications to allow multiple telephone calls to be carried out through a single wire. Telephone carrier multiplexing which was invented by George Owen, ensured that multiple data signals transmitted via the telephone reached their destination within the shortest time possible.

The combined data signals are sent through a transmission media such as a simple cable. The transmission medium is basically divided into multiple logical channels through which each data signal is transmitted.

For multiplexing process to be conducted, a special equipment referred to as a Multiplexer is required to carry out the task of combining multiple data signals into a single set of data signals.

A multiplexer divides a single media into several transmission channels for each data signal to be transmitted from source to destination (Jiang, 2018).

5.3. TYPES OF MULTIPLEXING

There are two main types of multiplexers used for multiplexing purposes. They include analog multiplexers and digital multiplexers.

Analog multiplexers earned their name for combine multiple analog signals into a single analog signal for the purposes of transmission from source to destination via small logical channels in a single large medium.

The analog signals are combined according to their processing speed and wavelength.The analog multiplexers are further divided into several sub-divisions.

The frequency division multiplexing uses different processing speeds of data signals so as to combine them and to be able to come up with a single stream of data, to be sent via a communication medium from source to destination.

It allows multiple users to access and share a single physical transmission medium to transmit data from different sources to different destinations. Dense wavelength division multiplexing simply determines the different wavelengths of different data signals and combines them for the purposes of transmission from source to destination.

Increase in wavelength of data signals does lead to decrease in the frequency rate of a data signal which in turn reduces the processing speeds of different data signal modules (Jiang, 2018).

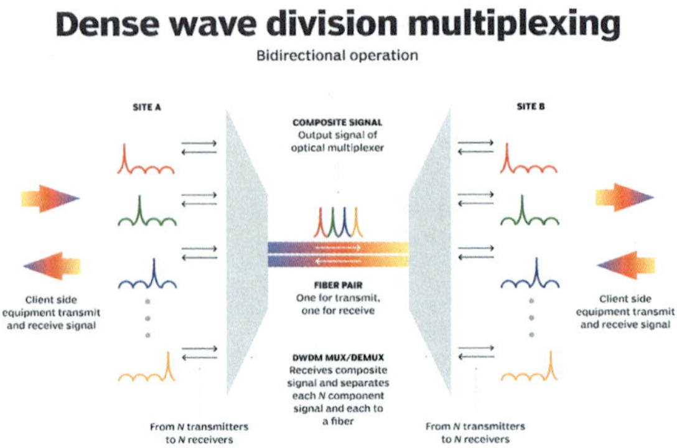

Figure 5.2. Illustration of the dense wavelength division multiplexing technique.

Source: https://searchnetworking. techtarget. com/definition/dense-wavelength-division-multiplexing-DWDM.

The second main type of Multiplexing is the digital multiplexing. These multiplexers earned their name because they are a set of different data packets which are discrete and since digital devices are mainly composed of components which are discrete in nature, hence the name digital multiplexers. They are further subdivided into different subdivisions.

Time-division multiplexing uses the technique of time division. The required time frame for multiple data signals to be transmitted from source to destination is divided into different slots. Each time slot is used to transmit data signal from source to destination via a single transmission medium. It is further categorized into several categories.

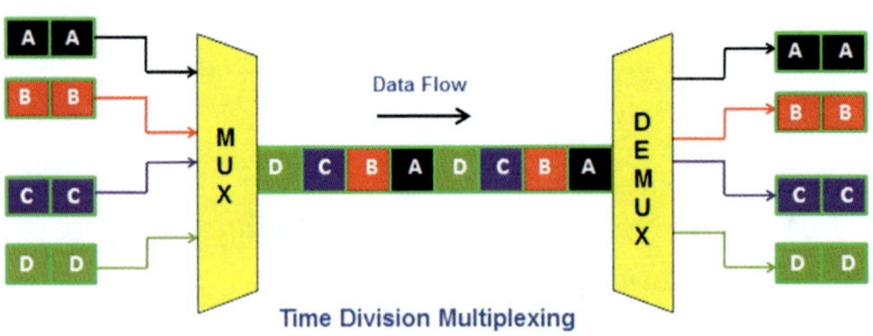

Figure 5.3. Illustration of the time-division multiplexing.

Source: http://www.physics-and-radio-electronics.com/blog/multiplexing/.

The first category is the Synchronous time-division multiplexing. In this category, the data signal input source is connected to a time frame. Based on the number of input source connections to the time frame, different slots are created such that each data signal from one input source is being transmitted via a single time slot. This technique ensures that the sampling rate for different data signals is the same and that the same transmission rate is being applied to each transmission medium at all times (White, 2015).

Asynchronous time-division multiplexing is the second category which does not use the number of data input sources to divide the time frame into different slots. A common clock is not required for each time slot is not allocated to a specific data source hence any slot can be allocated to any data input source so long as it is not transmitting any data signal.

Integrated Service Digital Network (ISDN) multiplexing which is the third category of time-division multiplexing is a set consisting of all transmission requirements for sending and receiving voice, video, data, and other network services all at the same time via ordinary telephone copper wires. Multiple devices, more so telephone devices, can be attached to a single copper wire for the purposes of transmission for ISDN does support a large bandwidth (White, 2015).

The fourth category is the Transmission 1 multiplexing famously known as the T1 which refers to a type of data transmission medium that relies on division of time frame into different slots for transmission of data signals across private point-to-point connections of different computers that have been set up and interconnected to provide a common way of sharing information across multiple locations and allow access to the internet.

Synchronous Optical Network (SONET) Multiplexing famously known as SONET Multiplexing is the fifth category of time-division multiplexing. It involves use of laser beams and a single clock for handling timing, control, and the functionality of different transmission devices. SONET multiplexing combines different data signals into corresponding Optical signal for transmission from source to destination.

The sixth and the last category of time-division multiplexing is statistical multiplexing. It divides a communication medium into multiple logical channels randomly without any pre-assigned specific criteria. The number of bits or data signals conveyed via the channels keep on changing with every transmission.The last type of digital multiplexing is the Code Division Multiplexing. It combines multiple data signals into a single data signal for the purposes of transmission via a common transmission medium which transmits data based on its processing speed from source to destination. It can also be referred to as Code Division Multiple access once it allows multiple users to share a single communication channel.

5.4. CHARACTERISTICS OF MULTIPLEXING CATEGORIES

5.4.1. Frequency Division Multiplexing

In this type of multiplexing, the combined multiple signals are transmitted all at the same time from source to destination. Between each signal, there is a suitable gap so as to increase the processing speeds during transmissions for if the space is quite large, the transmission rate will be slow and if the space is small, the transmission will increase. The transmission medium is divided into several logic channels which are determined by the frequency of each data signals such that each data signal is transmitted via a specific channel.

5.4.2. Dense Wavelength Division Multiplexing

Involves the process of combining different data signals onto a single fiber with the same wavelength for the purposes of transmission. The signals are transmitted via a transmission medium divided into different optical channels which aid in transmissions use of light wavelength through a parallel technique of transmission from source to destination.

5.4.3. Time Division Multiplexing

In time-division multiplexing, data signals which are being transmitted through a medium at a high rate compared to their generation rate from the source are allocated a definite slot of time in the time frame. The slots are quite small such that the transmissions of different data signals seem to be parallel to each other.

5.4.4. Synchronous Time Division Multiplexing

For this type of time-division multiplexing, the slots are assigned to different input sources of data signals even before the transmission process is initiated. Once a certain input source is allocated a slot, that slots remain fixed to it throughout all transmission processes to be carried out.

5.4.5. Asynchronous Time Division Multiplexing

The time slots are allocated randomly to different data signals sources depending on the rate at which they are being generated from the source. This saves the channel capacity of transmitting data, for a certain input source is not fixed to only one-time slot channel.

5.4.6. Integrated Service Digital Network Multiplexing

It is more of a circuit-switched telephone interconnection of different computers deigned to allow transmission of mainly voice and data signals over normal telephone copper wires which results in transmission of quality voice. ISDN does also offer a platform for transmission of data signals via a transmission medium. Multiple devices can be connected to a single transmission medium which makes use of the ISDN multiplexing technique for the purposes of transmission of multiple data signals from different sources to different destination. The multiple data signals are all combined into a single large data signals which are transmitted via a large transmission medium divided into logical channels. At the destination, the combined data signals are separated into original individual data signals through the process of demultiplexing. The entry level access to ISDN multiplexing is referred to as the Basic Rate Interface which is a service availed via a pair of standard copper wires. The Basic Rate Interface is used to specify different network interfaces which include:

The U interface is a two-wire connection point between the source and the destination for data signals. The T interface is a continuous connection point or device between a computing device which mainly acts as the source and a terminal adapter which connects to the destination. It mainly acts as the digital equivalent of a modem. S interface is a four-wire pathway for data signals that a user making use of the ISDN multiplexing technique uses to plug a device into. The last network interface is the R connection point which defines the point between a non-ISDN source device and a terminal adapter which connects to the destination and provides translation of various data signals which are being transmitted from source to destination.

5.4.7. T-1 Multiplexing

T-1 Multiplexing is basically a physical requirement for carrying out different combination of a multiple set of data signals which is transmitted via a single four-wire transmission medium which has been divided into different time frame slots. They mostly used the twisted pair copper wired cables as the main transmission medium which is further allocated different time frame slot channels. This type of cables employs one pair for sending and one pair for receiving information. Signal repeaters are used in between the transmission distance so as to clean and boost the data signals being transmitted from source to destination to avoid delivering data whose content has been distorted or data with a low attenuation rate.

5.4.8. SONET Multiplexing

SONET Multiplexing is basically an optical-based transmission medium connecting different computers. It combines different data signals into a single optical signal which is transmitted at a very high speed from source to destination. The different communicating nodes in a SONET network are connected to each other under a very accurate timing technique that ensures data is delivered within the specific allocated time to its destination without any distortion or with low attenuation rates.

In cases of any errors occurring during transmission, SONET multiplexers have the capability of reversing the transmission process back to its source to avoid any data signal loss from taking place. This makes the SONET multiplexing technique more reliable.

SONET multiplexers do also make use of simple but powerful multiplexing and demultiplexing techniques during transmission of data signals from source to destination. SONET multiplexing transmissions are immune to noise and other damages which occur to different communication channels.

5.4.9. Statistical Multiplexing

Statistical Multiplexing is facilitated mainly through packet-oriented transmission techniques which mostly make use of the packet-switched interconnected computers.

The transmission medium is divided randomly into different streams of channels without having to follow a certain criterion. The logical channels which have mostly been divided randomly according to different time slots are assigned to specific data signals for transmission purposes depending on the rate at which the data signals are generated from the source. Statistical Multiplexing mainly operates based on the technique of the rate of demand for a transmission medium rather than having a certain logical channel being fixed to a specific data signal input source.

5.4.10. Code Division Multiplexing

Code Division Multiplexing does make use of the technique for combining data signals based on their frequency rate. In this type of transmissions, a single data signal is composed of different sub-elements of data signals with varying processing speeds. This type of multiplexing is less susceptible to interference since its combination of multiple data signals results to a strong single data signal hence providing a better way of communicating data signals from source computer device to the destination device. It allows multiple data signals from multiple users to be transmitted via a common transmission medium. In this mode of transmission where multiple users share a common transmission medium, each set of multiple signals is encoded in a specific discrete sequence such that only end-users at the destination point with a specific decoding code can access a specific set of data signals. These sequences assigned to different data signals are carefully generated codes commonly referred to as chip sequences for they hold properties which allow sharing of information to take place.

5.5. APPLICATION AREAS OF MULTIPLEXING TECHNIQUES

5.5.1. Frequency Division Multiplexing

This technique of multiplexing is mainly sued in television networks for transmission of data signals from source to destination depending on the frequency of data signal being transmitted.

It is used in television networks for it transmits data signals by broadcasting them from source to destination. At the source the data signals are converted into an analog format which is continuous in nature and transmitted via the transmission medium. At the destination, the data signals are then converted from the continuous format to a digital format through a process referred to as demodulation.

Frequency Division multiplexing can also be used in the transmission of radio waves or signals from the radio station to the radio device.

The multiple signals from the source which is the radio station are combined and transmitted via a transmission medium, the air, which is divided into multiple logical channels based on the frequencies of the different combined signals to their destination which is the device airing a specific radio frequency channel (Jiang, 2018).

The first-generation cellular phones utilized the frequency division multiplexing. This is because, cellular communication is composed of two devices, the receiving end, receiver, and the calling end, the transmitter. Once the signals to be transmitted have been combined and transmission via the frequency-based logical channels has been initiated, they are converted into an analog format and then at the receiving end, they are converted back into digital format by removing the carrier signal to be left with only the original signal to be communicated.

Most frequency division multiplexed transmission are carried out either through the coaxial cables or the fiber optic cables for they are immune to electromagnetic interference and have a high bandwidth rate avoiding the risk of transmitting signals with low attenuation (Jiang, 2018).

5.5.2. Dense Wavelength Multiplexing

This technique of multiplexing is trending mostly in large organization which comprise of a collection of entities connected together to perform a specific goal. They are being used to curb the practical problem of cable frequent damage or exhaust due to transmission of large amounts of data signals. Dense Wavelength multiplexing does offer a new way of having an ever-reliable transmission medium which has services of recovering data in case of any loss at the physical layer during transmission. It allows data signals to travel for earlier thought to be impossible distances initiating the death of distance as a problem during transmission of data signals from one point to another.

Dense wavelength multiplexing allows for fast transmission of data signals via a transmission medium mostly set up in optical networks. This is because the combining of different data signals is based on the fact that data signals with the same gap in between them (wavelength) are all combined together into a fiber optic cable through the light technology of refraction and then transmitted to their destination depending on the different wavelengths of the combined data signals.

5.5.3. Time Division Multiplexing

The main application of the time division multiplexing technique is the offering of a common means of sharing access to commonly used transmission mediums across multiple users with multiple signals which need to be shared via a common medium and at a fast way from source to destination.

5.5.4. Synchronous Time Division Multiplexing

They are the basic transmission technique in many networks. This is because they connect data traffic from end receiver to end transmitter where the number of signals being transmitted is maintained at a constant speed. They also provide high levels of data recovery in this network for the logical channels of the transmission medium in between the receiver and transmitter are strictly fixed reducing the risk of data loss in any way.

5.5.5. Asynchronous Time Division Multiplexing

Asynchronous time division multiplexing is used in networks which need to interconnect different devices with different speeds. For example, interconnection of two devices whose speeds vary might be an issue while transmitting multiple combined signals from source to destination for their speed vary. But with asynchronous multiplexing, one can combine signals which are being generated at a lower rate from multiple sources with signals which are being generated at a higher rate from their source to come up with a single multiplexed signal. This is made possible because, during transmission, time slots on the logical channels are allocated randomly based on which data signal is on high demand.

5.5.6. Integrated Service Digital Network Multiplexing

Most Integrated Service Network multiplexing techniques are used in the combination of signals being transmitted via interconnected computers which have been setup to communicate using the Open Systems Interconnection model. This is because it combines voice signals and data signals to be transmitted via the same transmission medium in different logical channels without having any transmission problems due to the combination. It does allow combination of different communication rules to govern its transmission for itself it is a combination of different signal types which require different rules to govern their transmission.

In videoconferencing, this multiplexing technique is used widely for its special features of combining different signals types to be transmitted via the same transmission media all at the same time. It does use special coding technique to create different data signals in a way that will not be prone to any transmission complication such as mixing of signals different components. This ensures that at the receiving end, it will not be difficult to separate the signals.

5.5.7. Transmission System 1 Multiplexing Technique

Transmission System 1 multiplexing technique is mostly used for the transmission of signals directly from one computer device to another by broadcasting method via a network which has mostly interconnected different devices using telephone copper wires or the famous twisted pair copper wires. Signal Repeater stations tend to be placed in between the transmission distance if the distance separating the two communicating nodes is quite large.

This repeater station receives a signal from either the transmitting node or the receiving node depending on the direction the signal is traveling in, cleans it using special techniques to remove any type of distortions whatsoever, boosts it to a higher attenuation rate and then transmits it to its final destination. This ensures that information is communicated in the most effective way possible without having any connection problems (Jiang, 2018).

5.5.8. Synchronous Optical Network Multiplexing

Synchronous Optical Networking multiplexing technique is being widely used nowadays by telecommunication companies. It utilizes light technology to combine a set of multiple signals into one large signal which is also later transmitted via the logical channels of a transmission medium by use of the same light technology. They also use time frame slots which ensures that signal transmission is firmly fixed to a specific data input signal source. The SONET multiplexers which carry out the combination of signals into a single signal for the purposes of transmission do offer the redundancy of data service which ensures that incase one optical path, the next path which has the same data as the current failed path will be able to deliver the whole data signal to its destination in good condition.

5.5.9. Statistical Multiplexing

This type of multiplexing is used to allow video, audio, and data signals of different processing speeds to be transmitted via the same transmission medium in a logical channel. In this multiplexing technique each channel has a specific identification number, commonly referred to as the program identification number (PID). The number of signals being transmitted via this channel is limited most of the times such that, each logical channel transmits a specific number of signals and it cannot surpass its limit.

5.5.10. Code Division Multiplexing

Code Division Multiple Access is mostly used as the main access method in many mobile phone devices. It allows access to a single transmission medium to several users transmitting different sets of multiple signals all at the same time from source to destination. For example, in an auditorium filled with lots of people and most of them are trying to communicate using their phones either by sending messages or making phone calls, most of their signals use the same transmission medium availed to them to reach their destination.

5.6. ADVANTAGES AND DISADVANTAGES OF DIFFERENT MULTIPLEXING TECHNIQUES

5.6.1. Frequency Division Multiplexing

Advantages: Frequency Division Multiplexing does not need to set up time frame slots between its receiving and transmitting end in order to make transmission process effective. With this multiplexing technique a large number of multiple signals can all be sent at the same time. The separation of the combined signals at the receiving end is easy and does not require too much effort for signals to be returned to their original setting.

Disadvantages: Most of the Frequency Division Multiplexing logical channels in a transmission medium are affected by the high rates of attenuation. This happens because of the distance between the two communicating computing devices. A large number of devices for converting digital signals to analog signals is required so that frequency division multiplexing sends multiple number of signals all at the same time. The logical channels must be able to support a large number of signals being transmitted all at the same time. This type of multiplexing suffers from high rates of electromagnetic interference and intermodulation errors.

5.6.2. Dense Wavelength Multiplexing

Advantages: This multiplexing technique does offer fair combination processes hence it can support many signal formats. Dense Wavelength multiplexing is scalable and can reduce the costs of setting up its multiplexer components. It provides users with a simple way of accessing the network which enables them to send information with ease.

Disadvantages: Dense wavelength multiplexing is not cost-effective because it offers few logical channels for transmission of signals from source to destination. It does mostly use very complex transmitting devices and receiving devices for the propagation of signals. The main disadvantage of this multiplexing technique is that, as the wavelength of the signals increases, the transmission rate does decrease.

5.6.3. Time Division Multiplexing

General Advantages: Time Division multiplexing techniques are more flexible for their setup is not that complex. It rarely does suffer from electromagnetic interference problems. The logical channels in the transmission medium do not have a limit to the number of signals to be transmitted.

General Disadvantages: The setting up of frame time slots in time division multiplexing technique is a kind of a complex process and time consuming.

5.6.4. Synchronous Multiplexing

Advantages: It is easy and simple to setup the synchronous time division multiplexing technique and also encouraging for they do guarantee the users with maximum rates of performance.

Disadvantages: Time slots in logical channels of a transmission medium may be wasted if the user does not send any data signals through them.

5.6.5. Asynchronous Multiplexing

Advantages: Asynchronous time division multiplexing technique ensures that it utilizes the transmission capacity provided by the logical channels in the transmission medium.

Disadvantages: It is difficult to guarantee that the transmission process will be complete and effective.

5.6.6. Integrated Service Digital Network Multiplexing

Advantages: Integrated service digital network multiplexing technique does present the user with multiple logic channels of the same transmission medium which can send multiple signals from source to destination all at the same time. The number of signals to be transmitted by this technique is limitless. ISDN multiplexing does take the shortest time possible to launch a connection between the transmitting device and the receiving device.

Disadvantages: This multiplexing technique is costly to set up because it requires specialized digital devices to operate efficiently and effectively.

5.6.7. Transmission System 1 Multiplexing Technique

Advantages: The main advantage of Transmission System 1 multiplexing technique is the fact that it limits its access to outsiders are not within the set range of users. During setup, it can be set to only offer a certain bandwidth to its users to avoid its wastage. The multiplexing services offered by T-1 multiplexers are all time hence not limiting its users to only a specific access time.

Disadvantages; It is really costly to setup a network using Transmission System 1 multiplexing technique because it requires complex and expensive equipment for its operations. Turmoil does mostly occur during the purchase of transmission system 1 multiplexers for some of them allow transmission of only one signal at time through the transmission medium while others offer transmission of several signals from source to destination all at the same time. This emphasizes the fact that a user should be very careful when selecting the type of transmission system 1 multiplexer to purchase depending on their transmission needs.

5.6.8. Synchronous Optical Network Multiplexing

Advantages: This technique of multiplexing does reduce the cost of operation because it does offer high network surveillance features to its end users. It can be setup in any type of network hence it is quite flexible. The rate of operation is high for it allows transmission of all forms of signals. The separation of the combined signals at the receiving end is quite easy and less complicated. It can be operated remotely from any location hence no need of being physically available at its multiplexer location during the combining of different signals for transmission from source to destination.

Disadvantages: With SONET multiplexing technique, there is no standard for its multiplexer to operate well with other devices. The cost for setting up multiple logic channels in a transmission medium is quite high. The interconnected devices are not well equipped most of the times with appropriate resources for its effective operation for its complete setup cost is quite expensive. The number of data signals to be transmitted via a specific transmission medium per specific duration of time is not completely set hence its varying number every now and then might be a problem to its operation.

5.6.9. Statistical Multiplexing

Advantages: With statistical time division multiplexing technique, there is no specific division of time frames into slots for the transmission of data signals hence transmission is carried out one demand. This does also make it to be a more cost-effective methodDisadvantages: The transmission of data signals in statistical time division multiplexing technique can be quite slow. For example, in periods when the rate of transmission for data signals is quite high, data signals fight for their entry into the transmission medium slowing down the whole transmission process.

5.6.10. Code Division Multiplexing Technique

Advantages: The code division multiplexing technique does not require any time slots to be setup for the logical channels in the transmission medium hence saving on time. It does allow multiple users to share the same transmission medium despite the number of signals to be transmitted. The rate of electromagnetic interference during transmission is low. The transmission rate is well utilized ensuring that multiple number of data signals are transmitted within the shortest time possible.Disadvantages: The collection of all the entities required for efficient functioning of this multiplexing techniques sums up to forming a complicated structure which is quite hard to repair damages in case of any errors. As the number of users accessing the same transmission medium for transmission of data signals increases, so does the overall quality of services (QoS) being delivered to users decrease.

5.7. COMPARISON BETWEEN DIFFERENT MULTIPLEXING TECHNIQUES

Frequency division multiplexing techniques use the rate of frequency for different signals to determine the way they will be combined and transmitted via the transmission medium. In dense wavelength division technique, the wavelength of the signals is the main component which determines the multiplexing of different data signals for the purposes of their transmission. With the time division multiplexing techniques, which are divided into several categories, the main thing which governs their multiplexing is the setup of different time slots in some for the purpose of transmission while in others which do not support time slots mechanism, the selection of different signals which are governed by one- or two-time components, be it fixed or randomly, for the purposes of transmission.

CHAPTER

6

Computer Networking and Communication: Errors, Error Detection, and Error Control

CONTENTS

6.1. INTRODUCTION

In coding and information theory, the detection, correction, and control of errors involve techniques that are able to provide the delivery of digital data over communication channels in a reliable manner.Many communication channels are subjected to noise and thus may lead to errors which can occur when signals are being transmitted from the source to the receiver. Error detection techniques are normally used for the detection of errors and the error correction techniques allow for the original data to be reconstructed. Error detection involves detecting errors that occur due to noise or different impairments while signals are being transmitted.

All schemes for detecting and correcting errors normally lead to the addition of some redundancy to the message. Receivers are able to use this to check for consistency in the message that is being delivered, and also for the recovery of data that is considered corrupted. These schemes can either be non-systematic or systematic.In a scheme that is systematic, the original data is sent by a transmitter, which also ensures that a fixed number of check bits are attached. These check bits are derived from the data bits through the use of a deterministic algorithm. If one only needs the error detection technique, the receiver is able to use the same algorithm for the data bits that have been received and use this to make a comparison of its output with the check bits that have been received. If the values are not matching, it means that there is an error that has occurred during the process of transmission.

In a scheme that is non-systematic, the original message undergoes transformation into a message that is encoded, which carries the same information, and the number of bits is equal to those in the original message.

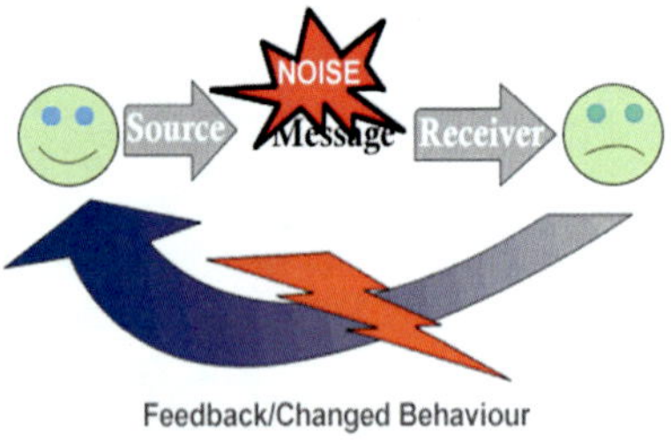

Figure 6.1. Noise is one of the factors that can change the behavior of a transmitted message from the source to the receiver.

Source: http://communicationarticless.blogspot.com/p/communication-noise.html.

To ensure good error control, the scheme needs to be chosen based on the characteristics of the channel of communication. Some of the channel models that are commonly used include: memory less models where there is a random occurrence of errors and also with a certain probability; and dynamic models where the errors primarily occur in bursts.

In general, error correcting and error detecting codes can be distinguished between burst error detecting and correcting, and random error detecting and correcting. There are some codes that make it possible for there to be a mixture of burst errors and random errors.

If it is not possible to determine the characteristics of the channel, or the characteristics are highly variable, it is advisable to combine an error detection scheme with a system that allows for erroneous data to be retransmitted. This is referred to as automatic repeat request. Hybrid automatic repeat request it an alternate approach for controlling errors. It is a combination of error correction coding and automatic repeat request (White, 2015).

6.2. TYPES OF NOISE IN COMPUTER NETWORKS

Noise, in electrical terms, refers to a form of energy that is not wanted, which makes it difficult to properly receive and reproduce transmitted signals (White, 2015). There are several different noise types. We observe acoustic noise when there is conversion of signals into sound, which is referred to as snow in video or TV images.

We consider computing or processing noise as data that is random and unwanted, which means that it is data that is not being utilized for the transmission of a signal, but it is being produced as a by-product that is not wanted, from other different activities. Sometimes, the signal to noise ratio refers to the ratio of Information that is useful to information that is irrelevant in an exchange (White, 2015).

There are a couple of ways in which noise can be classified. The main mode of classification classifies noise as either internal noise or external noise.

6.2.1. External Noise

Thus refers to noise which is generated externally because of the communication system. This noise is normally quantitatively analyzed. There are three types of external noise: atmospheric noise, industrial noise, and extraterrestrial noise. These are explained below:

- Atmospheric Noise – this is also referred to as static noise. It is the natural source of interference that is due to discharge in thunderstorms, lightning, and other disturbances that naturally occur due to the nature.
- Industrial Noise – this noise is due to aircrafts, ignition of electric motors, automobiles, and changing gears. This noise is mainly caused by high voltage wires. In general, industrial noise is produced by the discharge that normally occurs during the operation.
- Extraterrestrial Noise – this normally depends on the source of origin. It can be divided into cosmic noise and solar noise.

6.2.2. Internal Noise

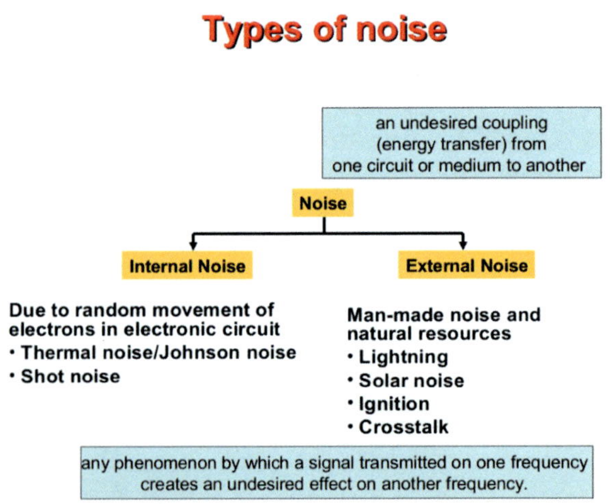

Figure 6.2. The first classification of noise into external and internal noise. Internal noise is due to electrons randomly moving in the electronic circuit, while external noise is man-made or natural noise

Source:-https://de.slideshare.net/alexantrine92/noise-22506040?nomobile=true.

These types of noises are those that are created internally or inside of the receiver or in the communication system. They can be treated in a quantitative manner, and there can also be reduction or minimization of the noise by designing the system properly. They can be classified as:

- Shot Noise – this normally happens in the device while it is active, because of the random behavior of the carries or the charge particles. When an electron tube is being used, this noise is normally created because of the tube's ability to randomly emit electron form cathodes.
- Noise – in this situation, there is a circuit dividing two or more paths. It is created due to having a fluctuation that is random in this division.
- frequency Noise – this is also referred to as flicker noise. For this noise to occur, the range of frequency needs to be under 5kHz. In this noise, there is an increase in power spectral density when the frequency decreases.
- frequency noise – these are also referred to as transmit time noise. They are normally seen in semiconductor devices when the charge carrier's time of transit whiles it crosses the junction is compared with the signal's period of time.
- Noise – these noises are normally random and they are normally referred to as Johnson Noise or White Noise. This noise is normally seen in the components of a complex impedance, that are sensitive resistive, or in the resistor, because of rapid and random movements of atoms or electrons or molecules.

There are also other different types of noises that are not included in the classification above. These include:

- Crosstalk – this occurs when there is transmission of a signal, through the transmission system, in one of its channels or circuits, causing an effect that is undesired in a different channel or circuit. It is normally caused by undesired conductive, inductive, or capacitive coupling from one channel or circuit to a different one.
- Impulse Noise – this is a part of acoustic noise which includes noise that is sharp, instantaneous, and unwanted. This noise is normally caused by gunfire, electromagnetic interference, explosions, when the recording disk is scratched, and poor synchronization in digital communication and recording.
- Echo – in terms of the acoustics and audio signal processing, this occurs when sound is reflected and it reaches the position of the listener after the direct sound, with a delay. This delay is normally directly proportional to the distance of the surface that is reflecting the sound from either the listener or the source.

- Jitter – in telecommunications and electronics, this occurs when a periodic signal deviates from the true periodicity, and it is normally referenced from a clock signal. It is referred to as a timing jitter in clock recovery applications. This noise is normally undesired and it is significantly considered in most of the communication links.
- Delay distortion – this is media phenomenon that involves the guided transmission of network data signals through a certain means of communication at a specific speed and frequency. It occurs when there is a variation in the signal frequency and velocity. This variation causes the signals to arrive at separate times. This leads to the signal distorting. It mainly occurs in fiber optics.
- Attenuation – this is a term that generally refers to a situation in which the strength of a signal reduces. It may happen with either analog signals or digital signals. It is sometimes referred to as loss and it is a natural consequence of the transmission of signals of a long distances. In fiber optics and conventional cables, this noise is specified with the number of decibels for every kilometer. The lower the level of attenuation for each unit distance, the better the cable when it comes to efficiency. It is advisable to insert one or more repeaters along the cable length when transmitting signals over long distances. These repeaters help in boosting the strength of the signal so as to prevent attenuation. They help in increasing the maximum attainable range of communication.

6.3. ERROR PREVENTION TECHNIQUES

There are many different techniques that can help in either preventing errors or reducing the chances of errors occurring. The technique used is all dependent in the situation (Banzal, 2007). Below are some of the techniques.

6.3.1. Shielding

This is a method that helps in protecting cables from crosstalk, intermodulation noise, and impulse noise by covering them with a coating that is insulating. It normally surrounds the conductors of the cable that are carrying the power, and ensures the cable is protected by picking up the noise and ensuring that it is conducted to the ground, or by making sure the signal interference is reflected. There are a couple of options for shielding cables and they each have a different degree of effectively shielding the cables.

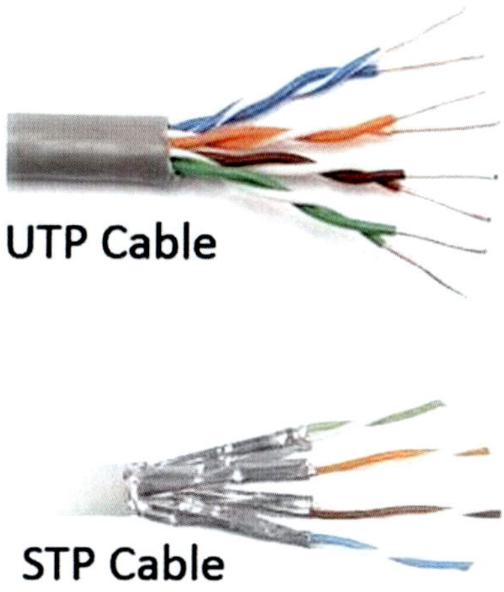

Figure 6.3. A good example of unshielded and shielded Ethernet cable

Source: https://www.fomsn.com/copper_cabling_solutions/sun2002/shielded-vs-unshielded-ethernet-cable-which-should-you-use/amp/.

There are a couple of things that one needs to consider when choosing the amount or type of shielding. These include:

- The signal interference type – ESI, RFI, or EMI;
- The level of the noise;
- The configuration of the system;
- The cost of the cable; and
- The weight, flexibility, and diameter of the cable.

Here we discuss three main forms of shielding: foil shield, braid shield, and multi-shield.

Foil Shield – this is used for protecting cables that are transmitting signals that are more than 15 KHz. They are not expensive, and they are also lightweight. In comparison to core conductors, they provide 100% coverage. It normally uses polyester and aluminum or Kapton foil and aluminum, all with 100% coverage and it is normally continuously in contact with tinned copper drained wires that are helically served. The drain wire is normally utilized for creating a connection that is electrical between the circuit ground and the shield. This method of shielding can be used for twisted pairs or triads or individual conductors.

Braid Shield – this provides protection to the cables that transmit signals that carry up to 15 KHz, protecting against RFI and EMI resistance in data, control, and power applications. These have a high physical strength. This shield is made from a mesh of tinned, bare, nickel-, or silver-plated copper wires. The shield is able to provide a minimum coverage of 85%. It also helps in providing a path that has a low resistance to the ground, in addition to being able to terminate it much easier when it is being attached to a connector. Due to the fact that copper has a higher level of conductivity in comparison to aluminum, and the fact that it is woven provides more mass for the noise conducting, the braid is one of the most effective shields.

Multi-shield (Braid and Foil) – this shield helps in providing protection across the whole range of frequency. It also has a high physical strength and it is much easier to terminate. This type of shield is recommended for environments that are very noisy, and also in a situation where the physical strength is a factor. It uses a triple laminate that includes aluminum, polyester, and then more aluminum foil, having drain one American wire gauge size smaller than conductors that are insulated, in addition to a copper braid that is tinned so as to increase its superior shielding and physical strength from noise, which would interfere with the signal.

6.3.2. Moving the Cables Away from the Noise Source

When cables are moved away from the noise source, especially a power source, the level of crosstalk, intermodulation noise and impulse noise is reduced. It is possible to reduce impulse noise by avoiding heavy machinery and lights. It is always advisable to locate communication cables far from power cables (GUPTA, 2006). Crosstalk can be avoided by separating the cables physically from different cables for communication.

6.3.3. Proper Multiplexing

Most cases of intermodulation and crosstalk are due to improper multiplexing. Both digital and analog communication systems require communication mediums to transmit signals. These mediums can either be wireless or wired. It is not possible to provide each user with an individual channel. It is much more efficient when there is combination of a group of signals which are then sent through the same channel. This is achieved with the use of multiplexers, which is a device that allows for routing of digital information from different origins, onto one transmission line and to one destination. The reverse of this operation is achieved by the demultiplexer, which takes a single line of digital information and then distributes it to different lines of output.There are two ways to ensure proper multiplexing. Firstly, one can change the technique of multiplexing, for example, changing from frequency division multiplexing to time division multiplexing. Frequency division multiplexing works by dividing the channel into two or more ranges of frequency without overlapping, while the time division multiplexing works by dividing and alternatively allocating specific periods of time to each of the channels. This means that time division multiplexing makes sure that at some of the time, each signal fully utilizes the bandwidth, while frequency division multiplexing only uses a small portion of the bandwidth for each signal, all of the time (GUPTA, 2006).

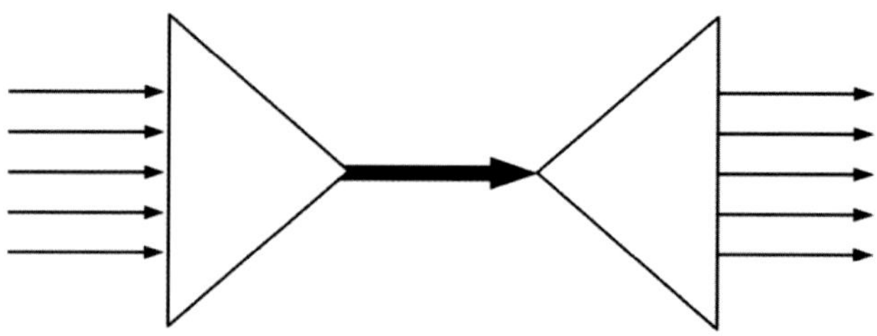

Figure 6.4. A visual representation of multiplexing with the combination of digital or analog signals

Source: https://en.wikipedia.org/wiki/Multiplexing.

Secondly, proper multiplexing can be achieved by changing the size or frequency of the guard-bands in frequency division multiplexing. A guard-band works by separating two ranges that have a wider frequency. It is able to achieve this because it has a narrow frequency range. This helps in ensuring that communication channels that are working simultaneously do not experience a decreased signal quality due to noise interference.

6.3.4. Proper Maintenance of Equipment, Poor Connections, and Spliced Cables

Harmonic distortion, jitter, white noise, echoes, and other types of noises can be due to poor maintenance of equipped, spliced cables, and poor connections. Echos in fiber-optic cables normally occur mostly due to poor connections. This can be fixed by tuning the transmission equipment and also redoing the connections. When wire casings are spliced, this allows for unwanted signals to penetrate into the circuit, thus causing crosstalk.

6.3.5. Using Repeaters or Amplifiers

These are electronic devices that are utilized for the enhancing the power of signals that are being transmitted. The major difference between the repeater and the amplifier is that the repeater is used as a device for reproducing signals and also for eliminating signal interference. On the other hand, the amplifier is only used for enhancing the signal's waveform amplitude. However, the amplifier does not consider the noise that is being amplified together with the signal.

To prevent attenuation, telephone circuits are normally equipped with amplifiers or repeaters equally spaced out all through their length. The distance between the repeaters or the amplifiers is dependent on the amount of power that is lost for every unit length of the line for transmission (PAL, 2013).

The amplifier normally takes in the signal and causes it to increase in strength, and then later on retransmits it onto the next portion of the circuit. These are mostly used on analog circuits. The amount of attenuation is what helps in determining the distance between the amplifiers. The most commonly used interval is 1 to 10 miles intervals. When using analog circuits, one needs to consider that the distortion and noise is also amplified together with a signal. In this situation, the noise that comes from a previous circuit undergoes regeneration and amplification every single time the signal is amplified. For analog circuits, it is advisable to use repeaters instead of amplifiers, especially if the noise level is high.

Figure 6.5. Amplifiers are used to increase signal power, current, and voltage. These, however, normally generate noise and the noise can be amplified as the signal is being amplified.

Source: https://www.whathifi.com/best-buys/hi-fi/best-stereo-amplifiers.

6.4. ERROR DETECTION TECHNIQUES

Anytime there is storage of data in a computer with the intention of transmitting it, it is important to make sure that the data is not corrupted. If there was a situation where corrupted data was sent, the data that is transmitted would be inaccurate and it may also not be able to work in a desirable manner. This is why data detection systems are important for checking that all the entered data is not corrupt before it is encrypted or transmitted (Prasad, 2004)

There are a couple of error detection techniques that help in providing a very high error detection performance. It is only possible to perform error detection by sending extra data every time a message is being sent. The error detection data is normally sent together with the message through the sender's data link layer, based on an algorithm that has been used on the message. There are situations in which the techniques are built inside the hardware.

After the message is received, the receiver is meant to use the same algorithm on the message and crosscheck it with the error detection data that was sent together with the message. If they match, then the message did not go through interference and is correct. It they do not match; this means that there was occurrence of an error.

Generally, if the amount of error detection data sent is larger, the higher the chances of detecting the error. However, with an increase in the error detection data, comes with a reduction in the throughput of useful data, due to the fact that the more of the amount of available capacity is utilized for transmitting the error detection data and a lower amount is used for transmitting the message itself. This means that the data throughput efficiency varies inversely with an increase in the desired amount of error detection (Prasad, 2004).

There are three main techniques that are used for the detection of errors: Parity checks, Cyclic redundancy check, and checksum. These will be discussed below.

6.4.1. Parity Checks

This form of checking normally uses parity bits for checking if there has been accurate transmission of data. It works by adding a parity bit to every data unit this is being transmitted. Normally, 7 or 8 bits are added. For each unit, the parity bit is set so as to ensure that the bytes either have an even number or an odd number of set bits.

In a situation where the two devices are having communication with parities that are even, which is very common, as the devices for transmitting send data, the number of set bits will be counted in each group of 7 bits. If the set bits are of even number, the parity bit is set to 0; if the set bits are an odd number, the parity bit is set to 1. This allows for every bit to have an even number of set bits (White, 2015).

On the side that is receiving, each byte is checked by the device so as to ensure that the set bits are of an even number. If the set bits are an odd number, that means that the receiver can detect an error that occurred during the transmission process.

Both the receiver and the sender are required to use the parity check and they are supposed to come to an agreement on whether the parity is meant to be even or odd.

If the receiving side and the sending side don't configure the bytes with the same parity sense, it will not be possible to communicate.

In communication, parity checking is the most commonly used technique for error detection. Despite the fact that is detects many errors, it is not 100% efficient, because it is not able to detect when the number of bits in the same data unit, that are supposed to be even, are altered due to noise (electrical) (White, 2015).

So as to ensure transmission accuracy, there are many other efficient protocols, such as CCITT V.42 and MNP. Not only is parity checking used in communications, but also for test memory storage devices. There are many personal computers (PCs), for example, that carry out a parity check on the memory every time there is reading of a byte of data.

Due to its simplicity, it is used in many different hardware applications, where it is possible to repeat an operation in a difficult situation, or if it is just helpful to detect the error.

For example, the Small Computer System Interface and the Peripheral Component Interconnect buses normally utilize parity for the detection of errors that occur during transmission, as well as many instruction caches for the microprocessor including parity protection. Due to the fact that the I-cache Data is considered a copy of the main memory, it is possible to re-fetch it and disregard it if it is corrupted (White, 2015).

Parity bit examples

sequence of seven bits	with eighth ecen parity bit:	with eighth odd parity bit:
0100010	01000100	01000101
1000000	10000001	10000000

Figure 6.6. The major disadvantage in this form of error checking is that it is only able to detect errors are odd in number in the sequence. It is not able to catch an even number of bits that have been flipped.

Source: https://www.computerhope.com/jargon/p/paritybi.htm.

In the transmission of serial data, the seven data bits is a commonly used format, in addition to the one or two stop bits and an even parity bit. This format is able to accommodate all the 7-bit ASCII characters in an eight-bit byte that is convenient. It is also possible to use some other formats such as the eight bits of data including a parity but which can help in conveying all eight-bit byte values.

In the context of serial communication, there is normally generation and checking of parity by interface hardware, and after it has been received, the result is made available to a processing machine such as the central processing unit, in the interface hardware, through a status bit in a hardware register. Retransmission of Data helps in recovering from the error, all which is normally done by the software, such as the input and output routines of the operating system (OS) (White, 2015).

Odd parity normally has an advantage in that the patterns of all-zeros and all-ones are both detected as errors, when the total number of bits that have been transmitted, together with the parity bit, is even. If the total number of bits that have been transmitted are odd, either the all-zeros pattern or all-ones pattern is detected as an error, but not both of them. The decision is normally made on the basis of the most expected common error to occur.

The advantages of this technique are its efficiency and simplicity. On the other hand, some of the disadvantages of parity checks include:

- They do not have the ability to detect all the errors;
- They only can detect errors that are of an odd number;
- There may be changes in the parity bit;
- They lead to an increase in the length of the transmission; and
- They only state that there has been the occurrence of an error without showing exactly where the error is.

6.4.2. Cyclic Redundancy Check

This is a technique that is used for detecting errors, mainly used in storage devices and digital networks for the detection of changes to raw data that are accidental. A short check value is attached on the blocks of data that are entering the system. These are based on the polynomial division of the contents that remain. After they have been retrieved, there is repetition of the calculation, and in a situation where the values being checked do not match, it is important to take the corrective action to avoid data corruption (Banzal, 2007).

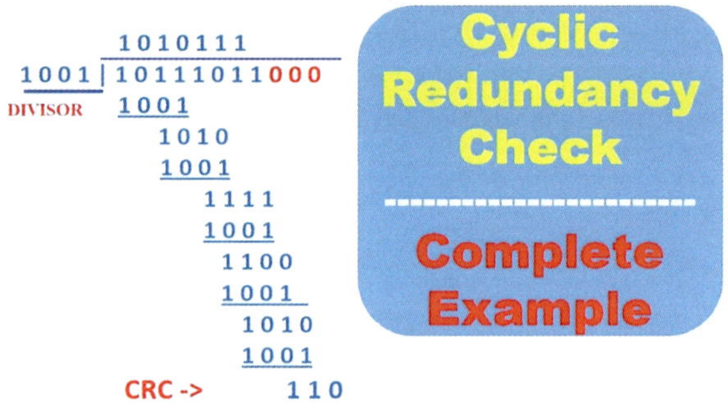

Figure 6.7. This check is popular because it is easy to implement in binary computer hardware, mathematical analysis. It also quite good for detection of common errors caused by noise

Source: https://en.bitcoinwiki.org/wiki/Amp/Cyclic_redundancy_check.

Cyclic Redundancy Check (CRC) is created on the basis of cyclic codes and the check value is able to expand the message without additional information. CRC is used very often these days because it is easy to implement in binary hardware. Additionally, it is good at detecting common errors caused by noise in the channels during transmission. Due to the fact that the check value has a length that is fixed, the function that is used to generate it is normally utilized as a hash function.

W. Wesley Peterson invented CRC in 1961. In 1975, the 32-but CRC function, normally used in Ethernet, was created by a group of researchers. CRC is based on the cyclic error correcting codes theory. In 1961 W. Wesley Peterson proposed the use of systemic cyclic codes that added a fixed length check value for encoding messages so as to ensure that errors are detected in communication networks.

Not only are the cyclic codes easy to implement, but they also have an advantage of being able to effectively detect burst errors, which are sequences that are contagious and contain erroneous data symbols in the messages. This is very important considering the fact that the burst errors are very common in many different channels of communication including optical and magnetic storage devices (Banzal, 2007).

In general, an n-bit Cyclic Redundancy Check that is used on a data block that has an arbitrary length will help in the detection of any burst error, as long as it is not longer than n bits. The definition of a generator polynomial is important for the specification of a cyclic redundancy check code. This polynomial tends to become the divisor in long division equation that is polynomial, which works by taking the message as the dividend and therefore leading to the discarding of the quotient and the result becomes the remainder. The important factor is that the calculation of the polynomial coefficients is in accordance to the arithmetic of a field that is finite. This means that the additional operation can always be performed in a bit-wise parallel manner.

A device that is cyclic redundancy check enabled helps in calculating a short-fixed length binary sequence that is referred to as the check value, for each data block that is supposed to be either sent or stored, and later on forms a codeword through appending it to the data. When the codeword is read or received, the device is either able to make a comparison of its check value with a codeword that has previously been calculated from the block of data, or, perform a CRC on the entire codeword and then make a comparison of the resulting check value with a residue constant that is expected (Banzal, 2007).

If the CRC does not match, then the block of data has an error. This means that the device is required to take a corrective action, for example, requesting for the data block to be sent again, or rereading it. If they match, the device assumes that the data block contains no errors. It may, however, contain errors that may not have been detected, which is a common problem of most error detection techniques.

CRC can also be used to store data in storage drives. Despite the fact that data inside a storage drive is structured to look like a normal folder and file, they are, however, tons of bit and byte binary values that have been combined. When there is creation of data in the hard drive, it will look like the files, folders, file system, etc., in the upper level. In the lower level, it will just be represented by ones and zeros built in a group of hush tables. Due to the fact that the smallest file can carry many zeros and ones that are binary valued, this means that the chance of data loss and data mislay is increased. When a single value is lost, it can lead to the complete alteration of the internal arrangement of a file's raw level (White, 2015).

This means that there is a need for a resourceful and legitimate mechanism for ensuring that trails of data loss in the hard drive raw data are discovered. This is now the work of the cyclic redundancy check. Because the data is normally written in a high speed, wherever there is possible space in the Hard Disk Drive, is where the data will be scattered and stored. The index of the data that is scattered will be made and stored in a different part of the memory. In addition, there will also be saving of a few additional data that is calculated by the cyclic redundancy check.

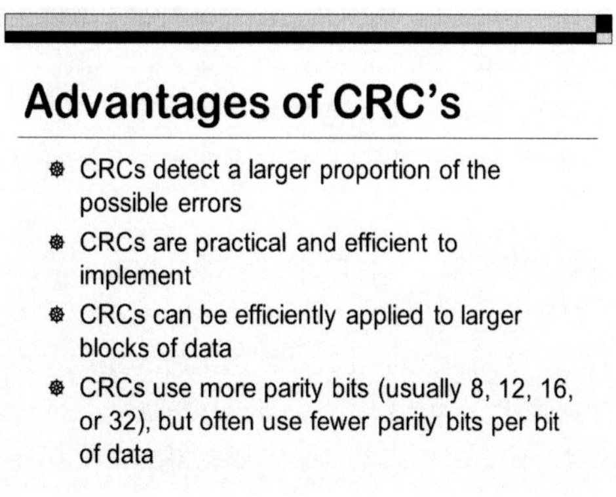

Figure 6.8. Above are some of the advantages of CRCs.

Source: https://slideplayer.com/amp/6048221/.

Some of the advantages of CRC include:

- It can detect a larger part of the errors that may possibly occur. This means it can detect many different combinations of errors that may occur, such as burst errors, any odd number of single bit errors, errors in two consecutive bits, and single bit errors.

- It is very practical and easy and efficient to implement in both software and hardware. It is also very fast when it is implemented in hardware.
- It can be applied to larger data blocks.
- It uses a larger number of parity bits (either 32, 16, 12, or 8), however, it uses a lower number of parity bits per bit of data.
- It is not expensive and it is also portable.
- It helps in breaking down the barriers of communication.
- Based on how severe and complex the error is; it is possible to generate an error correction mechanism. This mechanism is mainly located in utilities and software for repairing files.
- Due to how simple the code is, it is able to fit in all versions of and any form of OS, inclusive of the latest.

Some of the disadvantages include:

- It is not suitable for the purpose of security. Despite the fact that CRC looks like a mechanism for authentication, it is easy to crack and it is not trivial.
- Using CRC without a mechanism for correcting the errors is useless.

6.4.3. Checksum

This is a type of redundancy check that is simple and used for the detection of data errors. There is a frequent occurrence of errors in data when the data undergoes transmission across a network, written to a disk, or otherwise undergoes manipulation. Typically, the errors are quite small, such as one incorrect but, however, it doesn't matter the size of the error cause the smallest error can cause a negative effect on the data quality, or even make the data completely useless.

A checksum in its simplest form is created through the calculation of binary values, in either a block of data or in a packet, with the use of the same algorithm, and also ensuring storage of the results with the data. When there is retrieval of the data from memory, or when it is received at a different network end, there is calculation of a new checksum, and this is compared with the checksum that already exists. when they do not match, this is an indication of an error, however, a match does not always mean that there are no errors, but it does mean that the simple algorithm probably did not detect any error (White, 2015).

Within the error types that cannot be detected by these checksum algorithms that are simple are: multiple errors that are able to cancel each other out, deleting zero valued bytes and reordering of the bytes. On the other hand, it is possible to use sophisticated methods for the detection of such errors, for example, cyclic redundancy checks. Despite the fact that such methods have a disadvantage of needing better system resources when it comes to bandwidth and processor speed, this has proven not to be important as a consideration in the recent years. This happens due to the continued increase in bandwidth and processor speed.

For the detection of errors using checksums, the data is separated into fixed size segments:

- Sender's End – so as to get the sum, the sender adds the segments with the use of 1's complement arithmetic. So as to get the checksum, it complements the sun, and then sends it together with the data segments.
- Receiver's End – so as to get the sum, the receiver adds the segments that are incoming together with the checksum using 1's complement arithmetic, and then complements it.

If the resulting value is a zero, the segments that have been received are accepted. If not, they are discarded. Some of the advantages of checksum include:

- They do not use a large number of bits.
- They are easily implemented in software.
- The algorithms are simple to calculate.
- In comparison to the size of the frame, the checksum has a small overhead.

Some of the disadvantages include:

- Compared to CRC, Checksum is not a strong algorithm for error detection.
- It normally does not catch the common small errors.

6.5. CYCLIC REDUNDANCY CHECK VS. CHECKSUM

One of the main differences between CRC and Checksum techniques is that the cyclic redundancy check normally uses a math formula that is created on the basis of 32-bit or 16-bit encoding. The Checksum technique uses a math formula that is created on the basis of 8 bytes, when it comes to checking for anomalies in the data.

CRC/Checksum Seven Deadly Sins (Bad Ideas)

1. Picking a CRC based on a popularity contest instead of analysis
   - This includes using "standard" polynomials such as IEEE 802.3
2. Saying that a good checksum is as good as a bad CRC
   - Many "standard" polynomials have poor HD at long lengths
3. Evaluating with randomly corrupted data instead of BER fault model
   - Any useful error code looks good on random error patterns vs. BER random bit flips
4. Blindly using polynomial factorization to choose a CRC
   - It works for long dataword special cases at HD=3 or HD=4, but not beyond that
   - Divisibility by (x+1) doubles undetected fraction on even # bit errors
5. Failing to protect message length field
   - Results in pointing to data as FCS, giving HD=1
6. Failing to pick an accurate fault model and apply it
   - "We added a checksum, so 'all' errors will be caught" (untrue!)
   - Assuming a particular standard BER without checking the actual system
7. Ignoring interaction with bit encoding
   - E.g., bit stuffing compromises HD to give HD=2
   - E.g., good 8b10b encoding seems to be OK, but lax decoding may not be; results depend on specific CRC polynomial

Figure 6.9. There are some things that one has to consider before choosing either the checksum or CRC technique. Above is a list that can guide you in this decision making

Source: https://www.slideshare.net/PhilipKoopman/crc-and-checksum-presentation-for-faa.

The cyclic redundancy check is used based on a hash approach, while checksum normally attaints its values by adding all of the data that is truncated which may come in 16 or 8 beats. This means that the cyclic redundancy check normally has a higher ability for the recognition of data errors due to the fact that a single bit missing in the hash system can lead to a change in the overall result.

On the other hand, checksum needs a lower level of transparency and works by providing an ample amount of error detection, as it is able to employ additional bytes together with the variable. This means that the cyclic redundancy check has the main purpose of catching a wide range of errors that may occur during the data transmission process in analog mod. On the other hand, checksum was mainly designed for detecting regular errors that may occur during the implementation of software.

Cyclic redundancy check is considered to be an improvement over checksum. Checksum is one of the first techniques used for error detection in computing and cyclic redundancy checks have been created by advancing the arithmetics of the checksum code, so as to increase the computation complexity. This helps in increasing the number of patterns that are available for use, and therefore making it possible to detect more errors with CRC. Checksum has mainly helped in detecting single bit errors. CRC, however, can detect any Double-bit errors that are seen in the computation of data. Being able to understand these differences helps in understanding why it is important to use the two methods hand-in-hand when it comes to Internet protocol, where it helps in reducing the occurrence of vulnerability of internet protocols (GUPTA, 2006).

In summary:

- Checksum is the oldest of the two;
- CRC does a better job of checking for and reporting errors compared to Checksum;
- CRC has a computation technique that is much more complex than that of Checksum;
- Checksum is well known for the detection of single-bit changes, while CRC is able to detect and also check for double-digit errors;
- Due to the much more complex function of CRC, it is able to detect many more errors;
- Checksum is mainly used in validating data when it comes to the implementation of software; and
- A Cyclic Redundancy Check is mainly used for the evaluation of data when transmitting analog data.

6.6. PARITY CHECK VS CHECKSUM

When making a comparison, parity checking is a method that is used to check for errors when data is being transmitted, with the help of an additional bit referred to as a parity bit. When the parity is odd, it is necessary for the number of 1s in the nine bits to be odd. If there has been occurrence of an error in single bit, this means that there will be a difference in the parity, which indicates that there has been occurrence of an error.

Checksum is a method of error detection that checks for errors in data that has been transmitted by being able to count the number of bits found in one packet of data. If there is a match in the count, then the device assumes that the data was correctly transmitted and received (Prasad, 2004).

Despite the fact that these two methods are quite similar, they each have their own pros and cons. Parity checking is, however, the better choice, due to the fact that the checksum technique can have a bit that is not in place, and the end that is receiving will not have the ability to determine the misplaced bit.

6.7. ERROR CONTROL

Controlling errors in the data link later involve being able to detect and correct corrupted or lost data frames during the process of transmission. In a situation where frames are either corrupted or lost, the receiver receives a data frame that is incorrect, and the sender will not be able to know about the loss. This whole technique involves the detection of transit errors and taking the required corrective actions, which involves the retransmission of frames in case of an error detection or losing a frame. This process is referred to as Automatic Repeat Request.

In the process of controlling errors, the mechanism has the following phases:

- Detection of the error – the sender or the receiver of the data should be able to detect any errors that may have occurred during the transmission process.
- Acknowledging – there might be a positive or negative acknowledgment. Positive showing that there are no detectable errors, and negative showing that an error may have occurred.
- Positive Acknowledgment – if the frame is received without any errors, the receiver is expected to send back a positive acknowledgment to the sender.
- Negative Acknowledgment – if the frame received is damaged or duplicated, the receiver is expected to send back a negative acknowledgment.
- Retransmission – the sender is expected to maintain a clock and set a specific period to call for a timeout. If there is no positive or negative acknowledgment for a frame of data that had been sent previously by the timeout, or when the sender receives a negative acknowledgment, the sender is expected to retransmit the frame.

6.7.1. Error Control Techniques

There are four main techniques for controlling errors. Below is a description.

Stop and Wait Automatic Repeat Request: This is also referred to as alternating but protocol, and it is a telecommunications method that is used for sending information between two devices that are connected. It makes sure that there is no loss of Information because of packets being dropped, and also in making sure that the packets are received in an order that is correct. Of all the automatic repeat request mechanisms, this is the simplest.

The sender sends a frame at a time. After each frame is sent, the sender is not supposed to send any other frames until an acknowledgment for the sent data is received by the sender. The receiver is expected to send an acknowledgment after receiving a frame that is valid. If the sender does not receive an acknowledgment before the time out period, the sender is expected to send the frame again. This time out period is normally set again after the transmission of each frame. This is a good example of this top and weight. However, the implementations that are used in real life have variations when it comes to its design (Prasad, 2004).

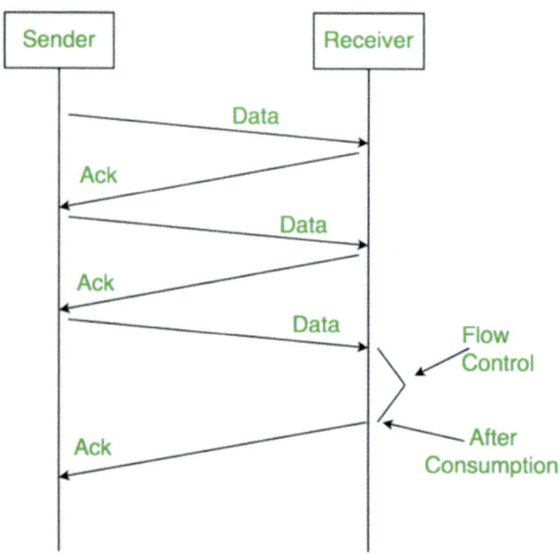

Figure 6.10. Performance issues may arise when a sender has to wait for acknowledgment even if it is ready to send the next packet

Source: https://apachecn.github.io/geeksforgeeks-zh/docs/en/net/40.html.

In general, the transmitter normally includes a redundancy check number to each frame's end. The receiver is expected to use this check number to detect for any damages that may have occurred during transmission. If the receiver notes that the frame is valid, it is supposed to send an acknowledgment. If it notes that the frame has errors, the receiver gets rid of it and does not send an acknowledgment, thus acting as if the frame was not just damaged but completely misplaced.

One of the main issues is that when the acknowledgment that the receiver sends is lost or damaged, the sender does not get to receive the acknowledgment and therefore it times out, and the frame is sent again. This means that the receiver will have two copies of the same frame, and the receiver will not be able to determine if the second one is a duplicate or a part of the sequence as the next frame that carries identical data (GUPTA, 2006).

Another issue may occur when the medium of transmission has a latency that is long meaning that the time out period for the sender runs out before the receiver receives the frame. In such a situation, the sender then sends the same frame again. In the end, the receiver will now have two copies of the same frame, and have to send an acknowledgment for each copy. The sender, will receive two acknowledgments and this may cause problems if the sender assumes that the second acknowledgment is meant for the next frame in the same sequence.

To prevent the occurrence of these problems, it is possible to define a 1-bit sequence number in the frame's header. In the subsequent frames, the sequence number alternates from 1 to 0. This means that when the receiver sends an acknowledgment, the sequence number of the next packet that is expected is included. In this way, the receiver is able to note if there are any frames that have been duplicated by checking if there is an alternating factor in the frame sequence numbers. If two frames following each other have the same sequence number, the receiver is able to detect this as a duplicate, and gets rid of the second frame. In the same way, if the receiver receives two acknowledgments with the same sequence number, the sender is able to know that they are acknowledging the same frame (GUPTA, 2006).

In comparison to other ARQs, the stop-and-wait ARQ has proven to be left efficient due to the fact that amount time between the packets, is twice that of the transit time, that is if the data and the acknowledgment are successfully received. This means that the channel has a throughout that is a fraction of what is could be. So as to fix this issue, it is possible to send more than one packet at a time, with a sequence number that is larger, then use one acknowledgment per set. This is the method used in the Selective Repeat ARQ and the Go-Back-N ARQ.

Sliding window protocol: This is a feature of data transmission protocols that are based on packets. These protocols are used when there is a need for reliable in-order package delivery such as in the transmission control protocol and in the data link later. When the channel has a high latency, they are also used for improving the level of efficiency.

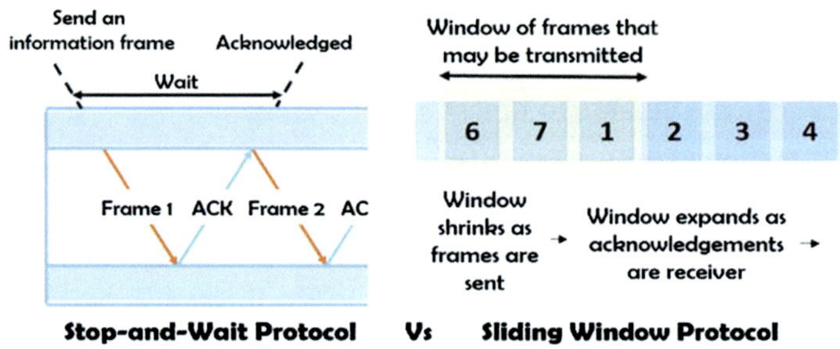

Figure 6.11. Above is a visual representation of the difference between the stop-and-wait protocol and the sliding window protocol.

Source: https://techdifferences.com/difference-between-stop-and-wait-protocol-and-sliding-window-protocol.html.

Systems that are packet based are created on the basis of the idea of having the ability to send a bunch of data, the packet, together with data that is additional for providing the receiver with the ability to make sure that the data is received correctly. This could be a Checksum. When the data is verified by the receiver, the receiver then send an acknowledgment signal to the sender, so as to communicate to the sender that it can now send the next packet in the sequence. In a simple ARQ, the sender has to wait for the receiver to send an acknowledgment signal after every packet has been sent. This helps in making sure that the packets are received in a correct order, because only one can be sent at a time.

The amount of time that it takes to receive the acknowledgment signal may be much longer than the time it takes for the sender to send the packet. In this situation, this may lead to a lower throughput than is possible theoretically. So as to deal with this issue, the sliding window protocols make it possible for a select number of packets, the window, to be sent by the sender without the sender having to wait for an acknowledgment. A sequence number is attached to each packet, and the acknowledgment is supposed to include that number when it is being sent to the sender. The sliding window protocol helps in keeping track of the packets that have been acknowledged, and after they have been received, the protocol is able to send more packets. Sliding windows are a major part of several protocols. It is very important in the Transmission Control Protocol, which allows for the packets to arrive in any order. It is also used in many protocols for the transference of files, such as ZMODEM and UUCP-g, as a method of ensuring that the efficiency is improved in comparison to protocols that are not windowed, such as XMODEM (White, 2015).

Go-Back-N ARQ: This is a specific instance of the automatic repeat request protocol, whereby the process of sending continues to send a specific quantity frames which have been specifically picked by a window size, even without having to receive an acknowledgment signal from the receiver. It is a specific case of the generally used sliding window protocol with N as the transit window size, and 1 as the receiver window size. It is able to ensure the transmission of N frames to the receiver before having to receive an acknowledgment.

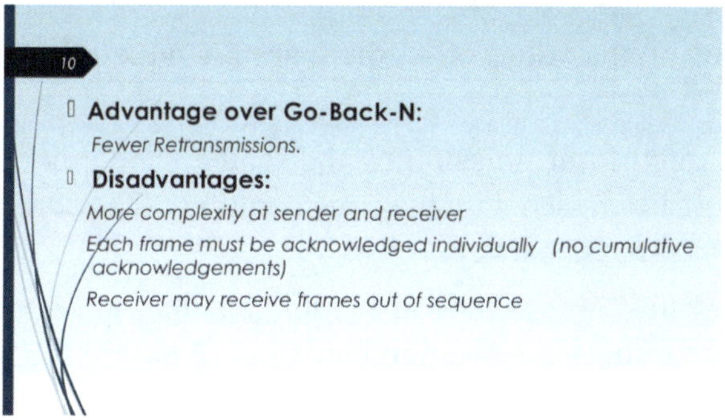

Figure 6.12. Above are some of the advantages and disadvantages of this protocol. It has proven to have a higher level of complexity at the level of the receiver and the sender.

Source: https://pt.slideshare.net/manushadilan/selective-repeat-protocol-49828840/10.

Receiver works by keeping track of the next frame's sequence number that it is expecting to receiver, then with every acknowledgment it sends, it attaches the number. The receiver then gets rid of any frame that does not have the expected sequence number because this frame is either a duplicate that had already been acknowledged, or a frame that is out of order because it is expected to be received at a later time, and it then resends an acknowledgment for the last correct frame that was in order. Once all the frames have been sent by the sender in the window, it is then able to make a detection that there is an outstanding number of frames since the first lost frame. It will then go back to the sequence number of the last acknowledgment that it had gotten from the receiver process and ensure that the window is filled starting with that frame, then go on all over again with the whole process.This ARQ Is much more efficient in comparison to the stop-and-read ARQ because the connection for the go-Back-N ARQ is still being used as packets are being sent, unlike having to wait for an acknowledgment for each packet. This means that, there are more packets being sent during that time that would otherwise be spent waiting. However, the go-Back-N ARQ normally ends up sending the same frame a couple of times. This normally happens if there was loss or damage of a frame, or the acknowledgment was either damaged or lost, then the ARQ will re-send that frame and all the frames that follow in the end window, even if those frames had previously been received without an error. This can be avoided by using the selective repeat ARQ (PAL, 2013).

When choosing the value of N, there are a couple of things one needs to consider:

- The rate of transmission by the sender should not be too fast. N should be chosen with the consideration of the ability the receiver has to process packets.
- The value of N needs to be smaller than the numbers that are used for the sequence number, so as to ensure the verification of transmission in case of a packet being dropped.
- When you consider the two factors above, N should be the largest number possible.

Selective Reject ARQ: This is used for solving sequence number dilemmas in communications. It is a part of the automatic repeats request. It allows the sender to send a number of frames that have been selected by the window size without having to wait for the acknowledgment sent by the receiver, such as in Go-Back-N ARQ.

In this ARQ the receiver is able to reject a frame selectively, which may be transmitted again alone. This is different from the other forms of ARQ, which are expected to send each frame from that specific points all over again. In this ARQ the receiver is able to accept frames that are not in the correct order and then buffer them. The sender then only retransmits the individual frames that have been timed out. It is possible to use it as a protocol for the acknowledgment and also for delivering the message units, and it may also be used as a protocol for delivering message subunits that have been subdivided.When it is utilized for delivering messages, the process of sending works by continuously sending the number of frames that had been specifically selected by the window size even after losing a frame. Compared with Go-Back-N ARQ, the process of receiving continuously accepts and acknowledges frames that have been sent after an error that had initially occurred. This is something that normally occurs in the sliding window protocol when the window size for transmitting and receiving is greater than 1 (White, 2015).The process of receiving works by keeping track of the sequence number of the earliest frame that had not yet been received, and then it sends that number together with every acknowledgment that it sends. If by any chance a frame that has been sent does not reach the receiver, the sender still proceeds with the process of sending the frames that come after it, until the window is fully empty. The receiver them continually fills its window for receiving with the frames that come after, while still sending an acknowledgment for each frame, each containing the sequence number of the frame that was missing earlier. Once all the frames in the window have been sent by the sender, it then resends the frame number that it had been receiving together with the acknowledgments and then goes back to where it had left off.

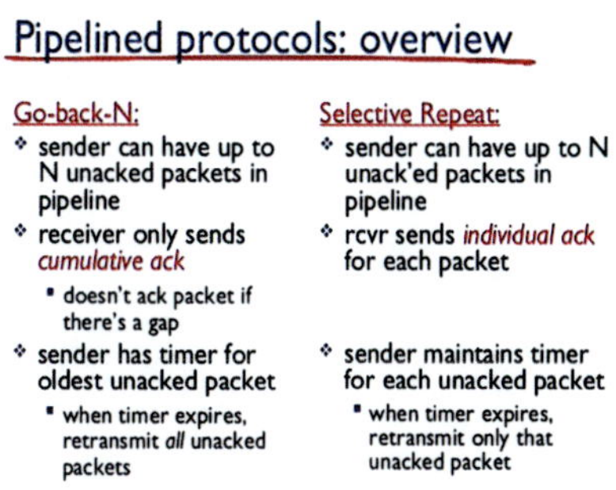

Figure 6.13. These are some of the differences between the Go-back-N protocol and the selective repeat protocol. The selective repeat protocol is the most efficient of the two.

Source: http://torun.rsd7.org/sliding-window-protocol/.

The size of the windows that are used for sending and receiving have to be equal. Additionally, there needs to be a half of the maximum sequence number to prevent miscommunication in all the situations of dropping the packets. If the receiving window is greater than one half the maximum sequence number, most or all of the packets that are available after that time out period will be duplicates. The sender is only able to move it window for every acknowledged packet.

When it is utilized as a protocol for delivering messages that have been subdivided, the ARQ works differently. Whenever channels are not continuous, the hybrid ARQ or Standard ARQ protocols may end up treating the message as a single unit. It is also possible to have a selective transmission in conjunction with the basic ARQ mechanism whereby, there is first the subdivision of the message into sub-blocks, through a process that is referred to as packer segmentation. This means that the original message that varies in length is the represented as sequence of a number of sub-blocks that vary. This is different from the standard ARQ, where there is either acknowledgment or negative acknowledgment of the message as a whole. When there is selective transmission in the ARQ, the acknowledgment response will also carry a bit flag that shows that there has been successful receiving of each sub-block. When there is selective retransmission of messages that have been subdivided in the ARQ, there is a reduction in the length with each retransmission, because they only need to contain the linked sub-blocks (White, 2015).

CHAPTER

7

Local Area Network: The Basics

CONTENTS

7.1. INTRODUCTION

The (MAC) or medium access control is a data link sublayer that uses the open structure interconnections (OSI) reference system for data transmission. It's useful for flow control as well as multiplexing for the transfer medium. This controls the transfusion of data packets through remotely shared medium, while sending data through the network interface slot. As for (LANs) local-area network, it's a computer network spanning a fairly small area. Typically, the LAN is restricted to just one room or building, but, one LAN may be linked to other LANs across vast distances through technologies like radio waves and telephone cables.

7.2. PARTS OF THE OSI

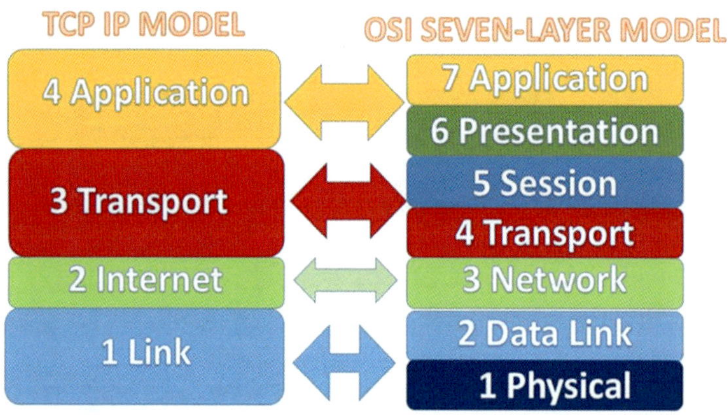

Figure 7.1. All the 7 parts of the OSI model are interconnected.

Source: https://thetechlogy.com/osi-and-tcp-ip-model/.

The (OSI) Open System Interconnection system describes an interactive framework to execute protocols in seven different layers. An OSI system is not even tangible to begin with, but rather a networking concept. It also does not perform any specific roles in the networking stage. The International Standardization Organization (ISO) was the one that created (OSI) model.

This program partitions network communication into seven different layers. Layers 1 to 4 are regarded as the lower levels and are responsible for transferring data. Layers 5 to 7 are known as the top layers and feature application-data details. Networks work on one key principle, known as "pass it on." Every layer handles very specific tasks and transfers the information onto the next level. In the OSI system, control is moved from one level to the next, beginning at the application level (Layer 7) at one point, and continuing to the bottom level, over the network to the subsequent station and way up the chain. The OSI system takes the role of inter-networking and splits that up into vertical piles that number 7 in total (Robertazzi, 2017).

7.2.1. Layer 7: Application

Layer 7 is responsible for supporting application and final-user processes. Contact partners are detected, service quality detected, operator authentication and confidentiality are also regarded, plus any limitations on data syntax get identified. Every process in this level is application-specific. The layer offers application solutions for file transfers, network software services, and e-mail facilities. FTP and Telnet are programs that exist completely in the application stage. Tiered application structures are part of the level.

7.2.2. Layer 6: Presentation

This level provides independence from variances in data representation (e.g., encryption) by converting from application to networking format, and contrariwise. The presentation level works to convert information into the format that the application level can accept. Additionally, this layer sets up and encrypts information to be delivered across a network, giving freedom from compatibility issues. It's sometimes known as the syntax level.

7.2.3. Layer 5: Session

The session level establishes, supervises, and terminates links between applications. This session layer is responsible for setting up, coordinating, and cutting conversations, exchanges, or dialogues occurring between the applications found at each end. The layer addresses session and connectivity coordination. Some common examples are RPC, SQL NFS, and NetBios.

7.2.4. Layer 4: Transport

Layer 4 offers transparent exchange of information between end structures, or hosts, plus is the cause for terminal-to-terminal error recovery and movement control. It ensures total data transfer and some of its common examples are UDP, SPX, and TCP.

7.2.5. Layer 3: Network

Level 3 is responsible for providing switching and routing functions, developing logical routes, called virtual circuits, for transferring data from one node to another. Forwarding and routing are the main roles of this level, including addressing, internet-working, error management, packet sequencing, and backlog control. Some popular forms include IP, IPX, and AppleTalk DDP.

7.2.6. Layer 2: Data Link

At Layer 2, the data packets get encoded and decrypted into bits. It supports transmission protocol data and management, apart from handling errors found in the physical level, flow management, and frame synchronization. Besides, the data link level is further divided into other dual sub-layers: The Logical Link Control (LLC) and Media Access Control layers (MAC). The MAC sub-level determines how a computer found on the network can gain easy access to the information and permission for transmitting it. Meanwhile, the LLC layer determines frame synchronization, error inspection, and flow control.

7.2.7. Layer 1: Physical

It's the final part of OSI Model. This layer transmits the bit stream – consisting of light, radio signals, and electrical impulses – via the network both at the mechanical and electrical levels. This provides the hardware medium of sending as well as receiving data through a carrier, including labeling cables, cards, and physical elements. A few protocols found in the physical layer components include RS232, Fast Ethernet, and ATM.

7.3. MAIN ROLES OF LOCAL AREA NETWORKS (LAN)

The key function of local networks is connecting devices for improved proficiency and productivity, particularly in the workplace, while reducing costs. Whereas computers and other appliances, which serve as workstations in the office setup can run using their own programs, they're capable of access information resources about shared data apart from sharing the usage and functionality of productivity devices which are equally connected to the LAN system, such as fax machine or office printer.

Developed to facilitate a simple and efficient way of exchanging and retrieving data, the LAN system allows workstations and devices found in the computer network to easily share software, firmware, and files between the interlinked nodes. It's based on a server which connects every node closely therefore, forming a shared working setup for these distinct workstations. Both the wired or wireless networks are capable of providing networking function between proximal devices.

LAN joins the computer firmware in a localized zone, such as at home or office. Normally, LANs make use of cabled connections to attach computers to one another, including a variety of other secondary devices like printers. Instruments connected to the LAN network are capable of accessing data from whichever machine that's linked to the network. Besides, LAN operators can connect with each other through chat and email channels (Cowley, 2012).

7.3.1. Features

LANs are defined by various characteristics which help to differentiate one LAN from the other. The linear placement of devices attached to LAN is called the topology, referring to how machines are linked to the network. Basically, a LAN's media function refers to the tangible connections of the machines to the network. Normally, devices are attached to LAN systems through co-axial cables, fiber optic lines or twisted-double wires. The network's protocols determine the specifications for transferring data through the LAN. These particular protocols define if the network operates as a client-server or peer/peer LAN.A client-server LAN, also known as dual-tier LAN, comprises of powerful computers, called servers, which perform the role of handling disk drives, network traffic as well as printers. The clients found in this kind of LAN consist of personal computers (PCs), or processors running applications. As for peer/peer LANs, they are networks whereby each workstation, or node, shares correspondingly in the operation of the LAN. Whereas peer/peer LANs are easier to establish, they don't work as well under great workloads, and this is what client-server LANs are particularly developed to handle.

7.3.2. Capabilities

Typically, LANs transmit data at quicker rates compared to phone-line connections, though are limited in terms of the number of computers to transmit data. LANs can easily connect with other LANs through networks, such as telephone cables, satellites, and radio waves, thus creating wide-area network (WAN). The world's leading WAN system is the Internet. In overall, LANs are made up of several wires and cables referred to as a bother. Wireless LANs or (WLANs) perform the same tasks as the LAN without any clutter.

WLANs use radio signals to transfer data rather than cables and wires. One common standard applied in WLANs is the Wi-Fi system founded on the IEEE's (Institute of Electrical and Electronics Engineers') 802.11 principles for cordless data transmission. The Wi-Fi principles support similar kinds of interfaces applied in LANs, such as printing and Internet access.

7.3.3. LAN Infrastructures

The local area network might not consist of a definite variety of devices being the network's limit, yet the same elements are still required to create a LAN. The following are components of the required infrastructure:

- Connective Devices: A LAN connects appliances found within a particular proximity. This connection may be accomplished only when particular connecting devices are present. Originally, computers were connected to each other via wired connections. Nevertheless, a variety of devices, such as desktop computers, tablets, smartphones, and laptops may be linked onto the same local framework. Sharing functions of a device may be controlled through the server or the appliance itself from its configuration settings.
- NIC and Drivers: Network Interface Card (NIC) allows for easy connections between the LAN and linked device. Operating as a means of fostering communication within the network, a majority of modern devices consist of integral NIC systems that permit them to connect directly to a network. Organizations that have specialized needs might choose to offer their devices using a specialized NIC so as to enhance individual PC performance across the network. Driver software also helps to simplify communication between the appliance's operating system (OS) and the NIC. Same as the NIC, drivers typically are built within the system. Nevertheless, when integrating a modified NIC into your instrument, installation of a fresh driver for integrating it into the structure might be necessary.

- Mutual Hardware: There are two types of hardware found in LAN systems. The first one is necessary hardware, which includes routers, switches, and hubs, which work together to connect the appliances in your network. The hardware are crucial components of the LAN physical structure since without these appliances, no connection can be formed. The second group is optional hardware, consisting of hardware that can easily be shared together with other users across the network. Even though these are not strictly necessary, devices such as fax machines and printers may be shared across a network for the purpose of creating a more advanced work environment.
- Network OS: In order to build a functional LAN network, the system must be established to fully manage the nodes found on the network. This OS offers a network manager the ability to effortlessly check all devices connected to the network, choose what resources must be shared, plus be able to troubleshoot both firmware and software glitches on the network.
- Connection Channel: Contemporary LANs are able to use both wireless Wi-Fi connections and wired Ethernet cables to create a connection between different nodes found on the network. It is also possible to implement both methods concurrently. Wireless LANs depend on Wi-Fi waves that can handle wireless access points coming from any devices that's connected to it. The Wi-Fi signal comprises of a limited range, plus can be secured through an access code which allows operators with permissions to link up to the network. The Supervision of an access spot is typically a role of broadband routers. Regular cabled LANs depend on Ethernet cables to link up devices.

7.4. ADVANTAGES AND DRAWBACKS OF (LANS) LOCAL AREA NETWORKS

7.4.1. Benefits

LANs are effective since their transfusion capacity is higher than any particular terminal on the grid. Therefore, every station terminal may be provided a certain portion of time from the LAN, such as a time-sharing structure. To derive the best from this opportunity, it is necessary for stations to arrange their messages into compressed packets which can be quickly transported.

While challenging for access, the station with content to send records its data packet inside a buffer up to the point that the LAN becomes clear. At that moment the message is dispatched.

At times, two stations might perceive the opening concurrently and dispatch their messages simultaneously. Oblivious that another message may have been dispatched already, these two signals shall end up merging on the LAN. In case this happens, it's the software's role to decide the user who should have priority access, while requesting both connecting appliances to try again.

In busy LANs crashes may happen more often, slowing down the system significantly. To resolve the issue, the LAN software transmits a token. This functions like a ticket which is distributed just to one posting at a time. Rather than waiting so that the LAN can clear, this station waits to accept the token.

Once it processes the token, this station proceeds to send out its packet across the LAN. Upon completion, it returns back the token into the stream so that the next operator can access it. Tokens, applied in both bus and ring topologies, practically remove the issue of collisions by giving orderly, non-contention admission.

The transmission processes found on LANs can either be broadband or baseband based. Typically, baseband medium makes use of high-speed virtual signal comprising of square signal DC voltage. Though it's fast, the system can accommodate just one message per time. Consequently, it's ideal for much smaller networks in which contention is minimal. It equally is quite simple, needing no tune ups or frequency control circuits. Therefore, the transmission channel may be linked openly to the network accessibility unit and is appropriate for use over curved wire pair facilities.

Alternatively, the broadband medium adjusts signals to unique frequencies, more or less like cable TV. Stations are directed by signaling data to focus on a particular channel for receiving information. This information that's found in each single channel within the broadband medium might also be digital, though they're distinct from other messages in terms of frequency. Consequently, the medium broadly requires greater capacity cables, like the coaxial cable. Suitable for high capacity LANs, broadband units need the use of special tuning appliances in the system access unit which can sieve out all but one channel that it needs.

7.4.2. Drawbacks

LANs are vulnerable to many forms of transmission errors. For instance, electromagnetic disruption from power lines, motors, static sources and shorts from corrosion, have the potential to corrupt data. Furthermore, different types of wires are more prone to these issues than others. Besides, software bugs as well as hardware failures may introduce certain errors, so can anomalies in wiring and networking.

Normally, LANs recompense for these particular errors by functioning off a reliable power source, like batteries, and applying backup software to recollect most recent activities while also keeping unsaved content. Equally, some systems can be developed for redundancy, like keeping a pair of file servers and alternative cabling for routing around failures.

Furthermore, as computer software progresses requiring quicker processors and quicker rates of transfusion, LAN technology should also evolve with it. Multi-media and film applications particularly force businesses to upscale their LANs, so as to use these applications within a network setting. Accordingly, LANs increasingly must transmit information at gigabit level, not megabit, meaning speeds and therefore older technology should be up-scaled or even replaced (Toral-Cruz et al, 2015).

7.5. COMMON (LANS) LOCAL AREA-NETWORK TOPOLOGIES

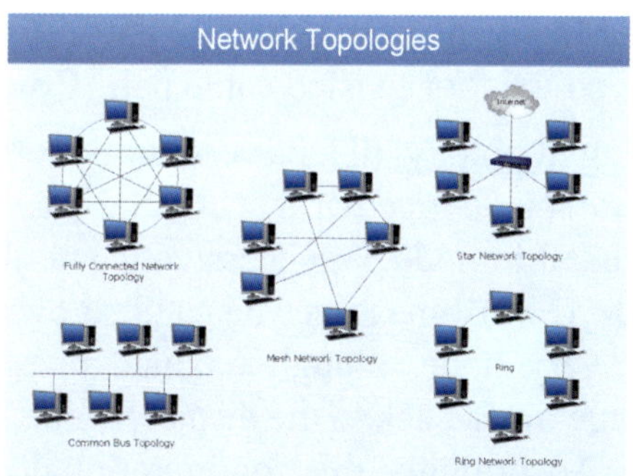

Figure 7.2. There are various ways to connect a LAN network based on the user's needs.

Source: https://www. kullabs.com/classes/subjects/units/lessons/notes/note-detail/6969.

LANs are developed in various unique topologies linking terminals. The most widespread topology is bus, whereby multiple terminals are linked directly to one another over one transmission track.

LANs layout is also linear and looks like a street having multiple driveways. Not to mention, the bus setup which requires cables allowing waves to move in either direction, known as the full-duplex medium.

Every terminal found on the bus-LAN competes with other different terminals for accessibility to the system. Upon securing access to the network, it transmits its message to every terminal simultaneously. The message is chosen by a single terminal or set of terminal points for which it's meant to reach. Moreover, the bus network's unavailability of routing as well as central control makes the structure quite reliable, since failure of a particular network's computers normally won't disrupt the movement of another network circulation (Cowley, 2012).

Another second topology, called the star network, similarly works just the same as bus with regards to contention and broadcast. However, within the star, stations get connected to one single, center node which controls access. The center node understands the route to every other node, therefore making routing a rather easy process.

Furthermore, the central node allows for easy access control while also setting up a priority rank for users. Multiple of these nodes can be linked to one another. Case in point, a bus that serves 6 stations could be linked to another different bus serving up to 10 stations, including a third bus that connects 12 stations. Mostly, it's star topology that's widely used where the linking amenities are co-axial or twisted cable pair (Cowley, 2012).

Basically, the ring topology links every station to its unique node, besides these nodes are joined together in a circular way. Node I is linked to node 2, that's also linked to node 3, successively, and the ultimate node is linked back onto node 1. Most messages dispatched over the LAN network are regenerated by every node, though retained just by the addressees. Ultimately, the message flows back to the dispatch node, which eliminates it from the mainstream. Accordingly, this configuration doesn't need any type of routing.

7.5.1. Bus/Tree Topology

The bus topology relies greatly on one unique communication line to transfer data in both directions. The central cable, commonly known as the backbone, links up to every node found on the network. Meanwhile, bus topology is also used in establishing Ethernet connections, which forms the standard for connections in the technology sector.

Among the reasons why the bus topology us a widely used method of setting up LAN systems is its basic design, which requires a continual cable length that finishes with terminating resistors found on either end. Both Installation and recalibration of this kind of LAN topology forms a rather simple and straightforward process. Nevertheless, some difficulty may be encountered while troubleshooting since data transmission relies on one specialized cable.

Tree topology is also closely related to bus. It refers to a mix of technologies used to establish bus/star topologies, where work stations which are linked to central hubs consequently are linearly supported through a singular cable which acts as the pillar in data broadcasting. Tree networks are typically known as the hybrid network (Ibe, 2017).

7.5.2. Star-Wired Bus Topology

The Star is a simple computer network topology whereby all nodes (PCs and peripheral devices) within the network are attached to a central hub or switch, having a terminal-to-terminal link up, constituting a physical network section. Such network section can work separately or in form of a multifaceted network topology.

The switch doubles up as a server, while the peripherals function as the clients. Massive workload and roles of network administration are entrusted on one primary computer; all data exchange passes through it. Therefore, it's by all means the most significant network.

Additionally, the star network system is a basic topology for both design and application. Its benefits are high performance, dynamic administration functions, simplicity of adding extra nodes and inspection of errors, including the fact that disruption of one workstation won't affect the functioning of the entire network. However, interruption of the central hub may cause failure of entire network or even network segment, which is its key disadvantage (Ibe, 2017).

7.5.3. Star-Wired Ring Topology

The star-network ring topology has a central connection spot known as the "hub" which could either be a router, switch or hub. Appliances normally attached to the hub have a (UTP) Unshielded Twist Pair Ethernet. There are many different forms of this particular topology which support 1024 contact nodes on one logical network. The star-ring carries one major advantage of being easy to move, separate, or interlink with other networks. In case of any technical issue with the cable, it shall generally not have any impact on the other aspects of the network.

Moreover, sets of nodes are linked to hubs that are then attached onto one bus. These networks are useful for covering longer distances, but the main downside is that they are relatively expensive to install since they require additional cabling and more hubs. The network is also considerably slower compared to Ethernet networks, when exposed to normal data load.

7.5.4. Wireless LANs

Wireless Local Area-Network (WLAN) refers to a computer network which permits devices to be connected and communicate cordlessly. Different from a conventional wired LAN, devices on WLAN systems communicate over Wi-Fi. Even though a WLAN may appear different from a conventional LAN, it works in a similar principle.

Modern devices are normally added and configured through DHCP. They can interconnect with other instruments on the network similarly as they might on a cabled network. The main difference is on how the information is transferred. In a typical LAN, the data is transferred over physical lines through a sequence of Ethernet packets that handle it.

As for WLAN, information is transferred over the air through any of the IEEE 802.11 connection protocols. While wireless instruments have increased in popularity, the same also applies to WLANs. Generally, most routers being sold today are the wireless routers. These cordless routers act as a control station, supplying wireless connections to whichever Wi-Fi-allowed devices found within proximity of the router's cordless signal (White, 2015).

It includes devices such as tablets, smartphones, and laptops among other wireless appliances, like smart gadgets and smart home-based controllers. Wireless routers regularly link up to cable modems, or other Web-connected devices for purposes of providing Web access to linked devices.

Both WLANs and LANs and may be connected together through a bridge which joins up the two networks. A number of wireless routers further have Ethernet ports, offering connections for a certain limited number of wireless instruments. For most cases, cordless routers function as a bridge, by connecting the Wi-Fi and Ethernet connected devices into one main network. This permits wired and wireless instruments to easily communicate with one another through one main router.

Benefits of using WLANs: The clearest advantage of connecting to WLAN network is that, instruments can connect cordlessly, therefore eliminating the requirement for cables. Eventually, this allows households and businesses to develop local networks, without having to wire the entire building using Ethernet.

Additionally, it provides a means for small-scale devices, like tablets and smartphones, to link up to the computer network. WLANs aren't limited at all by the amount of physical ports found on the router, meaning they can support multiple or even 100s of devices. Besides, the scope of a WLAN may easily be extended through adding one or multiple repeaters. Lastly, a WLAN may easily be upgraded through replacing its routers with other newer versions — a simpler and affordable solution compared to upgrading of old Ethernet wires.

Shortcomings of WLANs: Wireless networks are normally less secure compared to their wired networks. Just about any type of wireless device can try to link up to the WLAN, therefore it's key to restrict accessibility to the network in case security is an issue.

This is normally done through wireless authentication devices, such as WPA or WEP, which are responsible for encrypting the communication. Besides, wireless networks are prone to interference emerging from other different signals or physical obstacles, like concrete walls. Considering that LANs provide the greatest performance and security, they are applied in many corporate and state-sponsored networks.

7.5.5. Comparison of Bus, Star-Networked Bus, Star-Networked Ring and Wireless Topologies

Computer networking has rapidly grown over the recent few months, forming the backbone of web technology and the Internet as it's understood today. The Web is basically a network made up multiple connected computers, meaning there isn't anything like a standalone PC on this network. For operators or host workstations to engage in data or resource sharing, the system must be linked to some kind of networked topology. This has inspired the development of computer networking so that it can include more appliances, which shall further improve the activity of data transmission across diverse geographical spots.

Many individuals are already accustomed to words like LANs, meaning computers found within a particular geographical area or building. As for (WANs) Wide Area Networks, these are devices which are detached based on geographical distance. Besides, there are many other terminologies applied in computer networking like Metropolitan Area Network (MAN), and Personal Area Network (PAN).

Merits and Demerits of Bus Topology: Bus topology consists of a network structure where nodes utilize one line of communication for data transfusion. Most networks at the start of the computer-networking age utilized this topology because of simple implementation. One of the key advantages is because there's only one communication line, it means that the same networking channel is shared. Hence, the main advantage of utilizing this topology is the simplicity that it provides. It's also simple to establish and extend, less expensive and requires minimal cabling. On the contrary, having one communication channel for data transfusion makes it simpler for collision to happen, which is considered a disadvantage of utilizing this particular network topology. In case one network cable is the one with an issue or disconnection, it means then the entire network breaks.

Pros and Cons of Star Topology: The star system topology is among the most widely used topologies nowadays due to its ease of use and efficiency. For this type of topology, the centralized node is situated at the center of the network architecture, whereby all the different nodes need to communicate from. This topology is regularly used in the house and office settings today. For instance, the typical Ethernet LAN networks connect through the Star Topology. This network features an Ethernet Button (centralized node) through which all processors and network systems are connected to. One key advantage of star topology is that it is simple to install and launch with cabling etc. furthermore, the configuration is simple to troubleshoot as well as detect any hitches in the network. In case one device fails, then it won't affect other devices connected to the network. It is possible to easily add or eliminate devices without necessarily influencing the remaining part of the network. It also allows for integrated management and monitoring from a central hub/switch. As for disadvantages, the primary disadvantage of implementing this particular topology is that the system has one main stage of failure, that is, when the core switch node malfunctions, there shall be a disruption in communication targeting all connected appliances. Additional cabling is required since you attach each specific device to a central node. The performance of this entire network will depend on the activity of the center node.

Advantages and Disadvantages of Ring Topology: Ring topology features devices which are structured in a circular way, or same as the ring. Even though the device's layout is the same as bus topology, for the most part ring topology works as a shut/closed loop. The ring networks aren't widely much nowadays. The primary benefit of using ring network topology is its capacity to have quick network throughput, minimal packet collisions and top speed transfers. The token is implemented between nodes therefore making this system to perform better compared to bus topology. The disadvantage of ring topology lies at its point of failure, since a single node may break the transfusion of data across the network.

7.6. MEDIUM ACCESS MANAGEMENT PROTOCOLS

7.6.1. Contention-Based Protocols

The contention-based protocol (CBP) refers to a communications protocol used for running wireless telecommunication appliances which allow several users to utilize the same radio frequency without pre-coordination. Moreover, the "listen before dialog" operating process in IEEE 802.11 is a renowned CBP.

According to U.S. Federal Communication laws, a protocol which allows several users to connect through a similar spectrum, by describing the events that should occur when at least two or multiple transmitters try to concurrently access the same network and establishing rules through which a transmitter offers reasonable prospects for other receivers to work (Cowley, 2012).

This type of protocol can comprise of procedures for instigating new transmissions, processes for determining the condition of the channel (accessible or inaccessible), and techniques for handling re-transmissions in case of overloaded channels. This description was included as part of Policies for Cordless Broadband Services, which was captured in the 3650 to 3700 MHz Band.

In this network, the carrier handles several access points with collision aversion (CSMA/CA), these are used together with cordless networking technology for purposes of mediating media contention. Moreover, the Carrier sensor multiple access and collision detection (CSMA/CD) program is used together with cabled Ethernet technology, for purposes of mediating media contention (Cowley, 2012).

7.6.2. Round Robin Protocol

Round Robin (RR) is among the algorithms used by process and networking schedulers for computing. Since the phrase is broadly used, time slices (commonly referred to as time-quanta) often get assigned to every procedure in equal measure and in circular format, handling all procedures without any particular priority (also called cyclic executive).

The RR scheduling technique is basic, simple to execute, and starvation-free. Not to mention, RR scheduling may also be used for other scheduling issues, such as data packet planning in computer networks (CS). It is an OS concept. Additionally, the algorithm name originates from the RR standard known from other disciplines, where each individual takes up an equal portion of a product in turn. The RR load balancing technique is a rather simple means of distributing client requests along a set of servers. Typically, the client request gets forwarded to every server in equal turns (Cowley, 2012).

The algorithm directs the load balancing system to reverse back to the uppermost list and replicates again. Simple to implement and understand, RR is among the most extensively used load balancing algorithms. Through this technique, client requests are directed to accessible servers on a cyclic manner. The RR server load balancing system functions best when the servers have almost identical computing functions and storage abilities.

The largest drawback of utilizing the round robin procedure in load balancing remains that, the algorithm accepts that servers are same enough to process equivalent loads. In case certain servers possess more RAM, CPU or other stipulations, then the algorithm doesn't have any means of distributing additional requests to the servers. Therefore, servers that have less capacity might overload or fail much faster, whereas the capacity for other different servers remain idle. A weighted RR load balancing configuration allows site officials to assign weights for every server depending on criteria such as traffic-handling ability. The servers with greater weights receive an advanced quantity of client requests.

In RR networks a load balancer, which preserves sticky sessions, shall create a special session item for every client. Upon receiving requests from a client, load balancers manage the request for the similar web server whenever information is stored and updated so long as the data session persists (Cowley, 2012).

Sticky sessions may be more resourceful since exclusive session-based data doesn't require to be transferred from one server to another.

Nevertheless, sticky sessions may become ineffective in case one server gathers different sessions with massive workloads, distracting the balance among multiple servers. In case sticky load balancers get used for load balancing RR style, the operator's initial request is routed towards a web server through the round robin process.

Consecutive requests are then directed to this similar server up to the point that the sticky session terminates, when the RR algorithm gets reused to develop a fresh sticky session. Equally, in case the load balancer becomes non-sticky, then the RR algorithm will be used for every request, irrespective of whether or contrary that requests travel from the similar end client (Quirke, 2000).

7.6.3. Differences between Load Balancing and Round Robin DNS

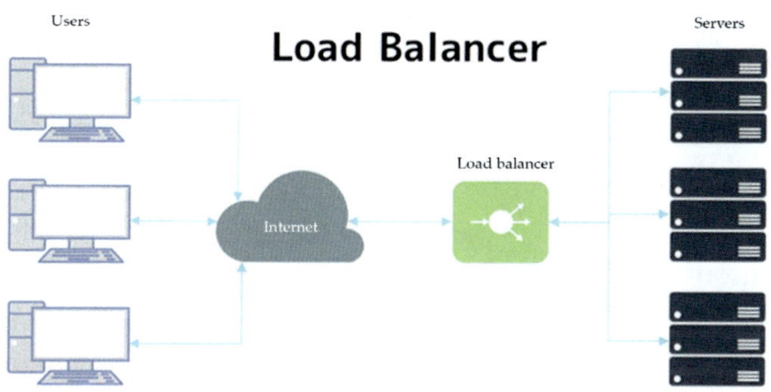

Figure 7.3. The Load Balancer controls data access rate to prevent transmission blockage.

Source: https://gbhackers.com/load-balancer-reverse-proxy/.

Normally, RR DNS utilizes a DNS server, instead of a committed hardware load balancer, for load balance applying the RR algorithm. Through round robin DNS, every website or solution is hosted on multiple redundant internet servers, which are typically geographically distributed. Every server dispenses an exclusive IP address targeted for the same site or server.

Through the round robin sequence, the DNS server can move through these particular IP addresses, harmonizing the load existing between different servers. As highlighted above, RR DNS is a unique load balancing instrument with a special DNS server. Contrarily, network load balancing mostly is a generic phrase that means network traffic supervision without complex routing protocols such as the Border Gate-pass Protocol (BGP).

7.6.4. Reservation Protocols

Reservation protocols form a class of protocols whereby the stations interested in transmitting data broadcast themselves prior to the real transmission. These particular protocols work in the medium accessibility control (MAC) level and transport level of the OSI system. These protocols have contention duration before actual transmission. During the contention phase every station broadcasts its wish for transfusion. Once every station broadcasts itself, a particular one will enjoy the preferred network resources depending on the agreed upon criteria (Ibe, 2017).

Considering that every station has full comprehension on whether other stations need to transfer or not before real transmission, every collision possibility is removed. Some popular examples of modern reservation protocols are Bitmap Protocol, which operates at MAC level, and Resource Reservation Protocol (RSVP) which works at network's transport level.

In Bitmap Protocol, contention duration is categorized into N slots, whereby N represents the average number of stations that share the channel. In case a station has any frame to transmit, it establishes the matching bit within the slot. For the likely event there are 10 stations. It means that the overall amount of contention slots shall be 10. In case the channels 2, 3, 8 as well as 9 want to transmit, then they shall fix the equivalent slots to 1. Largely, the transfusion is performed in the sequence of the slot figures.

As for RSVP, a transport level protocol would be applied to preserve resources within a computer network, in order to enjoy a different standard of services when accessing Web applications. It works over (IP) Internet protocol and launches resource reservations directly from the receiver's side. It's applied both for uniform-casting (transmitting data from a particular source to destination) including multicasting (transmitting data concurrently to a set of destination processors) (Ibe, 2017).

Main concepts: The two main models of RSVP reservation system are filterspec and flowspec. The latter preserves resources which are essential for a flow, while the flow is defined by the protocol identifier, destination address, and, occasionally, the destination port. For multiprotocol label switching (MPLS), the flow is described as some label switched path (LSP). Out of every flow, RSVP further identifies the specific quality of service needed by the flow even though it doesn't comprehend the specific details of the data flow QoS.

The QoS-specific data is known as flow spec, besides RSVP transmits the flow spec directly from the application onto the hosts plus routers across the path. Those structures then inspect the flow spec to receive and reserve the data resources. Generally, a flow spec comprises of a Reservation spec which controls data flow, Filter spec defining the group of packets which will be influenced by the flow spec (such as data packets for receiving the QoS captured by the flow spec). This filter spec normally chooses a subset of different packets which are processed by the node.

This selection may depend on any aspect of the packet, for example the port or sender IP address. Some presently defined RSVP reservation forms are fixed filter (holds resources for a particular flow) and wildcard filter (preserves resources for an overall kind of flow without stipulating the flow). Both of these flows share their resources. The RSVP reservation request consists of a flow and filter specificatication. While the flow specification establishes the structures of the packet programmer at a node, the filter specification establishes the parameters within the packet classifier.

Networking Messages: There are two key categories of messages. The first is path messages (path) where the content is transmitted from the transmission host across the data path. Generally, the path state comprises the IP address from the previous node and other data items, such as transmitter template to define the setup of the sender information. The data elements in RSVP messages may be transferred in any sequence. You can reference the RFC 2205 protocol to obtain a comprehensive list of RSVP posts and date objects. The RSVP host must transmit data flow using a particular QoS which is passed after every 30 seconds. If the path message reaches a router which doesn't understand RSVP, then the router will forward that message without inferring the finer details of the message (Ibe, 2017).

7.7. MEDIUM ACCESS CONTROL SUB LAYER

7.7.1. IEEE 802 Frame Formats

The IEEE 802 frame structure is needed for every MAC implementation. As such, it is referred to as the IEEE 802.3 standard. Multiple optional formats can be applied to lengthen the protocol's fundamental functions. Ethernet frame begins with SFD and preamble, which operates at thc physical level.

Ethernet header comprises both destination MAC and source address, which guarantees that frame's payload is existent. The final aspect is CRC applied to distinguish the error. Additionally, the 802.3 frame has a start framework delimiter, which motions the receiving instrument that the real frame transfusion is almost starting. Below is a look at the elements of this basic frame format:

- PREAMBLE: The Ethernet frame begins with 7-Bytes Preamble. It is a sequence of alternate 0's and 1's that showcase the beginning of a frame, while allowing the dispatcher and receiver to create bit synchronization. Originally, PRE (preamble) was created to eliminate a few bits because of signal delays. However. today's top-speed Ethernet doesn't require preamble to safeguard the frame bits. PRE shows the receiver that a frame is coming and allows the receiver to latch onto the information stream before the main frame begins.
- (SFD) Start of the frame delimiter: This refers to a 1-Byte section continually set to 10101011. The SFD shows that impending bits are beginning of the frame that is the final destination address. Occasionally, SFD is regarded as a section of PRE, which is the main reason Preamble is defined as 8 Bytes for many situations. The SFD alerts station or stations with the message that this program provides the final chance for synchronization.
- Data: It's the spot where tangible data is slotted in, commonly referred to as the Payload. Both data and IP header are inserted here in case the (IP) Internet Protocol is applied over Ethernet. The greatest data present might be as extensive as 1500 Bytes. If the data length present is lower than minimum length, which is 46 bytes, it means padding 0's would be added in order to meet the lowest possible length.
- Length: This is a 2-Byte frequency which shows the span of whole Ethernet frame. The 16-bit field is capable of holding length values of around 0 to 65534, however, length can't be greater than 1500 due to some particular limitations of Ethernet.
- (CRC) Cyclic Redundancy Check: The CRC refers to a 4 byte field containing a 32-bits data hash code that's produced through the Destination Address, Data field, Source Address, and Length. In case the checksum calculated by destination isn't the same in comparison to the transmitted checksum value, then the data

attained is corrupted.

- Source Address: It's a 6-Byte field containing the source machine's MAC address. Since Source Address is often a personal address (Unicast), often the least substantial bit of original byte is typically 0.
- Destination Address: It's a 6-Byte field that comprises of the device's MAC address where data is transmitted.

7.7.2. LAN Standards for IEEE 802.3

If you consider Ethernet from the viewpoint of OSI, then it is evident that its origins stem from the data link layer. In case you check the different versions, such as IEEE 802.3U, you will realize that provisions allow for faster connection speeds.

This protocol is divided into two subcategories. The first one is media access control (MAC) sublevel that deals with media access and describe the MAC addresses in every device found in the Ethernet network. Furthermore, the logical link management sublayer addresses the issue of communication with higher layers. Therefore, as Ethernet modules process every packet, they make references to IP at higher layers through utilizing the fields found in the frame heading (Cowley, 2012).

7.8. LOCAL AREA NETWORK (LAN) SYSTEMS

7.8.1. Ethernet

Ethernet is commonly used as the preferred protocol by LANs. Essentially, it is a group of interlinked machines and located reasonably close together within a limited expanse. There are several factors that classify LANs. The first one is physical proximity within a limited geographic range. The second one is the resources for operating at fast speed rates.

The bandwidth covers anywhere between 100 Mb/s to 1 GB/s up to 10 GB/s, as seen in modern networks. Bandwidths don't require a lease line, telecom provider, or service provider to interlink the machines. LAN might be as tiny as one office, a teleworker's residential office, or a college campus with several buildings and fiber networks between the buildings (Cowley, 2012).

7.8.2. Ethernet Development

Being a LAN protocol, the Ethernet program was developed in the 1970s by Intel, Xerox, and DEC. As a matter of fact, it was known as the DIX Ethernet and later changed to thick Ethernet, due to the usage of coaxial cables. During the mid-80s, Ethernet was developed to support more functions and speeds. It was known as Ethernet 2, besides around the same period, IEEE was developing policies for Ethernet-based networks; these were known as 802.3. All through the years, Ethernet has progressed into 10-Mb/s, 100-Mb/s, and 1-Gb/s, including today's 10-Gb/s in the version of an IEEE protocol 802.3AE.

7.8.3. Ethernet Frame Configuration

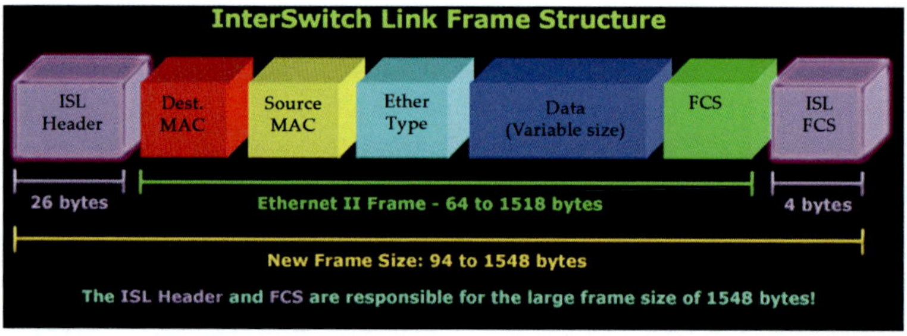

Figure 7.4. Ethernet frames can accommodate various data sizes measured in bytes.

Source: http://www.firewall.cx/networking-topics/vlan-networks/219-vlan-tagging.html.

Proper Ethernet frame configuration can reduce the chances of collision whenever two machines seek to transmit information at the same time. In Ethernet technologies, devices are able to automatically sense the frequency and decide if there are signals coming from other different transmitters. This defines the carrier section of the protocol. It allows equipment to easily sense the frequency and distinguish collisions, thereby making it a collision recognition aspect of the protocol.

How it functions: Whenever machines detect collisions, immediately they'll back off and reorganize transmission based on a random timer, this would be unique per machine ultimately. It increases the chances of machines seeking to retransmit concurrently again. This is exactly how it operates and forms a fair environment that in the long term must also be a system with good performance.

A few things might go wrong, typically with bad design, such as, a massive collision domain having too many machines which share one common channel. Something that may increase the possibility of machines transferring concurrently, or possibly increase the chances of collisions that consequently diminish or degrade output. Other issues are tied to malfunctioning firmware, which could be transmitting error frames or faults to the network, creating confusion with different machines and triggering frame and network malfunctions.

Header: The header comprises of both source and destination MAC addresses (every one measuring 6 octets in length), it also covers the EtherType scope and, optionally, the IEEE 802.1 and IEEE 802.1Q programs. The EtherType system measures two octets long, besides it can also be applied for two other purposes. Figures of 1500 or below simply mean it's applied to specify the payload size in octets, whereas values of 1536 or above show that it's applied as an EtherType, for showing which protocol is compressed in the frame's payload. When taken as EtherType, the frame length is typically determined based on location or spot of the interpacket space, including certified frame check sequence (FCS). Both IEEE 802.1adtag and IEEE 802.1Q tag, when in existence, represent a 4-octet field which specifies virtual LAN (VLAN) affiliation and IEEE 802.1p precedence. The original two octets captured in the tag are known as (TPID) Tag Protocol IDentifier, though they double up as EtherType fields as well showing that the structure is either 802.1ad or 802.1Q tagged. Generally, 802.1Q utilizes a 0x8100 TPID whereas the 802.1ad applies a 0x88a8 TPID. The least payload available is 42 octets whenever an 802.1Q tag has been present, plus 46 octets if lacking. In case the real payload is less, then padding bytes are included accordingly. The average payload amount is 1500 octets. Meanwhile, non-standard large frames permit for bigger maximum payload scale.

Frame check sequence: The (FCS) frame check series consists of 4-octet cyclical redundancy check (CRC) which allows for detection of degraded data within the whole frame as captured on the receiving end. The principle mentions that the FCS rate is computed in form of the secured MAC frame fields: covering origin and destination address, span/type field, padding, and MAC client data (which is, every field apart from FCS) utilizing the left shifting protocol CRC32 BZIP2. This standard stipulates that data is transferred in the least substantial bit of (bit 0) first, whereas the FCS is transferred in the most substantial bit range (bit 31) first (Carne, 2004).

The other alternative is calculating a CRC through right shifting, ultimately resulting in a CRC that is opposite of FCS. The code mentions that the receiver must calculate a fresh FCS when data is obtained, thereafter comparing the obtained FCS along with the FCS which the receiver has designed.

Another alternative is calculating a CRC covering both the obtained digital information and FCS, ultimately resulting in a permanent non-zero "verify" quotient. (The outcome is non-zero since the CRC is post supplemented during CRC generation). Considering that the data is obtained least significant bit originally, in order to avoid buffering octet's of data, normally the receiver applies the right-shifting CRC32, including the "verify" value (occasionally termed "magic check") which is 0x2144DF1C.

Nevertheless, hardware application of a right shifting CRC might employ a left shifting program Linear Feedback Shifting Register (LFSR), as main basis for computing the CRC, retreating the bits, and coming up with a verify rate of 0x38FB2284. Besides, since the supplementing of the CRC can be done post calculation or during transference. Eventually, what stays in the firmware register continues to be some non-complemented outcome (Carne, 2004).

End of frame – the physical level: End-of-frame layer is normally shown by the final-data-stream sign at the physical level, or loss of a carrier transmission; a good example is the 10BASE-T program, whereby the receiving side detects the finishing of a transferred frame through carrier loss. Subsequent physical levels apply an open end-of-data or final stream sequence or symbol in order to prevent ambiguity, particularly in cases where the carrier may be continually sending between frames; a possible example is the Gigabit Ethernet that carries a 8b/10b encryption scheme, applying special symbols that are transferred before and once the frame has been transmitted.

One of the common concepts is the Interpacket space-physical level. Generally, the Interpacket gap captures idle moments between packets. Once a packet is sent, transmitters would be needed to transfer around 96 bits or (12-octets) of idle line status before transferring the next packet.

7.8.4. IBM Token Ring

IBM Token-Ring Network refers to a high-tempo communications network used for linking data processing equipment within a local station (such as, building or campus). This network utilizes the IBM Cable System, as well as Type iii specified phone media, primarily for physical interconnection, including a token-ring accessibility protocol for system traffic control.

The IBM Cable System is commonly applied to offer physical interlinking between network attaching appliances and access units. Double twisted media pairs are applied to reserve the receiver and transmission path needs for ring transmission. Around 260 devices may be connected to the network through data grade media. A total of 72 devices may be connected to this network through Type III telephone media.

Wiring components are accessible for pre-cabling through the star-wired arrangement for connecting work areas to cabling closets. Furthermore, network attaching instruments are attached into work zone outlets, plus the outlets connected into a central network from the wiring closets (Carne, 2004).

Different access stations can be connected, as necessary, to accommodate every attaching device found on the network. The cable assemblies, or (patch cables), are accessible for use in executing networks without solid cable installation. Possible benefits from IBM's Token-Ring Network use are enhanced connectivity, interactive data communication, resource sharing, and structured building cabling.

The mechanisms of IBM's Token-Ring Network consist of a PC Adapter feature card, commonly used as a feature card for operating IBM (PCs) PCs. This adapter comprises of a microprocessor system working under management of the adapter resident-microcode. It transfers and receives data at a rate of 4-million bits a second through protocols that conform to ECMA 89 and IEEE802.5 principles.

This adapter offers logical link regulation functions that conform to IEEE 802.2 standards. Considerable reliability, accessibility, and serviceability roles are established both into the microcode and adapter. Moreover, Diagnostics applied during adapter initialization confirm the adapter operation, while checking-out the wiring to the access station. The adapter further detects long-term errors, like the loss of receivers' signal, while generating a notification signal for launching automatic network recovery. Certain recoverable errors, like bit errors within the transferred message, may be detected through the adapter for successive reporting to the ring diagnostic sequence (Carne, 2004).

There are various digital products available that allow for attaching of IBM (PC) PC to networks. However, for the program to be useable it must conform to Institute of Electrical and Electronics Engineers (IEEE) standard 802.5, including the (ECMA) European Computer Manufacturing Association standard89, which is used for token-ring, primary band (LANs) LANs.

Features: The IBM token-ring is an "open" structure architecture that accommodates both IBM attaching and non-IBM connecting devices, through technical interface provisions that were made available during the initial quarter of 1986 by IBM, also including semi-conductor components accessible from Texas Instruments, Incorporated for application in non-IBM machines.

The system allows for Physical interconnectivity of network modules through the IBMCabling Structural data grade transmission (Type 1 and Type 2 cable), as well as Type3 quantified telephone media. Furthermore, modular, and dynamic network configurations are available, which support between 2-to-260 connective devices through the IBM Cable System data-grade media, including from 2-to-72 equipment with Type 3 phone media capability.

7.8.5. Fiber Data-Distribution Interface (FDDI)

The FDDI is a group of ISO and ANSI standards applied for data transmission through fiber optic cables in the (LAN) local-area-network, which can spread in scope up to 200 kilometers (124 miles). Typically, the FDDI model is based upon the token-ring protocol. Apart from being massive geographically, FDDI LANs can support multiple users at a time. Besides, FDDI is normally used as background for the (WAN) wide area network. The FDDI network comprises of double token rings, the first is for potential backup just in case the original ring fails.

Additionally, the main ring provides up to 100-Mbps volume. In case the secondary ring isn't required for backup, then it can also transmit data, stretching overall volume to 200 Mbps. One ring can stretch the total distance; where a double ring can stretch up to 100 kilometers or (62 miles) (White, 2015).

The FDDI is defined as an invention of (ANSC) American National Standardization Committee X3-T9, which conforms to Open Structures Interconnection (OSI) principle of functional layering. This program can be applied to interlink LANs through other protocols. Moreover, FDDI-II is an edition of FDDI which adds the function of adding circuit-switched solution to the network, such that voice signals may also be addressed. Plus work is still ongoing for how to connect FDDI systems to the emerging (SONET) Synchronous Optical Network.

How FDDI Functions: FDDI is typically implemented in form of a double token-passing ring inside a ring topology (such as, campus networks) or even star topology (inside a building). Besides, the double ring comprises of both primary and secondary rings. The main ring transmits data. While the counter-rotating ancillary ring may transmit data in the other direction, though is more widely reserved in form of a backup just in case the main ring goes down.

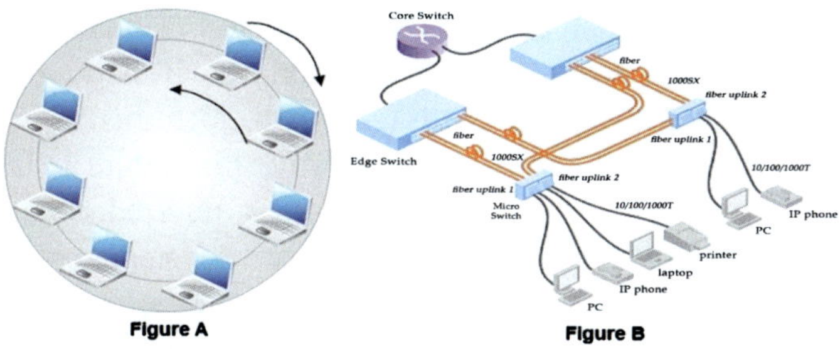

Figure 7.5. FDDI networks can be grouped into either single or double connections.

Source: http://ecomputernotes.com/computernetworkingnotes/network-technologies/fddi-network.

It provides FDDI some extent of fault tolerance that's ideal for network backbones. For the unlikely case of a primary ring error, FDDI mechanically reprograms itself to utilize the secondary ring instead. Errors can be identified and repaired through a fault isolation method known as beaconing. Nevertheless, the secondary ring may further be configured to carry data, lengthening the overall potential bandwidth to around 200Mbps.

Moreover, stations are linked to one (or multiple) rings through a media interaction connector (MIC). The two fiber ports may be either female or male, based on the implementation. Moreover, there are two unique FDDI implementations, based on whether stations get attached to a single or multiple ring. For Single-attached stations, also called Class B stations, it involves connecting to either the main or secondary ring through M ports. A single-attached FDDI applies just the primary ring, plus isn't as widely employed for network backbones like dual-attached FDDI. The Single-attached stations mainly are used for connecting Ethernet LANs, or personal servers to FDDI pillars.In Dual-attached or Class A stations, the configuration involves connecting to both rings simultaneously. The A slot is the point whereby the primary ring passes through while the secondary ring goes out, while B-port works is the opposite manner. Meanwhile, M ports offer attachment spots for single-linked stations. The FDDI utilizes a programmed token-passing technology that's same to that seen in token ring networks, described in IEEE 802.5 protocol. Most FDDI stations produce a token which manages the order whereby other stations can gain admission to the cable (White, 2015).

The token travels around the ring, going from a specific node to another. In case a station seeks to transfer information, it will capture the token, transfer as many data frames as it needs (within the identified access period), before ultimately releasing the token. Generally, this feature of transferring several data frames for each token capture is referred to as capacity allocation scheme, which is contrary to the priority system applied in IEEE 802.5 token-ring protocols. Each node available on the ring looks up the frames. Ultimately, the recipient station reads the data captured from the frames, then when these frames return back to the original station, they're automatically stripped off the ring. In general, the dual-ring FDDI structure can capture up to 500 stations (White, 2015).

CHAPTER

8

Computer Networking and Communication: Wireless Networks

CONTENTS

8.1. INTRODUCTION

These are computer networks (CS) that have no connection to any kind of cables. They use data connections that are wireless between network nodes. These networks are used with the purpose of avoiding the high costs that come with installing cables as a form of connection between different locations of equipment. Wireless systems are based on radio waves, which are an implementation that occurs at the network structure's physical level.

Some of the different wireless networks include satellite communication networks, cell phone networks, terrestrial microwave networks, wireless sensor networks, and wireless local area networks (LANs). Wireless communication has helped in enhancing our way of life. This technology has been improved over the decades, thus making their use much more widespread.

8.2. USES OF WIRELESS SYSTEMS

Figure 8.1. A network that is wireless allows devices to remain connected to networks while providing the ability to roam without having to tether to any wires.

Source: https://www.pcworld.com/article/2048052/6-mistakes-to-avoid-when-setting-up-your-small-business-wireless-network.amp.html.

There are different forms of wireless communication. This is inclusive of mobiles, satellites, Bluetooth, infrared, and wireless networks. There are many small businesses that have certain elements of wireless communication, inclusive of cloud-based activities, the Internet of Things, and even mobile applications. This means they are able to cause an impact in societies and companies generally. Some of the uses of this system are:

- The ability to make calls – globally, there are so many people, billions, who have subscribed to cellular communication. Wireless systems normally work by their ability to bounce radio waves from a certain cell tower to a different one. Cell towers help in creating a network from which waves can be directed. Therefore, the receivers of the cell then have triangulation of the waves to the antennae of their phones. Despite the fact that the internet is available, phone calls are still an important element of any business and even in communication with other people.
- Connection of devices – since the development of Bluetooth technology, people have been able to connect different devices to each other and to other devices. It is able to do this through radio waves that have a short range and low energy. Devices that are enabled utilize these waves to allow for the linking up with as well as provision of access to other devices that have been connected to Bluetooth. For example, people are able to enable the connection of their smartphones to headsets that are Bluetooth enabled. This is normally used by people who are too busy to make or receive a call such as drivers or business people. In addition, it is possible to enable the transference of data from a device to a different one with the use of Bluetooth. All this can be done using a computer, tablet or a smartphone. It is also possible to print documents in the office or schools using Bluetooth technology. Internet of Things also requires to be connected to Bluetooth for one to be able to connect electronic devices in the house. It allows for connection of phones, thermostats, light fixtures, cameras, and computers. It is also possible to link speakers and television sets. There are also some health enthusiasts who have the ability to pair their fitness devices to their phones or tablets. Doctors are also able to utilize them for acquiring data from devices that have been connected, such as a pacemaker.
- It allows one to access the internet – there are many people who know how to connect to the internet, however, they are not aware of how these connections occur. They are only possible through the use of wireless networks. The network systems are able to utilize routers for sending radio frequency signals to different devices. These devices should, however, be equipped with adapters that are wireless so as to have the ability to receive signals, in addition to being able to access the internet. This is what makes it possible for internet to be shared amongst companies.

- Enhancement of security – the different forms of this system are able to ensure the enhancement of security. For example, it is possible to transmit and receive radio signals with the use of a walkie-talkie. They have no disturbances with connection such as those that come up with cellphones. This allows for these walkie-talkies to be given to their guards. It is also possible for employees to use them for communication inside a building, especially if they are far away from each other.

Figure 8.2. Wireless security helps prevents damage or unautorized access to computers or data using wireless networks, including Wi-Fi networks

Source: https://solutionsreview. com/wireless-network/top-wireless-network-security-concerns/.

- • So as to be able to locate and track – satellites can be connected to devices that are here on the earth through the satellite communication technology. Therefore, we are able to call other people and also have an internet connection. The Global Positioning System (GPS), which is also referred to as GPS, is the most common use of this technology. This provides businesses with the opportunity to track and locate their employees as well as their vehicles.

8.3. ADVANTAGES AND DISADVANTAGES OF WIRELESS SYSTEMS

There are both pros and cons of wireless systems. Some of the advantages include ease of installation, reliability, mobility, cost, among others. Here are some of the descriptions of the advantages:

- Cost – wireless communication helps in eliminating the cost of installation for cables, wired, as well as other infrastructure that is involved, therefore reducing the overall system costs in comparison to communication systems that are wired. Installation of networks that are wired in a building involves having to dig up the ground for laying the cables as well as having to run the wires across streets, which is quite complicated and expensive, in addition to it being a task that consumes a lot of time. In buildings that are historic, it is not advisable to drill holes due to the fact that it could affect the importance and integrity of the building. This is also similar when it comes to old buildings, and these should use Wireless LAN or Wi-Fi.
- Mobility – this is one of the greatest advantages of wireless communication systems. Due to the fact that cables are not required for the connection, wireless communication systems allows for easier portability. It allows people to move around without losing the network connection.
- It is easier to install – installing and setting up the equipments for wireless communication networks as well as the infrastructure involved is quite simple, and it is also due to the fact that you do not need to install cables. In addition, the amount of time it takes to for setting up these systems, such as Wi-Fi, in much lower in comparison to having to set up networks that are full cabled.
- It is reliable – due to the fact that it does not need wires nor cables, the chances of a communication failure happening because of damages that may occur due to the condition of the environment, the metallic conductors naturally diminishing, and even cable splicing.
- Recovery from disasters – if by any chance there was an accident that may be caused by a fire, flood, or any other cause, wireless communication systems do not lose communication for a long period of time, and it also does not need to be fixed. The connection comes back on its own.

Despite the fact that there are many advantages of the wireless communication system, there are also some disadvantages. Health, security, and interference are some of the main disadvantages. Here is a description:Interference – these systems normally utilize spaces that are open as the mediums in which they can transmit signals. Due to this, there is a major possibility that the radio signals from a certain system or network for wireless communication, may cause an interference with the other signals. For example, Wi-Fi, and Bluetooth both normally use a frequency of 2.4GHz to communicate. When these two devices are actively being used at the same time, it is possible for their signals to interfere with the connection.

Figure 8.3. There are two common reasons why man-made interference may occur. These include: electrical equipments and transmitters. Interference can be generated by all communication systems that transmit signals.

Source: https://blog.global.fujitsu.com/fgb/2019–03–07/signal-interference-a-new-problem-in-the-age-of-wireless-communication-that-can-suddenly-disconnect-your-smartphone/.

Security – security of data is one of the greatest issues that come up when it comes to wireless communication. Due to the fact that the signals are normally transmitted in a space that is open, there is a high chance of enemies intercepting the signals and copying information that is considered sensitive.

Concerns to do with health – being exposed to any form of radiation continuously can be dangerous for the human body. Regardless of the fact that the levels of radio frequency energy that are able to cause any damage have not been established accurately, we are still advised against radio frequency radiation. This is more of a concern on the long term as no specific cases have come up yet.

8.4. TYPES OF WIRELESS SYSTEMS

These days, everyone uses a mobile phone, and different people use it for different reasons, such as multimedia, internet, talking, etc. These services need to be made available to the users in real time, which means that as the person is using the phone, so should the services be available. It is possible to transfer images, videos, data, voice, etc (Gast, 2005).

There are many other different services that are provided by wireless communication systems, such as paging, TV, cellular telephone, video conferencing, radio, etc. Because we require many different services for communication, there is development of many different forms of wireless communication systems. Some of the main systems that are found in our world today include:

- Television and Radio Broadcasting;
- Radar;
- Global Positioning System (GPS);
- Wireless LANs, also known as or WLANs, Wi-Fi, or WiFi5;
- Satellite Communication and paging;
- Bluetooth;
- Fixed wireless access;
- Radio frequency identification;
- Systems home RF; and
- Wide Area Wireless Data Services (WWANs).

There are also many others other than these. It is also possible to classify these systems as Full-duplex, Half Duplex and Simplex. Simplex communication refers to communication that is one way, for example, a system for making radio broadcasts. The Half Duplex communication refers to a communication that is two-way, however, it is not simultaneous, for example, a walkie-talkie. The Full-duplex communication refers to communication that is two-way, however, for this one, it is simultaneous, for example, using mobile phones.

Wireless communication devices are different in accordance to their uses. They may also be different in shape, size, cost, and even the data throughput (Gast, 2005).

Below we will discuss some of the wireless communication systems.

8.4.1. Television and Radio Broadcasting

Figure 8.4. The first form of broadcasting was Morse code and it worked by having to send telegraph signals over the airwaves.

Source: https://beonair.com/should-i-work-in-radio-or-tv/.

This is an example of the simplex communication system, seeing as the transmission of the information is one way and all the end-users receive the same data. Radios were the first devices that were able to broadcast. Transmitting television and radio programs from a television of a radio station to receivers at their homes through the use of radio waves is considered terrestrial broadcasting. In most countries, you need a license to broadcast, especially if it is using a wireless communication system. Transmitting with the use of cables or wires, such as cable tv, can also be referred to as broadcast, however, these do not always need a license. Using streaming digital technology to transmit radio and television programs has of this day started being considered as broadcasting (Rackley, 2011).

8.4.2. Radar

This is a system that is meant for detecting objects. It utilizes radio waves for the determination of angle, velocity, or range of the objects. It can help in detecting ships, motor vehicles, terrain, weather formations, guided missiles, and even aircrafts. These systems have a transmitter that produces waves that are electromagnetic in the microwave or radio domain, an antenna that is receiving, an antennae that is receiving, and a processor and receiver for the determination of the object's properties. Either continuous or pulsed radio waves from the transmitter are reflected by the object, and these waves then return to the person receiving, thus providing data on the speed and location of the object.

8.4.3. Global Positioning System (GPS)

This is a radio-navigation system that is based on satellites. The United States Government owns it, and the United States Space Force operates it. It helps in providing time information as well as geolocation to a receiver of GPS which can be anywhere on earth or near the earth where there is no obstruction of the line of sight to GPS satellites (either 4 or more). It is one of the global navigation satellite systems. Building blocks and mountains are obstacles that may block the GPS signals which are already relatively weak.This system does not need the user to make any transmission of data, and it is able to work in an independent manner without the help of Internet or telephonic reception, however, having Internet or telephonic reception can improve the usefulness of the positioning information that can be provided by the GPS. This system helps in providing important positioning capabilities to commercial, civil, and military users all over the world. It was created by the US government, and they also maintain it and ensure that it is accessible for free to users who are equipped with a GPS receiver (Rackley, 2011).The concept of the GPS is based on the known position as well as the time of GPS satellites that are specialized. These satellites are equipped with atomic clocks that are very stable, which are in synchrony with each other and also with the ground clocks. There is a daily correction of any drift from the time that has been maintained on the ground. It is in a similar manner that the locations of the satellites are accurately known. GPS receivers are also equipped with clocks; however, they are not as precise and stable.

Figure 8.5. The GPS that we use these days has three main sections. These include: a control segment, a user segment, and a space segment.

Source: https://afb.org/blindness-and-low-vision/using-technology/smartphone-gps-navigation-people-visual-impairments.

There is a continuous transmission of radio signals by GPS satellites. These signals have the data and current time about the location. Because the radio waves have a constant speed and they are also independent of the speed of the satellites, the delay in time between when a signal is transmitted by the satellite and the time in which the receiver gets it, is proportional to the distance between the receiver and the satellite. The receiver of the GPS signals is able to monitor more than one satellite at a time, and also solving equations for the determination of the exact location of the receiver as well as the level at which it has deviated from true time. For the receiver to be able to compute four quantities that are unknown, at a minimum, four satellites are required to be in view of it.

8.4.4. Wireless LAN (WLAN)

This is a wireless computer network that links many devices with the use of wireless communication. This makes it possible for users to move around in the specific area which still remaining in connection with the network. WLAN enables one to connect to the internet using a gateway.

Most of WLAN's are based on IEEE 802.11 standards and are referred to as Wi-Fi. These systems have become popular because of their simplicity and ease of installation. They are also widely utilized in commercial properties that provide internet access for their customers and employees (Gast, 2005).

There are different types of WLAN networks:-Infrastructure – this mode is mostly used for the deployment of Wi-Fi networks. In this mode, the base station represents the point hub for the wireless access, and it is through the hub that nodes communicate. Most of the time, the hub has a fiber or wired network connection, and it is possible for it to have wireless connections, that are permanent, to different nodes. They normally work by fixing wireless access points as well as providing services to the nodes of the clients that are within range. Smartphones and laptops are wireless clients that need to be connected to the access point so as to allows them to join the network. There are times that a network may have access to many different points, with the security arrangement and also with a similar SSID. In such a situation, being able to connect to any point of access on the network allows the client to join. In this situation, the software that the client is using will work by choosing the point of access so as to try and provide good services.

Peer to peer – in this network, the stations have peer to peer communication. These do not have a base, and no one has to be permitted to talk. They use the Independent Basic Service Set to accomplish this.

Another type of network with this type of communication is the Wi-Fi Direct Network. Peer to peer networks enable direct communication of devices that are wireless. It is possible for devices that are wireless to communicate and discover each other directly without the need of central points of access, as long as they are within range of each other. This methodology is mainly used by 2 computers so as to allow their connection in order to form a network. In this situation, using a signal strength meter may lead to lacking the ability to read the strength in an accurate manner, and this can mislead, due to the fact that it is only able to register the strength of the signal that is strongest, which may be the one closest to the computer (Gast, 2005).

Bridge – this can be utilized for making network connections that are of different types. It is possible to connect devices, using a wireless Ethernet bridge, on an Ethernet network that is wired to a network that is wireless. The bridge works as the point of connection to the WLAN.

Wireless distribution system – This system allows for wireless interconnection of the points of access in the IEEE 802.11 network. It provides the ability for the expansion of a wireless network with the use of many different access points, without having to link them using a wired backbone. The points of access can either be remote base station, relay base station, or main base station. Typically, the main base station works through its connection to the wired Ethernet. The relay base station is able to relay data between wireless clients, remote base stations, or different relay stations either to another relay base station or to a main base station.

Figure 8.6. Above is an illustration of how the wireless distribution system works. It works by extending a Wi-Fi hotspot to an area that is much larger without running wires to each of the access point.

Source: https://www.pinterest.com/pin/130956301643427824/.

8.4.5. Satellite Communication and Paging

This type of wireless communication is one of the most important. That are able to provide coverage all over the world without having to depend on the density of the population. This system is the one that provides broadcasting, internet, telecommunications, positioning, and navigation (GPS), etc. There are also other services that are wireless that depend on Satellite Communication Systems, such as television broadcasting, mobile, as well as other radio systems.

Paging is considered a form of technology that is obsolete, however, it was very successful before mobile phones became the main means of communication. A pager is able to provide information in message form in a simplex system, which means that it is only possible to receive messages without sending them back (Siddiqui, 2005).

8.4.6. Bluetooth

This is a wireless communication system that has a low range. It is a very important system in our modern time. It helps in providing data, audio, and voice transmission, having a 10-meter range for transmission. Roughly all of the laptops, tablets, and mobile phones have Bluetooth devices. It is possible to connect them to cameras, audio equipment, Bluetooth receivers, etc.

Bluetooth transmitters have a low power and therefore cannot interfere with other Bluetooth connection such as life support. The short-range transmitters in the Bluetooth devices makes it one of their biggest advantages. They hardly use any power and, due to the fact that they are not able to move far, they are them much more secure in theoretical terms, in comparison to wireless networks that are able to work over ranges that are longer, for example, Wi-Fi.

These devices normally work by detecting and connecting to each other in an automatic manner. It allows for up to 8 devices to communicate simultaneously. They do not cause interference amongst each other due to the fact that each of the devices utilize different channels from the 79 that are available. If there are 2 devices that want to communicate, they are able to choose one channel through random selection. If the channel they pick is already occupied, then they can pick a different one randomly. This process is referred to as spread-spectrum frequency hopping. So as to reduce any chances of any other electrical appliances causing interference, or even for improving security, the paired devices can frequently change the frequency that is being used (Siddiqui, 2005).

When there are two or more Bluetooth devices working to share information amongst each other, this forms a piconet, which is a mini-computer network. It is possible for other Bluetooth devices to join and leave the piconet that exists at any point in time.

8.4.7. FIXED WIRELESS ACCESS

This provides the ability to operate devices or systems for wireless communication by connecting two fixed locations, such as a tower to a building, using a wireless link, such as a laser bridge, or by using a radio. It is part of the infrastructure for wireless LAN. It is much cheaper to use Fixed Wireless Data links in comparison to having to lease fiber or install cables in between the two locations.

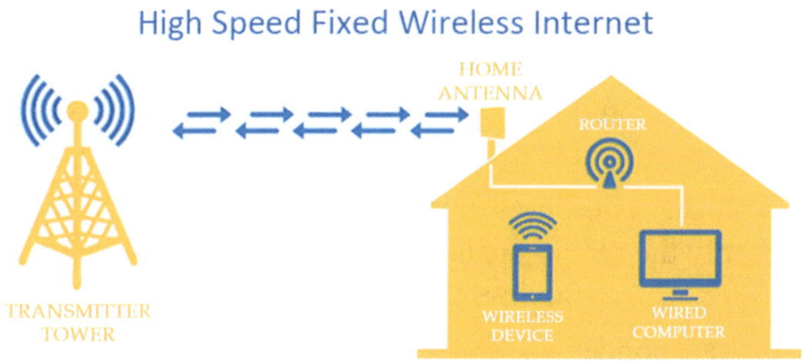

Figure 8.7. Fixed wireless internet is normally mainly installed in areas that are rural, where having to set this infrastructure up would be very expensive. It is also expensive to transport and bury cables in the ground. In addition, acquiring the required permits is also quite expensive.

Source: http://news.callapr.co.ke/zuku-loses-safcom-fixed-internet-rises/amp/.

Transmission of the signal from one point to another happens through the air, through a terrestrial microwave platform, instead of having to use optical fiber or copper. This means that fixed wireless does not need local telephone service, nor does it need satellite feeds, to work. One of the benefits of this system is that is makes it possible for users in remote areas to connect with each other, without having to lay new cables, and it also provides the capacity for broad bandwidth which is not obstructed by the capacities of cables or fiber. Fixed wireless devices normally get their electrical power from the utility mains that are public. This is different from portable wireless and mobile wireless which are normally powered by batteries.

8.4.8. Radio Frequency Identification

This is a form of wireless communication that works by incorporating the use of electrostatic or electromagnetic coupling in the portion of the electromagnetic spectrum that deals with radio frequency, so as to be able to make an identification of either a person, an animal, or an object. This technology is used in the household, retail sales, shipping, in managing inventory, in manufacturing, and also in healthcare.

It is used in a way that is similar to the barcode technology for tracking inventory, however, there are three main differences that one should consider before choosing wither one. These include:

- Radio frequency identification tags do not need to be read in a direct line of sight;
- The data that is stored in the Radio frequency identification tag can undergo updating in real time. The barcode, however, can only be read and it is not possible to change its data;
- Radio frequency identification tags need to have a source of power. Barcodes, however, do not need a power source to works, and only the reader needs to be connected to a source of power.

Each Radio frequency identification system has three main components. These are: a transponder, a transceiver, and a scanning antenna. A combination of the transceiver and the scanning antenna is referred to as a Radio frequency identification interrogator or reader.

The reader is a portable or permanently attached device that is connected to a network. It is able to transmit signals for activating the tags through radio frequency waves. Once the tag is activated, it is able to send back a wave to the antenna, where the wave then undergoes translation into data.

In the Radio frequency identification tags itself is where you find the transponder. T

here are variations in the range for reading the Radio frequency identification tags, and these are based on certain factors, such as the type of reader, the type of tag, interference in the environment surrounding it or from other Radio frequency identification readers and tags, and the frequency of the Radio frequency identification. In general,

Radio frequency identification tags that have a stronger source of power tend to also have a read range that is longer.

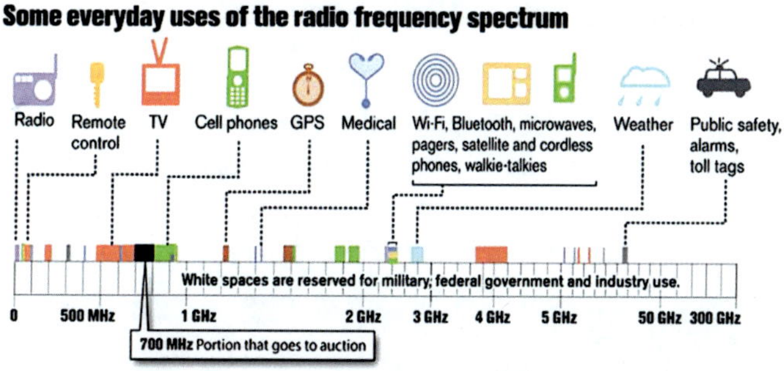

Figure 8.8. Above are some of the uses of the radio frequency spectrum. This system allows for many different devices to communicate without affecting the intercommunication of other types of devices.

Source: https://www.smartrayvision.com/news-1/what-is-radio-frequency/.

8.4.9. Systems Home RF

The systems home radio frequency is a standard for home networking that works by combining the Digital Enhanced Cordless Telecommunication and 802.11b portable phone standards into one. It was developed by Proxim Inc. it uses a technique of frequency hopping for the delivery of speeds as high as 1.6Mbps which can travel up to 160 ft. This range is quite short for use in the workplace, however, it can work in the household which was its main market (Rackley, 2011).

This system is amongst the two standards that are competing for the market share of the home network. Wi-Fi is the other, and it works by using a direct sequence spread spectrum transmission method for the delivery of higher speeds that can go up to 11Mbps. The home RF system has proven to have mechanisms that are much better in dealing with interference from home appliances such as microwaves. They are also able to handle video, audio, and voice data much better than Wi-Fi. However, Wi-Fi is still much faster that the home RF system but much more expensive.

Corporate Wide Area Networks (WANs) mainly use Wi-Fi products, which end up supporting the older standards for the networks at home. There are certain companies, such as Proxim and IBM, which started to support both standards despite the fact that most of the support from the industries is split between the two (Rackley, 2011).

8.4.10. Wide Area Wireless Data Services

These services provide high-mobility users with wireless data over a large coverage area. The specific geographical regions that are using these systems have base stations that have been mounted on mountains, rooftops, or towers. It is possible for the base station to either form a multi-hop ad hoc network that is wireless, or be connected to a backbone network that is wired.

Figure 8.9. Wide Area Wireless Data Services is wide area network that works by providing internet services to large separate areas that have coverage or cells through a wireless connection.

Source: http://www.lessons2all.com/WAWDS.php.

There is a wide area wireless data service that is overlaid on the cellular telephone network that is analog. It is referred to as the cellular digital packet data. This system is able to share the Description Frequency division multiple access voice channels of the systems that are analog, because most of these channels have been idle mainly because of the development of digital cellular.

8.4.11. Mobile Telephone Communication System

This wireless communication system is probably the most commonly used. There is no other technology that has changed the world as much as the development of the mobile cellular device. Due to the fast-paced development of technology, mobile phones these days do much more than just making calls. They have been equipped with many other features, such as GPS, Wi-Fi, FM Radio, and even Bluetooth. This makes it possible for mobile phones to incorporate many different wireless systems, making it the most effective and efficient wireless system.

8.4.12. Infrared Communication

This wire communication system is also commonly used in our day to day lives. It utilizes the electromagnetic spectrum's infrared waves. It is applied in remote control in audio equipment, cars, televisions, etc.

8.5. WI-FI VS HOME RF VS BLUETOOTH

8.5.1. Advantages and Disadvantages of Wi-Fi

Some of the advantages of Wi-Fi include:

It is easy to use – it is very easy to connect to a Wi-Fi network. All one needs to do is go to the settings, click on the Wi-Fi option, and turn on the Wi-Fi. If the network available has a password, all one needs to do is input the password and press connect. This is the same process in every device that can connect to Wi-Fi. After connecting, one is able to use the internet without any further complications. This process is easy even for those who are not computer literate.

It provides access to the internet – due to the fact that the Wi-Fi provides the opportunity for one to connect to the internet, it is possible to have access to the large amount of information that is found on the internet, while just sitting. This is very simple. It allows the user to solve any queries they may have, download movies, videos, news, audio, etc.

It allows for mobile computing – wireless connections have provided us with a level of mobility that was not possible in the past. Computers that have broadband cards are able to form an internet connection from almost any place. This level of mobility has helped in creating a large market for many different mobile applications including those that are able to track steps and even mobile banking.

It provides flexible computing – this is one of the greatest benefits of Wi-Fi. When offices are equipped with a Wi-Fi network, the users do not need to worry about finding a cable or a network jack. People can connect to the wireless network immediately and this allows them to maintain productivity at any time. As long as the Wi-Fi router has a range that can reach each end of the building, the users can use the internet at any point in time and at any position in the building. In addition, the Wi-Fi router does not only work for one person at a time. It allows for many devices to connect at a time.

It is not expensive to implement – because the network is wireless it does not need cables. The infrastructure for wiring an office or a house is quite expensive, and it accounts for a large portion of the funds needed for installing the network. This cost is eliminated due to the lack of wires.

It is efficient and effective –Wi-Fi is very effective. It allows people to perform many different functions at the same time. The user can pay their bills, shop, or transfer money online. It also brought a breakthrough in online communications via mail providers, such as Gmail or Yahoo. Being an effective and efficient means of communication, it saves everyone plenty of time.

ADVANTAGES AND DISADVANTAGES OF WI-FI		
	ADVANTAGES	DISADVANTAGES
1)	Freedom – You can work from any location that you can get a signal.	Speed – Slower than cable.
2)	Setup Cost – No cabling required.	Range – Affected by various medium.
3)	Flexibility – Quick and easy to setup in temp or permanent space.	Travels best through open space. Reduced by walls, glass, water, etc.
4)	Scaleable – Can be expanded with growth.	Security – Greater exposure to risks.
5)	Mobile Access – Can access the network on the move.	Unauthorized access. Compromising data. Denial of service.

Figure 8.10. Above are some of the pros and cons of Wifi. One of the greatest concerns is security. Cyber hacking has led many issues such as identity theft, spreading of malware, stealing private information for malicious intent, etc.

Source: https://computersciencementor.com/advantages-and-disadvantages-of-wi-fi/.

Despite the many advantages, there are also a couple of disadvantages, including:

They provide a shorter range – all Wi-Fi networks have a limited range. It is not possible to access the connection when the user is not within the range of the Wi-Fi. In addition, thick walls and concrete normally reduce the Wi-Fi signals. Locations in the building that are in the corners and surrounded by walls are not able to access a proper signal. In this situation, one need to add a Wi-Fi extender which will help in boosting the range of the signal.

It provides issues with security – Wi-Fi provides a huge opportunity for hackers to take advantage and perform malicious acts. It is possible for these hackers to crack passwords, which are meant to be the main form of security of any Wi-Fi. After cracking the passwords, they are able to utilize the internet. It is even possible for the hackers to track where the connection is coming from once they have cracked the password. This allows them to make extractions of Information that is valuable from devices that are connected to the router. Sometimes, when users connect to the router of a hacker, they can be accused of identity theft. This makes it very unsafe to use other people's Wi-Fi. It is also not advisable to perform any confidential transactions on an open network.

They have the possibility of causing cancer – smartphones have a chip that normally emits radiation from different devices that are wireless. Research has shown that exposure to this radiation for a long period of time can lead to one developing a tumor, leading to cancer. This, however, is not supported by strong evidence. The scientists believe that it is more of a chronic advancement, which means that is take a very long time period for the tumor to cause any effects.

It may cause insomnia – there has also been a discovery that people sleep in areas that have Wi-Fi signals have problems sleeping. The pollution that is caused by Wi-Fi normally changes the user's pattern of sleep, thus leading to insomnia. This can be dangerous as insomnia causes hypertension and depression. This, however, does not have much evidence backing it as well.

8.5.2. Advantages and Disadvantages of the Home RF

Some if the advantages of this system include:

- Based on its frequency, it is able to penetrate through building and house walls. This means that walls rarely tend to interfere with the strength of the signal. This means that it is best used for television and radio transmission, in addition to cellular mobile phone services.
- It can be used in the health sector for a couple of applications. It is normally utilized for taking images if the human body using the MRI. It can also be used for tightening the skin, and also as a diathermy instrument for surgery.
- It is utilized to detect an object in radar.

- It is also used in the microwave communication system that requires a line of sight.
- It is used for communication using a satellite.

Some of the disadvantages of this system include:

- The home RF system has emissions of radiations which are not controlled. These may cause a negative effect on pregnant women, children, patients with a pacemaker, small insects, fauna, and flora, the elderly, etc. This radiation can cause the growth of a tumor which can lead to cancer.
- It is a lightning attractor. According to research, any location that has an RF cellular tower has proven to have a higher level of lightening, in comparison to areas that do not have the towers.
- It has also shown to affect growing vegetation. Fruits and other crops that are growing around RF towers have developmental issues.

It is possible to find RF waves in both Line of Sight as well as non-line of sight regions that have the transmitters. This means that hackers are able to intrude the network and acquire information that is either personal or official. They can then end up using this information for negative reasons. So as to avoid this situation, radio frequency that is based on waves can be utilized together with algorithms that are highly secured such as WPA, WEP, AES, etc. It is also possible to modulate the RF signal with the use of spread spectrum techniques, or frequency hopping, so as to get rid of the possibility of having an enemy eavesdropping. This is one of the greatest disadvantages that come with the home RF system.

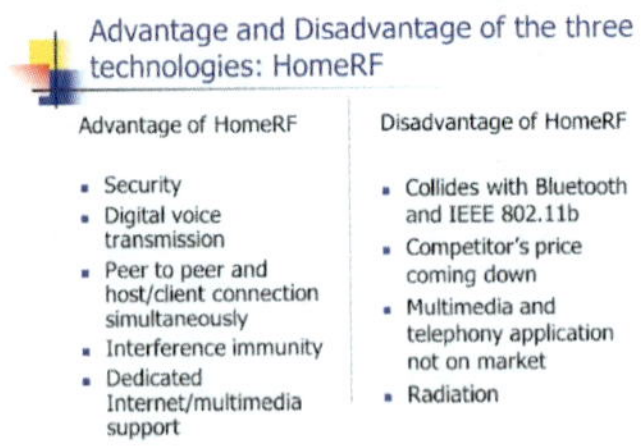

Figure 8.11. Above are a summary of the advantages and disadvantages of the Home RF system. This system is much more secure when compared to Wi-Fi. In addition, it also supports multimedia and the internet.

Source: https://slideplayer.com/amp/5919669/.

8.5.3. Advantages and Disadvantages of Bluetooth

Some of the advantages of Bluetooth include:

It is used widely – it has become a very popular form of wireless system. It still continues to gain popularity at a high rate. Almost everyone uses Bluetooth these days. It has become a very important aspect of new products that come up day-to-day.

Companies are using it to make our lives much better and easier. In the near future, almost every form of technology with be wireless because of the incorporation of Bluetooth. Bluetooth can be used on cell phones, headsets, printers, laptops, etc.

It is simple to use – one does not need to be computer literate to use Bluetooth. Anyone, as long as they have the device and instructions, is able to use Bluetooth, due to how easy it is to use. This is what makes is very popular. It is wireless and easy to use.

It does not need to be paid for – no one is required to pay any cost for the services.

It comes with the device you already own, and you don't have to pay for an extra router or device to have access to Bluetooth. All you need are the two devices, and you can connect them using Bluetooth.

It allows the user to go wireless – you do not need to carry a cord around to connect to Bluetooth. You also do not need to look for somewhere to connect the device so as to gain the connection.

The only cables you may need are those for charging the devices. When outside your home, it is also possible to connect to the internet with Bluetooth without having to use any wires.

It allows the user to remain in control – in spite the fact that it is possible to exchange information from one cell phone to another, it is still possible to make sure that the information is kept private.

One has to accept or reject requests using the device in question, so as to be able to transfer files, or even to allow someone to access certain files.

As long as the Bluetooth on the device is on, it is possible to receive requests from other devices to pair or share files.

Figure 8.12. One of main advantages of Bluetooth is that it is very efficient due to its wireless nature. However, its greatest disadvantage is that is can easily be hacked, making is not secure for private information

Source: https://techspirited.com/advantages-disadvantages-of-bluetooth-technology/amp.

Some of the disadvantages of Bluetooth include:

It uses excessive battery life – this is mostly on the smartphone, however, other devices such as Bluetooth speakers may experience the same effect. Leaving the Bluetooth enable on a device for a whole day means using up much more battery life. It is advisable to only switch it one when using it, then switch it off after the task is completed. This is not a lot of work because it only takes a button to enable and disable it.

Bluetooth internet is slow – with all devices that have Bluetooth, the Bluetooth internet runs very slowly. It does not have a good connection and thus not recommended unless it is extremely necessary.

8.6. BLUETOOTH: PICONET AND SCATTER-NET

Bluetooth is a Wireless Personal Area Network (PAN) open standard that helps in providing an ad-hoc way of being able to connect devices in a range of 10 meters. It is a radio technology that has a short range, it is not expensive, and it is very power efficient. It is able to support connections that are either point-to-multipoint, or point-to-point.

It aids in connecting devices that are handheld such as mobile phone, laptops, printers, as well as other accessories that are in a radius of 10 meters. Each radio channel uses a frequency hopping method and it also operational on the 2.3GHz. It allows devices that are Bluetooth enabled to locate each other. It, however, requires the action of the user so as to connect to other devices and also other networks.

In a Bluetooth network that is referred to as a Piconet, it allows connection of up to eight devices. One of the devices normally works as the master, and the other seven are normally referred to as the slaves. Within a piconet, it can only support a maximum of seven slaves. When there is a communication between a minimum of two devices, there is formation of a piconet.

A scatter-net on the other hand is formed by the connection of more than two devices communicate with the help of a bridge node. There can be a maximum of 255 nodes that are parked in the network, in addition to the seven slaves that are active, all which are only able to respond to a beacon signal that is initiated by the master. The master is the one that is able to give the slaves all the tasks and functions they are supposed to perform, and the slave do it. There is no communication that occurs between the slaves. All of it is between the master and the slaves (White, 2015).

There are some difference between the piconet and the scatter-net. In the piconet, it is possible to link many networks together with the help of some devices such as Bluetooth. A scatter-net is formed when there is a network of two or more piconet.

That means that it works mainly as a bridge between two or more piconet. Both the piconet and scatter-net are ad-hoc networks, and are used with Bluetooth devices. The piconet network can only allow for the connection of a maximum of seven devices, while the scatter-net allows for more than eight.

In the piconet, the devices normally function as slaves and their master. In the scatter-net, one of the piconet becomes the master, or even a slave in a different piconet, all from the same scatter-net.

There is a designated radio at the master which works by making a determination of the channel and phase being utilized each device in the piconet. It then provides a parameter that provides the devices with the channel they should tune themselves into. It is not possible for the slaves and the master to function independently; they all have to work together. The slave can only function without the master if it is given permission by the master to do so.

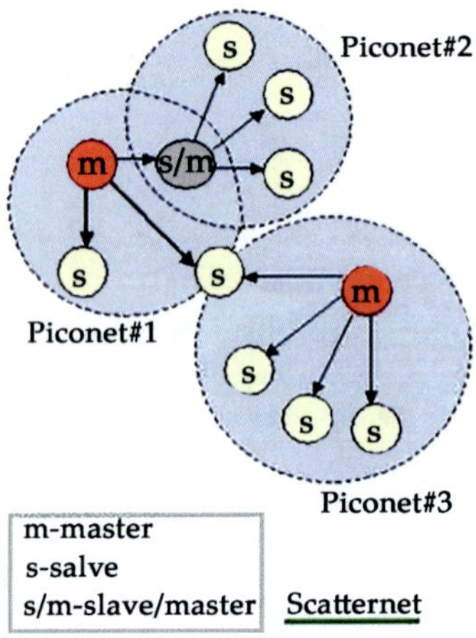

Figure 8.13. Above is a scatternet with three piconet within it. There is a good illustration of how the master and the slaves relate.

Source: https://www.rfwireless-world.com/Terminology/difference-between-piconet-and-scatternet-in-bluetooth.html.

In addition, piconet can cover only a range of ten meters. Scatter-net, however, is able to cover a wider range. While piconet has doesn't use the Bluetooth channel bandwidth, Scatter-net does by having a channel bandwidth that is efficient.

When it come to the ability they have to share data, in comparison to the piconet which has a limited sharing ability, the scatter-net has a network and sharing ability that is unlimited. It is possible to access both networks with the use of a smart phone, home appliances, and a small mobile. Piconet, however, is considered a network that is simpler in comparison to scatter-net, allowing it to serve devices and appliances that are smaller in size. Scatter-net has a network that is quite complex, due to its ability to work with more than 8 devices at a time, only allows it to work with newer home appliances and smartphones.

8.6.1. Wireless Ethernet

Wireless NICs: This is a wireless network interface controller which is a controller that has a network interface and works by connecting to a wireless computer network that is based on a radio instead of a network that is wired such as the Ethernet or Token Ring. A wireless network interface controller works on the Layer one and two of the Open Systems Interconnection model. It is able to communicate through microwave radiation with the help of an antenna.

A wireless network interface controller in a desktop computer was initially connected with the help of the Peripheral Component Interconnect bus. The ISB and the PC are other options of connection. It is also possible to find wireless network interface controllers that are integrated.

The wireless network interface controllers that were used previously require expansion cards so as to implement them. These expansion cards were plugged into a computer bus. The Wifi standards were cheaper and therefore it was possible to have wireless network interfaces that were installed in the motherboard in the newer mobile computers (Gast, 2005).

Access Points: A wireless access point in computer networking is a hardware device that is used for networking. It allows for the connection of Wi-Fi devices to a network that is wired. The access points normally connect via a wired network to a router as a stand-alone device, however, it is also possible for it to be a component of the router that is integral. There is a difference between an access point and a hotspot. A hotspot is a location that is physical, where one can find access to Wi-Fi which is connected to a WLAN.

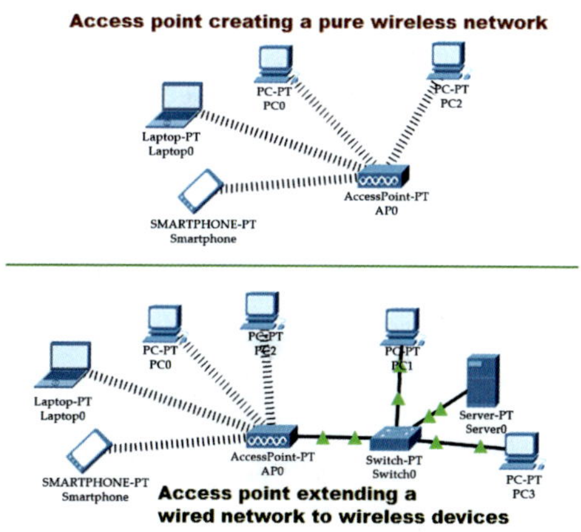

Figure 8.14. This is the difference between an access point creating a pure wireless network and extending a wired network to wireless devices.

Source: https://www.computernetworkingnotes.com/ccna-study-guide/access-points-and-wireless-lan-controllers-explained.html.

Base station: This is used to in wireless computer networking as well as other communications that are wireless, in land surveying, and mobile telephony. It acts as a GPS receiver in surveying, where it is found in a position that is known. It, however, works as a transceiver in wireless communications, allowing for the connection of several other devices to either a wider area, or to one another.

It works to provide a connection between the wider telephone network and mobile phones in mobile telephony. It works as a transceiver in computer network, where it acts as a switch for devices that are connected to the network, most times by being able to connect them to the internet and/or another network.

Ethernet bridge: This is a device that helps in connecting two separate LANs. It is required for the connection of the two networks to occur using an Ethernet protocol that is the same. This device can also be used for adding computers that are remote to a LAN. Most of these devices are able to make connections of many computers as well as other devices that are compatible either with the use of wires, or without wires.

Ethernet bridges come in two types. The first one is the Wi-Fi bridge which works by connecting a computer to a network without using a network adapter and also without wires. The second type in the power-line Ethernet bridge, which works by using the electrical system of a building for the connection of computers that are remote.

These devices are normally much cheaper and their installation is also much easier in comparison to installing routers. However, if there is a huge distance between the computer you are trying to connect and the network router, one may need to include an access point or a combination of an access point and a bridge, which may actually work better. The power-line bridge and the wireless bridge help in eliminating the need to install Ethernet cables through an attic or walls. This helps in making the installation process much easier. The bridge can also be used for the connection of a set top box or an IP telephone to a network. It is also possible to use the Wi-Fi bridge for putting a digital camera, Ethernet scanner, or printer on the wireless network (Gast, 2005).

8.7. AD HOC MODES

An Ad Hoc network is a wireless network that is decentralized. It is referred to as Ad Hoc due to the fact that it never relies on infrastructure that previously exists, such as access points in wireless networks that are managed, or routers in networks that are wired. Instead, each node is able to route through being able to forward data for different nodes. This means that determining the nodes that will work by forwarding data is done in a dynamic manner, on the basis of the routing algorithm that is used and the connectivity if the network (Gast, 2005).

Ad Hoc is a communication setting in the Windows operating systems (OSs), that makes it possible for computers to communicate with each other directly, without having to use a router. Ad Hoc networks that are wireless are able to configure themselves, and they are also dynamic, meaning that the nodes are free to move.

The fact that wireless ad hoc networks are decentralized makes them suitable for many different applications where it is not possible to rely on central nodes, and also when their use can help in improving network scalability in comparison to wireless managed networks.

Ad Hoc networks are very suitable for emergency situations, due to their quick deployment and minimal configuration. Some of the emergencies include military conflicts and even natural disasters. Ad Hoc networks can be formed quickly due to their adaptive and dynamic routing protocols (Gast, 2005).

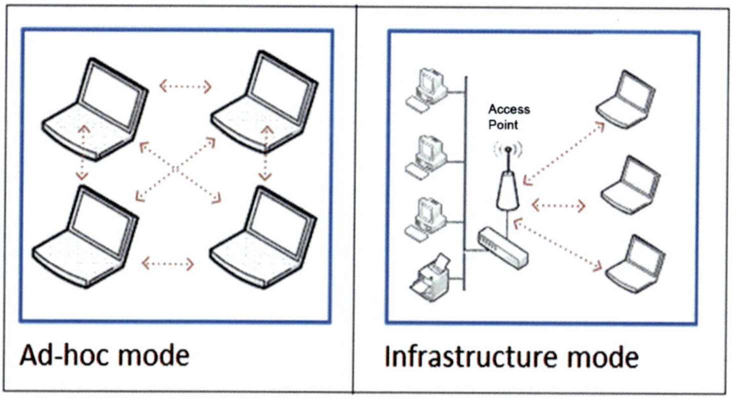

Figure 8.15. This is an illustration of the difference in functionality of the Ad-hoc mode and the Infrastructure mode. The Infrastructure mode requires an access point to connect to different devices.

Source: https://www.researchgate.net/figure/Ad-hoc-mode-vs-Infrastructure-mode-IEEE80211-introduced-many-types-of-the-Wi-Fi_fig1_316175326.

8.7.1. Infrastructure Mode

This is a 802.11 networking framework which uses an access point to establish communication amongst devices. In this mode, it is possible for wireless devices to communicate either with each other, or with a wired network. When an access point is connected to a set of wireless stations or a wired network, it is considered a Basic Service Set. A set of two or more Basic Service Sets that form one subnetwork is referred to as an Extended Service Set. Most of the wireless LANs that are used in corporate situations are normally in infrastructure mode, due to the fact that they need access to wired LANs so as to utilize certain services, such as printers or file servers.

8.7.2. Wireless Gateway

A wireless gateway works by routing packets from a wireless LAN to a different network, either wireless or wired WAN. This can be used either as a hardware or a software, and sometimes it can even be used as both. Wireless gateways work by combining the tasks of a router, a wireless access point, and they may also be able to provide a firewall function as well. They also allow for multiple users to the internet with one public Internet Protocol, through their network address translation. It may also work as a dynamic host configuration for assigning Internet Protocols in an automatic manner to devices that are connected to the network.

There are two types of wireless gateways. The one that is much easier to use needs to be connected to a cable modem or a Digital Subscriber Line modem, so as to connect to the internet through the ISP. The one that is more complex has a modem that is built in so as to allow it to connect to the internet without requiring a different device. This device that is converged helps in saving desk space, and also make wiring much easier by the ability to replace two electronic packages with one (Rackley, 2011).

It normally has one jack port for the LAN, a wired connection to the ISP, and for wireless users, an antenna.

All wireless gateways are able to use security encryption methods to protect the wireless network. Some of these methods include: WPS, WPA, and WEP. The most secure method is the use of WPA2 with WPS disabled. There are many different brands of wireless gateways, and the different models also offer different quality and features. They can also have differences on the wireless speed and range, extra functionality, number of LAN ports, and speed.

Some of the brands that are available in the market include linksys, Netgear, and Motorola. Most of the internet providers normally offer wireless gateway for free together with their services, therefore not giving the user much of a choice. The device that the ISP provides comes when it is already configured and that makes installation much easier, which is a major advantage. In addition, it is also possible for the ISPs to fix and troubleshoot any issues that may occur, via the remote access, making it quite convenient for the end user (Rackley, 2011).

8.7.3. OSI (open systems interconnection) Model

The OSI model is a theoretical model that standardized and characterizes the computing system's and telecommunications' communication functions, without considering its technology and internal structure. It aims to provide diverse communications that are interoperable, with standard protocols for communication. It works by partitioning a communication system into layers of abstraction. There are seven layers in the original version of the model.

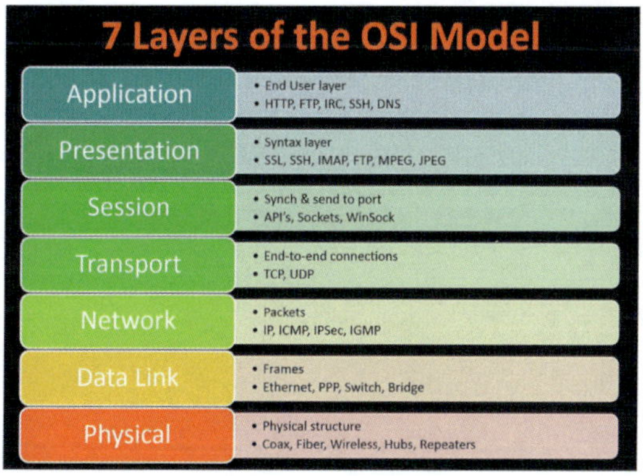

Figure 8.16. These are the seven layers of the OSI model.

Source: https://medium.com/@int0x33/day-51-understanding-the-osi-model-f22d5f3df756.

The top layer is served by the one below it, and that one by the one below it, etc. For example, a layer that is supposed to provide communication that are free of errors across a network is able to provide the path that is required by the layer above it, as it is calling the one below it to send and receive packs that have the path contents. In easier terms, one can visualize a horizontal connection between the two layers.

CHAPTER

9

Challenges Facing Computer Networking and Communication

CONTENTS

9.1. INTRODUCTION

A computer network is the connection of a set of computers forming networks called nodes. The connection of these computers is done using cabling by joining the computers together using cables. There are defend types of connecting the computers that include star topology, bus topology, and ring topology. These topologies bring about the different types of computer networking. Communication is information transfer from one person to another. The field of computer networking and communication faces various challenges, which include poor degradation, security issues, cost, or network performance issues.

9.2. SECURITY ISSUES

A major problem in computer networking and communication is security. The network should be secure such that it cannot be hacked or information cannot be stolen from it. It involves securing the denial of service attacks. His generally means protecting the network from malicious individuals who may try to infiltrating the networks and hence ensure that important information of the networks do no fall I the wrong hands. The dominant of how secure a network is, is the size of the network this simply means that networks which are large are more prone to insecurity of the network when they are compared with the smaller networks. This happens because a large network has a large number of users and passwords. The disadvantage of computer networking and communication system lacking security and therefore facing insecurity issues is that they will be prone and open to hackers who may hack the program and they steal information that may be vulnerable and very important and with this information they may form false documents and it may lead to the fall of the organization. Security is also key so as to ensure every user that have accounts in the computer network that they document is safe and it therefore leads to more users being attracted to the computer network and communication system. Lastly, security enables reduce the case of hacking and therefore hackers are eliminated as they do not have a Chace anymore of carrying out their malicious practices (Cowley, 2012).

Security in a computer network and commutation system is enabled by applying key measures that must be taken to ensure that the computer network and communication system is properly secured. These measures include employing the use of proxies and fire walls, ensuring that the passwords are secured appropriately, securing the assets of the computer network and communication systems, ensuring every device has a strict password policy, and ensuring all the devices have an antivirus system installed (Cowley, 2012).

9.3. COST

Cost refers to the amount of money that is required to design a computer system and make it operational. In short, cost is the total amount of money invested in a computer networking and communication system. When the cost is high, the system becomes unaffordable.

A computer networking and communication system involve more than one computing device put together by a medium. The computing devices that are connected together can be computers. They also need specialized software and hardware, such as routers or bridges to support these network systems and accommodate traffic (Cowley, 2012).

The other cause of the cost being high is the hardware that is required for the coming up of the computer networking and communication systems are also of high prices and therefore having to buy a lot of these hardware will cause them to be expensive and unaffordable. Though the buying of the hardware in bulk Is much cheaper than buying a single on at a time, it is still expensive when the total price is accumulated and hence it proves disadvantageous. For example, the price of a PC is quite high and it may prove disadvantageous.

The budget that is normally set for a computer networking and communication is very high because of the many requirements that are normally included and required and therefore they bring about many organizations being discouraged to start a computer networking system as the budget set most times is to even enough for the computer network and communication system. The computer networking and communication system is mainly more expensive when they involve the use of traditional information technology applications to offer their support to the computer networking and communication network.

By the cost of computer networking and communication system being high it has also led to the downfall of many computer networking and communication systems having a down fall because they fail to plan themselves in the appropriate way and therefore they lack the necessary amount of money that they require to maintain the systems and to ensure that the systems are running in the desired way. This therefore discourages many organizations from involving themselves in the developing of computer networking and communication systems as they have the fear of them lacking funds to run the system therefore leading to the final downfall of the network system (Cowley, 2012).

9.4. CONFIGURATION CONFLICTS

Configuration means the type of arrangement or how a certain thing are arranged such that how the parts and elements are put together to form a certain thing. Computer network faces several challenges that include configuration conflicts that is defined as follows. There is a difference between a large computer networking and communication systems when compared with a large on such that a small computer and networking and communicational system have a couple of IP addresses that have different host names that are different from one another and therefore there is a very small probability that the devices will conflict with each other but when a large network is involved the probability of conflicts is increased. Large networks often encounter conflicts along their way because they are busy networks and therefore, they have a lot of traffic happening along their way. The solution to this problem is that the networks should find many alternative routes to reduce the traffic and to make the route less busy.

The computer networks (CS) should therefore be designed in ways that ensure that they make sure that they can be able to avoid any conflicts along the way therefore they can be able to avoid the configuration conflicts that may arise. Since it is not easy to sway against these problems, the individuals therefore take a lot time having to find suitable solutions for the problem (Cowley, 2012).

9.5. PERFORMANCE DEGRADATION

Performance is how good is the output of a certain computer networking and communication system. Degradation is the lowering of quality of the computer networking and communication system. There are various causes that lead to the degradation of a computer networking and communication system which include:

- Hardware failure: this refers to the condition when hardware of the computer networking and communication systems fails to be functional. When the hardware fails it eats to the failure of the system since the hardware is connected together on the client end and server end hence the failure of the system is the result of a hardware failing

- Bandwidth congestion: this refers to the condition when the amount of data that is sent is too much for the network to deliver. This causes a congestion in the network and this leads to the failure and the degradation of the performance of the computer networking and communication system degrading.

Other causes of the network degradation include network switch configuration, network loop, network latency increase, shaping/ optimization/ filtering device, host resource outage, application server processing time, quantity of data, name resolution service, authentication service and application errors. The above factors cause degradation of computer networking and communication and therefore should be solved as soon as possible (Carne, 2004).

9.6. CONSTANT UPGRADES

In the networking and communication world there are constant upgrades being made in the networks. The constant upgrades affect the operation of the networks. The upgrades are made so that the networks offer better transmission services. The challenge of the constant upgrades is that some of the devices used are not capable to support the network being used. For instance, in mobile communication. Initially the mobile phones being used were not smartphones. With the advancements of using the wireless networks such as the Wi-Fi some phones are not able to support the use of such transmission networks. Therefore, they are not able to send or receive data rendering the transmission operation null.

There has also been an upgrade of the telecommunication network used. The transition from the 3G network to 4G network. This transmission will hinder the operation of the data. This may require the user to get an upgrade on the device being used. Therefore, the user may be forced to buy a device that supports the 4G network. Some of the upgrades have had an effect on the transmission process.

This can happen when the device is overloaded with the incoming signals and outgoing signals. This causes a jam and the device ends up hanging and it might take quite some time for the data to be transmitted. It may also be costly and time consuming when it comes to the changing of the cables. For instance, there are new type of fiber cables being introduced into the market. As they offer better services users will be forced to purchase them and it may be costly. Also, the cables might not fit the ports they are intended for.

The frequent coming up of the network configurations makes it hard to manage the configurations. The network configurations have to be unique numbers and therefore if several configurations are present in the networking world it becomes hard to keep record of the configurations present. Therefore, it may lead to a mix up of the configurations and therefore it may lead to difficulty in organizing the sequencing of the network packets and the IP addresses. This requires a system to be put in place to assist in the management of the network configurations (White, 2015).

The constant upgrades also involve changing the network configurations. This causes a challenge more so to the wireless media. In the wireless media the configurations have to be linked to the computer device the data is being sent to. Therefore, if the configurations are changed constantly it poses a challenge to the users as they have to keep up with the changes to the configurations to enable the wireless networks to connect to the devices. The configurations are also used in sending of emails. If the wrong configuration is used information may end up reaching a person it was not intended for and the information may be used for the wrong purpose leading cybercrimes.

It also contributes to poor communication in that it is a barrier as the individual may not get the data he or she was intended to have access to. This challenge has been taken up by computer scientist and some of the ways used in controlling it include regulating the upgrades to that they can be supported by the available devices. This ensures that there are no challenges are encountered during the data transmission process.

9.7. INSTALLATION

Installation refers to the putting in place of the media for its use. In computer networking there are challenges encountered during the installation process. Take the case of the fiber optic cables. They are made of glass in its structure and will therefore require much care for it to be installed. If the cable is mismanaged the transmission may not occur at all due to the damage on the glass which is the very important in facilitating the data transmission. This also make the installation process to be difficult for the individuals installing the cable (White, 2015).

Under installation a challenge that arises in the insufficient number of personnel that have the necessary skills required in media installation. The skills are a necessary requirement in ensuring that there is successful installation. Problem is that there are limited numbers of individuals who are capable of doing such. Due to this some of them have high charges for offering this kind of service. The limited number of the installers has brought about individuals known as quacks in the networking world. Quacks are individuals who have no experience or skill in a certain field of work yet they offer the service.

The presence of quacks has affected the computer networking and communication in that they make faulty connections rendering the network unable to work. Some of them are corrupt to an extent that they do not install the intended transmission media. Many are the cases where some individuals have the Wi-Fi connections made in the offices and homes but they are unable to transmit data because the connection was faulty. The quack tarnishes the CS as they have led to the production of fake transmission media. This includes the production of fake cables and Wi-Fi routers among others therefore destroying computer communication.

Some of the solutions used in solving the challenges in installation include the arresting of quacks among the installers. It also involves training individuals to have skills and experience in installing transmission media. Another challenge is the limited number of installation equipment. The limited number makes the purchase of the equipment to be expensive. The inadequate installation equipment also contributes to the faulty connections in the transmission media. This is solved by availing the installation equipment (White, 2015).

9.8. PACKET LOSSES

Data in most cases is transmitted inform of packets. Once the transmission media receives the data to be transmitted, it subdivided the data into small size packets so that the transmission process goes very smoothly. Though this is the cases on most transmission medias, there have been problems such as the loss of the data packets. During the transmission process, it is intended that all the data packets quality is transferred from the source to the destination through quite a number of routers and the data packets are each allocated to leave the source at a given time. The data packets are usually lost when they reach the routers.

The dropping of the data packets occurs due to the congestion of the routers. This is because the transmission routers receive data from several sources and when they reach the routers at the same time, they cause the congestion. The dropping of the signals leads to a distortion the multimedia signal transmitted. For instance, is the signal or data being transmitted was of the voice input, the drop of the packets would leave some of the parts of the voice input to be missing. It will therefore pose a challenge in trying to decode the meaning of the voice signal. The same case applies if the data was in video format or in image. Some of it parts will be missing and depending on the extent of the packet loss the parts of the image are lost.

If several of the data packets are lost, it may be extremely difficult for the brain to come up with a better decoding of the information as it is very challenging to produce the right reconstruction of the data. There are some solutions that have been provided to eradicate this challenge. It may involve rectifying the signal after transmission so that it regains the stature that it had in the beginning. This method is quite challenging as it requires one to have good quality skills in data reconstruction. It may also be costly as it will require hiring of data reconstruction specialists. Therefore, the most used method of solving this challenge is reducing the packet size therefore it focuses on reducing the packet loss.

The reduction of the packet loss may involve the compression of the packets so that their sizes. The reduction of the packet loss also involves making a network upgrade. The network upgrade involves increasing the bandwidth or changing the bit rate of the network. It also involves using ATM, SONETS for gigabit in transmission. Good wavelength is also required; the terabits. It also involves the regulation of the signals as they reach the routers. It involves use of time lapse which sequence the packets to reduce the congestion of the packets at the routers reducing the number of dropped packets. Though this is a quite effective method, it is quite expensive as it involves changing various things associated with the network. It is advantageous as this type of solution is readily available (Anttalainen and Jaaskelainen, 2014).

9.9. HOST IDENTIFICATION

Host identification refers to the network being able to identify the computer that will be hosting it. Hot identification greatly requires proper and correct configuration. The configuration in this case refers to the network address. Without the networking configurations the computer's hardware will be unable to send or receive data and messages. The challenge in host identification is usually experienced in the large networks. The small networks don't usually experience many problems as they can be configured with great ease with the use of manual addressing.

For the large networks this is a challenge because manual addressing is used, it may be an endless and tiring process. It may also require several individuals to be involved in the manual addressing. This increases the chances of the network being exposed to hackers who end up using the messages or data for the wrong purposes. Therefore, the larger the network the greater the probability of the information being obtained by hackers.

This requires that certain strategies be put in place to counteract this challenge. Some of the measures include use of networking software that assists in building a scalable computer network. It also required that domain controllers, DHCP servers as well as their addressing protocols are put in place to assist in maintaining a scalable network. By doing so the computer network will be able to handle the configuration of large networks.

The much emphasis put on proper host identification is due to the fact they proper host identification facilitates good or peak performance of the network. It also assists in ensuring the safety of the information from the hackers by allowing the network to properly configure and identify the host limiting the access to this information by the hackers (Toral-Cruz et al, 2015).

9.10. LACK OF NETWORK SIGNALS

This is a common problem in wireless networks. In most cases some devices, such as the computers, indicate that they have a strong signal whereas in reality they do not have any signal. They indicate a strong signal from the router but there was no connection that was made and therefore, the user cannot access the network. Most of the time, the problem usually occurs in the system hardware.

There are various measures to solve this issue. For some, they reduce the distance between the computer and the wireless router. In this case the signal might have not been there due to the over proximity on the distance. It may also involve checking the system hardware if it has any problem connecting to the wireless network.

For those who use the network card most at times they receive signals but they are unable to transmit effectively. In this situation it may require the user to update the network card drive or even replacing the card with another one (Jaffe, 2004).

9.11. NETWORK OUTAGES AND INACCESSIBLE FILES

Network outages are a common problem in computer networking. In most cases, the network outages occur at unpredictable times and this hinders the user from accessing some files. The network outages are usually as a result of conflict on the NETBIOS. The most common factor in this problem of the type of system used.

The network outage is a common problem in the windows systems. If one happens to receive a system update or if they get an upgrade to a different service pack, then they are most likely to be faced with this challenge and it may occur at a greater frequency. This problem may be solved by disabling the WINS/NetBT name resolution. This is only applicable if it is not required by a specific program. Another method is renaming the domain or the computer.

9.12. IP CONFLICTS

Depending on the type of system used in the computer, the number of IP addresses per device varies in the network. For instance, in windows in the manufacturer setting it allows only a single IP address per device placed in the network. In frequent cases two or more devices get assigned to a similar address. This is a challenge as the network may not be suited to support a large number of devices.

It ends up blocking the other devices leaving only the number of devices it can support to be functional. By blocking the devices, it hinders them from accessing various files as well as causing a lag in the network for both the connected and disconnected devices. This problem is mostly solved by reconfiguring.

In that the DHCP setup is reconfigured to facilitate the static IP address being exempted from the pool. By doing so the IP address will be reconfigured appropriately and in turn it will resolve the conflict allowing all the devices connected in the network being allowed access to the protected files; proper access.

9.13. SLOW APPLICATION RESPONSE

The slow application response is a major issue in computer networking. The poor application response is mostly in applications that require network access for them to run. Slow application response refers to the computer having a slow reaction time in its applications. It commonly occurs when the computer has just started and is getting connected to the network.The slow application response is usually due to the use of high bandwidth. For instance, if two devices are connected to a network then the other is starting while the other is using the network by dreaming videos, then it is most likely that the starting device will have a slow application response. This challenge is counteracted by ensuring good use of the network which will assist in controlling the bandwidth within a certain range.It can also be solved by upgrading the network so that it gets to support a larger bandwidth so that the applications are able to respond at a much better place.

9.14. POOR VOIP QUALITY

Problems of the VoIP affect how the network will be. Some of the problems with the VoIP include delays and stutters. These among others affect the productivity of the network. The stutters are the most common problem in affecting the quality of the VoIP. They are counteracted by installing jitter buffers. These buffers play a role of cache VoIP packets as well as allowing them to be easily accessed during the communication process facilitating a smooth stream.

The advantage of using the jotter buffers is that they can be tailor made. This means that they can be made to meet specific needs of the network in use. They are also easy and cheaper to install. The VoIP quality can also be improved by using a new or different playback codec that is equipped with a packet loss concealment feature. This feature is also useful in solving the issue of packet loss which is among the challenges in computer networking and communication. Also, by ensuring that the codes and the computer drives are up to date will help prove the quality of the VoIP.

9.15. ABSENCE OF CONNECTIVITY

Absence of connectivity means the failure of there being connectivity in a network. it is normally catastrophic when other CS are not detectable aside from following all the rules that are required to be followed. the absence of connectivity makes the whole network to be unavailable and therefore an individual cannot work on the internet and they cannot browse. it also hinders communication and this becomes a major problem as the passing of the desired information from one person to the other is hindered and therefore this issue is normally sorted as soon as possible.

9.16. IP ADDRESS ISSUE

The problem revolving around the IP address issue is the situation when two or more computers are given a similar IP address to each other. This is a major issue since the IP address on each computer is the factor that identifies the computer and therefore it may bring negative results if two or more computers are assigned a similar IP address. IP addresses are given erroneously and therefore the probability of two computers getting a similar IP address is high and with a similar IP address most computers will have a problem with the network and therefore this issue is solved by ensuring that different computers have different IP addresses.

9.17. NETWORK RELATED PROBLEMS

Network-related problems are when the computer networking experiences problems with the network which may include the network failing to reach some parts of the room or area. Even when using a WIFI router there are some areas that the network will not reach due to these problems and after installing a router they still don't solve the issue. The individuals must, therefore, select a central position to place the router so that it may ensure that the problem finds a suitable solution.

9.18. SLOW MOVING CONNECTIVITY

Slow-moving connectivity is the situation when the connectivity and the internet connection is very slow. When the network connection is very slow it means that a lot of time will be taken trying to load a page from the internet. This problem is mostly brought about by the presence of many users of the network a certain time that it makes the internet to be slow and to take a lot of time trying to serve each user of the network at the same time and therefore it tends to be slower than expected

The disadvantage of a slow-moving network is that it consumes a lot of time loading a page and therefore a person using the network at that time will waste a lot of time waiting for the page to load. The solution of this problem is that a faster network is installed for example, if it was 3G network a person will opt for the 4G which will tend to be faster and therefore they won't waste a lot of their time waiting for the page to load and they can carry their communication in a faster way.The other disadvantage of a slow-moving network is that many people get bored and discouraged when they are using the network. A slow-moving network, therefore, gets a lot of negative responses from people since it wastes a lot of time and this causes boredom. Many slow-moving networks are often neglected and are not installed since people will prefer the fast-moving networks s they will perform their duties in a faster way therefore when the network connectivity is slow it is most likely replaced with a faster-moving network that will show much better results at the end of the whole process (Jaffe, 2004).

9.19. DROP-IN INTERNET CONNECTIVITY

Drop-in Internet connectivity is also another challenge that faces computer networking and communication. Drop in the internet connectivity means that when one is using the internet smoothly then it is suddenly lost. An individual may be performing an important issue with the network and then when it is lost the lose their work especially if they had not saved their work. Also one may be sending a piece of important information to another individual and then when connectivity is lost their message fails to get delivered to the receiver and therefore the drop in connectivity hinders a lot of communication. The drop in the network connectivity may be a problem that may be caused with an issue at the router and therefore it may be solved by troubleshooting the router and checking for any configuration problems. It may also be a problem from the source of the network and therefore it is solved by solving the problem from the source. Drop in the network connectivity may cause loss of a lot of important piece of information and therefore it is solved before it leads to any more harm and then hindering this problem from arising hinders the loss of information in future.

9.20. PROBLEMS FACED BY FIREWALL STATUS

Problems faced by firewall status is another challenge faced by computer networking and communication. Firewall status is the situation where there is the allowing and provision of the necessary and required security in a network. This problem may arise when there is a hindrance in the sharing of files between different computers due to the firewall settings that may be put in place and therefore by hindering the sarin of files it hinders the flow of work and this must be solved so that the work may be performed as it is desired.

Although security is important in a network it must not hinder the flow of work and therefore the settings should be adjusted in such a way that it caused and leads to a positive workflow as it should not cause any hindrance.

Rigid firewall settings should be adjusted in a way that it ensures connected computers can share information smoothly and then the security should also be adequate as it is required. Therefore, when the security is okay and the flow of work is not hindered it means that the work will be done more efficiently than before.

9.21. INITIAL CONFIGURATION

The initial configuration is a challenge that is faced in the computer networking and communication system. Configuration stands for how the set-up is done in the most appropriate way that is desired. Initial configuration therefore means how the system is set up from the start. It is the initial problem that comes in mind of a person when they face glitches in the network and resources for use. A network is made up of many parts which range from how big the network is, the problems that it encounters to the probability of the problems occurring in future. In the past years up to more than 10 years ago, the world experiences the coming of telecommunication and with this, the hardware and software market has seen major growth in their sector. A lot of people have the capability of putting up the systems and networking them and they do not necessarily need the skills that are acquired from school and studies but they can perform these functions without having any formal education whatsoever (Periša, Cvitić, and Kolarovszki, 2016).

Whether an individual is only performing the function of putting up and configuring windows or a router they need to put everything in place and perform a lot of necessary functions and these functions must be performed perfectly and with a lot of carefulness to ensure the proper and required functioning. There are a lot of ways of ensuring that the function is completed and therefore the most appropriate way must be chosen before it is used. A good example is when one wants to connect a computer system to the internet several processes must be put in place to ensure that connections come out successful and as desired from the start to the end. The skills and information that one must have in mind before performing this function are the simple skills and information that revolve around IP addressing schemes that are given to every computer to mark as an identity to the computer. In the case of a similar IP address being given to more than one computer then there might be a hitch in the connectivity and therefore a lot of care must be taken and seriousness to avoid unnecessary troubles. Also, one must have the required knowledge of how the cabling is done so that they may avoid short-circuiting and other dangers and risks that may arise in the process. In the case of a wireless system, one must know how the connections are got and how the connections are made so that the system may be functional and work may be performed. There are a lot of processes that are required as networking is not a simple process and it is complex and therefore one must make themselves familiar with the complexity of networking and the fundamentals that revolve around networking (Periša, Cvitić, and Kolarovszki, 2016).

During the process of setting up a system, some problems may arise and among these problems, the most dangerous problem that may arise is when the power supply is lost. When there is the loss in the power supply, the process cannot take place without the presence of power and therefore the process comes to an end and it cannot take place any more. Other problems that may arise may include incorrect cabling such that the cables are not con net to the place where they are supposed to be connected and therefore connection cannot take place. For a wireless system, the problem will arise if the configuration is done wrongly and therefore connection will not be available. Another problem is IP problems that may arise for example, when a wrong IP address is given or giving more than one computer the same IP address as this may cause a failure in the network connectivity. The other problem that may arise is when the configuration of the computers does not allow access to shared resources. By this, it means that the computers cannot access resources that are shared for example, the printers and therefore it is important that it is dealt with.

Initial configuration, therefore, stands for how the system is set up from the start. How the settings are made. If the initial configuration is done as desired it is more likely that the system will operate as it is required but in case the system configuration is not thorough then several problems will arise as discussed above. Therefore, anyone who takes part in the computer networking and communication system configuration must have the necessary skills that are required to ensure the system runs as it is required and to ensure they avoid any problem that may arise due to improper configuration.

9.22. PROBLEMS IN COMPUTER SETUPS

Computer set ups are also known as network topologies. This refers to how computers are arranged to facilitate their communication amongst each other and therefore the network setup amongst them. Usually, there are two types of network technologies which consist of the logical topology and the physical topology. The logical topology is composed of the token ring and Ethernet topology. The challenge experienced in this type of topology is mostly encountered in the token ring topology. In this topology the devices are connected amongst each other and mass the signal from one computer to another.

In this kind of connection if a part of the cable connecting the computers is damaged then the whole network becomes dysfunctional in that there will be no transmission of the signals. The damage becomes a barrier to allowing the signal to be transmitted to another computer. This is a major challenge as it disrupts the whole transmission process. It is also difficult to identify the source of the problem in the setup. The devices are connected in a ring manner therefore if the whole network goes down, it makes it hard to troubleshoot the cause of the problem.

The physical topologies have several layouts. Each layout has a good and bad side. For instance, in the star topology provides in own problems. Its installation is time-consuming this is attributed to the fact that each node forms a segment on its own. In some cases, if the central device fails, then the entire network fails. This, therefore, means that no message will be incoming or outgoing. The cabling for such a layout is also expensive. In this layout, it is easy to troubleshoot the problem and also solving the problem. The damaged cable can easily be replaced.

There is also the bus topology. This topology involves the computers being connected to a cable in the form of being connected to a backbone. It is more of the illustration of the bus on roads and the bus stops. This network experiences challenges such as the entire network failing if there was a break in the cable. It is also quite a challenge trying to troubleshoot the source of the problem as it could be anywhere within the cable. Type of layout also limits the number of computers that can be connected to the network as well as limiting the addition of other devices into the layout. Hence this network setup can easily expand (Toral-Cruz et al, 2015).

The ring topology is almost similar to the token ring topology. The signals are transmitted in the same manner. They offer the same challenges as well. For instance, if one device breaks down then the whole network is affected. The solution for this layout is to use the multi-station access unit. This unit by passes the damaged device ensuring that even though the device fails the network still runs as it should. Troubleshooting for problems in the layout is also quite difficult. The cables are interconnected and it may be difficulty to identify the damaged cable. Modification in the layout is also quite difficult. This is because an addition of nodes into the network may cause a malfunction in the service of the computers.

In the mesh topology involves devices being interconnected at the nodes with several redundant. In this topology as it involves several devices connected with each other the devices the cabling becomes expensive. This is due to the redundant links which will require several cables to be used. For this topology there is no central device therefore the administration of such a network is difficult. This is due to the fact that it is a peer to peer connection.

There is also the hierarchical topology which is made up devices connected in bus and star topology. This layout also presents its own challenges. For instance, it requires a huge cabling therefore it may be expensive in the long run. It also requires a lot of maintenance which is quite expensive. Also if a cable has broken down the entire network will also break down rendering it unable to send or receive any signals. It also makes it difficult to trouble shoot.

All the network topologies present their own challenges. The layout is therefore chosen depending on the weight of the problems that may be encountered during its use.

9.23. CHALLENGES IN NETWORKING SOFTWARE

The challenges in the network software are brought about by the construction of the software. If the software was incompetently made it will disrupt the functioning of the network. If follows the principle of GIGO that means garbage in garbage out. Therefore, is the software was not properly made the software will in turn not be able to work properly. The networking software are classified into two: Network operating system (OS) and the network protocols. If the software is incapable it affects the functions of the OS and the protocols.

Under the OS, it affects it in that it limits access to network resources such as the printers. It also removes the effectiveness communication with each other at the nodes on the network. The poor software will limit the support on the inter-process communication therefore various processes in the network may not occur and the communication process becomes complicated. It may affect the OS in that it is unable to respond to requests from programs running on the network. It will also be unable to support networking services such as network protocols and network cards.

The OS will also be unable to install security features and therefore the network cannot be secured from unauthorized access. It will be unable to keep a log on individuals who access the network as well as track the network usage. It won't be able to properly monitor the performance of the network hence maximum quality of a network may not be attained.

A poor network software also affects the application protocols in the application layer affecting their performance. For instance, the email program may encounter challenges in composing and reading email messages. The simple mail transfer protocol may be unable to transfer the email to the receiver. The file transfer protocol may encounter certain problems in sending the files.

The network protocols may be unable to provide links between the services. It may be unable to handle the addressing and routing of information, check for errors as well as retransmit requests. This is a clear indication that a network software should be properly made for it not to encounter this challenge. For devices that are faced with some of these problems the proper solution would be to make upgrades to the currently existing software or even install a new software.

9.24. SIGNAL MODULATION CHALLENGES

Signal modulation refers to the process of changing the signals into a form that is more suitable to be used during the transmission process. In networking some computers experiences challenges in signal modulation.

The network may end up transmitting the signal in the wrong format. For instance, if a digital signal was required, it may end up sending an analog signal instead or vice versa. The same case may also apply in signal demodulation. The conversion of the signals may occur incorrectly such that the initial form of the signal may not be attained.

9.25. MULTIPLEXING CHALLENGES

The multiplexing challenges involve the network being unable to send multiple data signals within the same media. This makes it unable to generate multiple medium channels. The same case applies for the de-multiplexing where there is a challenge in separating the multiplexed signals. The network has to be properly modified to carry out multiplexing and de-multiplexing.

9.26. SOLUTIONS TO ALL THE COMPUTER NETWORKING AND COMMUNICATION SYSTEMS

9.26.1. Security Issues

Security issues are solved by increasing security by putting up measures that will ensure security in computer networking and communication systems. They need to put up measures that are going to discourage hacking in the system. Ways that they can employ is setting up passwords that cannot be easily hacked and these passwords should be unique such that they should not be passwords that can easily be guessed. The more secure the system is the more secure the pieces of information that are important to the organization are therefore it should be taken into consideration.

Security issues can also be improved by applying proxies and firewalls that ensure that the security is enabled. The organization must also ensure that by using the firewalls they do not interrupt the transfer of information between computers therefore being a challenge that is faced in computer networking and communication system. The workflow must remain the same and the firewalls must not interfere with the process in any way possible and therefore the security will be ensured and still the workflow will continue flowing just like it used to do before the use of the firewalls and proxies.

9.26.2. Cost

The cost of the computer networking and communication system is generally high because the amount of money that is normally invested in the organization that is manufacturing the computer networking and communication system is very high and therefore methods to reduce this problem is invented. The first way to lower the price of the computer networking and communication system is to ensure that the materials used are selected appropriately from the sources that are quite affordable to the organization at large. They should opt for the cheaper seller hence reducing the cost. The type of materials that are used should also be materials of good quality since they will need less maintenance.

They should therefore not buy the materials just because they are cheap but they should ensure they are of good quality. When the materials are of poor quality it will mean that they will get spoiled very easily and they will need to be changed from time to time but when the materials are of good quality they will last a long period and therefore the organization will reduce the amount of money they will spend on repairs from time to time. To solve the cost issue, the organization might also consider using cheaper hardware that may be found rather than using hardware that is way more expensive and one that may cause a rise in the budget of the computer and communication system. It must also be considered that the hardware used is still of good quality so that the organization is not forced to have to pay for the maintenance cost of the system all the time. They should select the affordable hardware.

9.26.3. Solving Configuration Conflicts

Configuration conflicts are solved by ensuring that the system is set up in the appropriate and desired way. when the system is set up appropriately it means that computer networking and communication will run smoothly. When the computer networking and communication system is set up in the wrong way it may lead to the fall of the system and therefore appropriate caution should be taken. To ensure that computer networking and communication system is set up and configured appropriately, individuals, and organizations need to employee trained and well-skilled individuals to carry out the duty of configuring the system.

9.26.4. Performance Degradation

Performance degradation is the falling of the computer networking and communication system as it reduces in quality. Every system must have the ability to keep the quality and standards high for a very long time. Failure to which it is considered as of a lower standard than expected. The solution to this problem is that they must ensure that the materials that are used to create this system must be of high-quality such that they do not degrade. The hardware chosen should also be of high quality and long-lasting hardware that does not degrade quickly.

9.26.5. Absence of Connectivity

Absence of connectivity is when the connectivity is not present despite their being the connection that is required. This problem can be solved by ensuring that the configuration settings are done in the required way and that all the settings are correct. They must also ensure that the router is connected appropriately and that all the connections are done correctly and appropriately in the computer network and configuration system. The absence of connectivity can cause major problems and therefore the organization must ensure the computer networking and communication systems are working in the desired way to ensure there is connectivity.

9.26.6. IP Address Issue

IP address issue is the situation where more than one computer is given an IP address that is similar to the other one.

The problem can be managed if the IP address is issued in a more chronological manner such that different IP addresses will be issued to different computers. Instead of giving the IP addresses erroneously they need to make it a more organized and orderly process that will involve record keeping and this will most definitely lead to the end of this problem and improvement in the computers connected to the internet.

9.26.7. Network Related Problems

By network-related it means that they face issues that are related in the network. the solution to this problem is to ensure that the network is configured appropriately.

Network related problems are solved also by troubleshooting the network to identify the source of the problem and find the necessary solution for it instead of wasting a lot of time trying to figure out where the problem is. Network related problems are Los solved by ensuring that the network that is put in place is of good quality to avoid any problems that may arise from this network.

9.26.8. Slow Moving Connectivity

Slow-moving connectivity is when the network is moving very slowly such that it takes a very long time before it loads a page.

It is mostly caused by many people being connected to the network at a certain time and therefore it can be solved by ensuring that the number of people using the network at a certain given time is the appropriate amount of people that the network can support.

Having this in place we can also choose a faster network that can support more people and it is faster than the slower network and therefore the problem is solved.

9.26.9. Drop-in Internet Connectivity

The problem of a drop-in internet connectivity can be solved by troubleshooting the router to find the source of the problem and by this they can find a suitable solution for the problem. The organization can also have a separate source of the network such that when one drops they have an alternative root. This will be of great benefit since it will enable the organization to always have an internet connection and therefore their processes cannot be disrupted at any one time and if one network fails they simply switch to the other one.

These solutions when applied that enable solve the challenges that are facing computer networking and communication systems more easily as desired.

CHAPTER 10

Trends of Computer Networking

CONTENTS

10.1. INTRODUCTION

With the advancements in technology increasing rapidly current technology will soon be obsolete. In late 1990s modems were being used in transferring files and communicating with other computers. A lot of hardware was required in the connection process like wires but with the current system, computer networking is using wireless connections. There has been increased flexibility in the usage of internet. Engineers and experts are constantly working to improve the computer networking and communication system and some of the futuristic trends are taking shape in design. For example, software-defined networking (SDN), 5G and supported applications, microservice architecture, open network switches, wireless data link for drones, ambient backscatter, expressive internet architecture, quantum computing, diamond semiconductors, artificial intelligence expansion, the continued acceleration of IPv6, continued usage of IoT and 100% uptime and sub-millisecond second transfer rates. We are going to discuss the trends and future of computer networking below and see how they can impact and improve the technology in the era of communication advancements.

10.2. SOFTWARE-DEFINED NETWORKING (SDN)

Due to the increasing manufacture and design modification of communication devices, you will notice that the world is moving further away from using a static computer placed on the desks in offices. This is because people have the ability to travel with communication devices like phones and due to this, it is also important for business people and customers to comfortably use their applications where ever they are. In order to enable bandwidth usage flexibility in these devices, SDN in gaining popularity in design and research Industries. SDN is a network management model that uses a cloud computing software that will enable a central management of all network devices separate from the physical aspect of the device in order to improve the performance of network systems. Another definition is the physical separation of the network control plane from the forward forwarding plane and where the control plane has control of several devices (Erol, Ufuk, and Tuna, 2005).

The objective of coming up with a software-defined network is to enable the decentralization of CS and get farther away from the static architecture of traditional networks. This will enhance flexibility and easy troubleshooting. The kind of Architecture being applied in software-defined networking that is, it is cost-effective it is manageable, it is flexible and it can adapt to different situations. Due to its adaptability, it can be ideal to be used will high bandwidth frequency. It will decouple the network control and the forwarding functions which will enable the network to be directly controlled from a central point using a cloud software. The open flow protocol is a core component in the software-defined network design. The concept behind the software design network architecture is Direct programmability, agility, central management, programmability configured.

- Direct programmability: Due to the process of decoupling the network control from the other control, it has enabled the networks to be directly programmable because the configuration can be fully done.
- Agility: The flow of network traffic can dynamically be adjusted by the manager from the control central office.
- Centrally-managed: The control of artificial intelligence has been centralized in software-based controllers in order to enable the administrators to maintain a wide-scale view of the network connection. This technology is being applied in other applications and policy engines as a single logical switch.
- Programmatically configured: Automated programs found in the software-defined networks have the ability to write themselves because the programs do not depend on proprietary software and this enables administrators to have a better management, configuration, security, and optimization of network resources.
- Open standards-based and vendor-neutral: Because of the centralization of all computer functions, there will be the improvement of network design and operation because of the commands being directly given from the software-defined network controllers.

10.2.1. Benefits of Software-Defined Networking

Provision of Central network control: The centralization of the whole view of the entire network enables administrators to supervise and manage the network flow smoothly. This will hasten service delivery and provide more agility in provisioning both virtual and physical network devices from a central location.

Holistic management of the Enterprise: Business Ventures have incorporated the concept of software-defined networks and their operations in order to accommodate for complicated requests such as those of for big data. Software-defined networks will enable engineers and software designers to perform tests on the network configuration without necessarily affecting the operations of the network outside. The hardware and software components of devices will also be able to be centrally controlled.

Because of the operations being control central security has been heightened in the networks and communications system. The use of virtualization in managing network systems had a lot of challenges because of the inability of separating the physical and the software component of the communication systems. With the incorporation of software-defined networks, communication companies can consistently configure firewalls and content filtering policies in their communication networks.

Reduced cost of operation: Centralization enable for increased efficiency in operations, utilization, and a better control of virtualization. All these lead to a reduction in operating costs. Although there is minimal usage of software-defined networks, it has been projected by statisticians that the operational costs of management will significantly drop with the proper implementation and configurations of software-defined networks.

Hardware saving and reduced capital expenditure: Software-defined networks will make it easy for hardware devices to be customized from the central office. Commands can be put on the hardware's which will reconfigure its function and this will reduce the costs of purchasing expensive hardware.

Cloud abstraction: Cloud resources can be unified with the usage of the cloud resources in the utilization of a software-defined the network. The software-defined network controller will have the power of managing all network components.

Consistent and guaranteed delivery of content: One of the main objectives of software-defined networking (SDN) is to have the capability of controlling and shaping data traffic. With such capabilities there will be the implementation of high-quality services otherwise known as quality of services (QoS) for voice over IP and multimedia transmissions. With the improvement of the network response, there will be high quality videos being streamed which will enhance and improve the quality of user experience.

Although the benefits of a software-defined network are revolutionary, don't necessarily apply to other networks and because of this it is important for institutions to assess the network and evaluate whether its advantages and beneficial to configure a software-defined network. It should be able to address the difficulties in availability of resources, security of the network and virtualization.

10.3. 5G AND SUPPORTED APPLICATIONS

In order to clearly comprehend how 5G will revolutionize the technological world of networking data transmission rates, it is important to discuss the other generations of CS which include 1G, 2G, 3G 4G and 4G LTE in which last two are commonly used. The analog 1G offered telephone transmission services without data, 2G had the capability of delivering digital signals of speeds of up to 250 kilobits per second and also supported voice, text, and data services. 3G is slightly better compared to 2G as it has data transmission rates of up to 3 megabits per second. In mobile phones, 4G provides speeds of up to 100 megabits per second and in wireless networks, speeds of up to 1 gigabit per second is reached. Internet service providers (ISP) who use wireless carriers offering high high-speed packet access of up to 6 megabits per second, also claim to be using the 4G network technology. The 4G LTE (long term evolution), TLE is a different packet that is also being offered within 4G and WiMAX. It is particularly known for its download link speed of up to 300 megabits per second and uplink speeds of up to 75 megabits per second (Elleithy and Sobh, 2014).

5G is a concept that was introduced to create a framework that will enhance the general mobile broadband services which will facilitate the expansion of mobile network services to support diverse hardware devices by generating an ecosystem that has optimum performance, efficiency, and cost in management. The 5G technology has been deemed to be so revolutionary that is being compared to the transformations brought about by electricity and automobile. This is because it can redefine a vast horizon of industries with connected services in every department. In the research department, experts have projected that the full benefits and impact of 5G will be felt before 2036. Findings from the study also suggest that the value chain which include the content creators, operators, application developers, consumers, and OEMs have the potential of generating revenues of up to 3.5 trillion dollars by 2035 and have the ability to support 20 million jobs.

10.3.1. Services 5G Will Be Able to Provide and Modify

- Enhanced mobile broadband – 5G will be able to boost the functionality of Smartphone's by enabling the configuration of virtual reality (VR) and AR which will enhance the overall user experience. With enhanced mobile broadband, Smartphone's consumers will bc able to get a faster, more uniform data rates, low latency and cost per bit benefits.

- Broad internet of things – there will be a smooth system of connecting devices all over the world by the configuration of sensors in virtually everything with its ability to lower the charges of data, power, and flexibility therefore providing Solutions that are cost-effective.
- Enhancing and enabling the compatibility of vast network devices – another possible benefit of 5G is to comfortably support future services that are not yet known to man.
- Mission-critical communications – with the development of 5G technology the revolutionization of industries will be witnessed due to the ultra-reliable and low-latency links that 5G enables such as having full control of critical infrastructure, vehicles, and medical processes.

10.3.2. 5G Data Transmission Speed

Currently there are modems, which have the ability of achieving speeds of up to 5 gigabits per download link peak data rate Qualcomm Snapdragon X50 5G modem. 5G technology is expected to bring speeds of up to 20 gigabytes per second. Connectivity in smartphones will be significantly advanced with the new 5G new radio mobile which is intending to configure a gigabit LTE long-lasting foundation. 5G will also provide low latency which will generate quick responses and finally, 5G will provide much more network capacity by expanding into new spectrum such as millimeter-wave (mmWave). Some of the major differentiating upgrades that 5G will bring are; scalable OFDM numerology with 2n scaling of subcarrier spacing, advanced spectrum sharing techniques, advanced massive MIMO antenna technology, advanced flexible LDPC channel coding, and flexible, dynamic, and self-contained TDD subframe design.

The principle used during the design of 4G LTE is also being followed when designing 5G. They are OFDM based. But with the objective of enhancing the scalability and flexibility of devices, the new 5G new radio air interface is designed to enhance the OFDM based principle. 5G is also aimed at broadening the services it can provide in areas such as mission-critical communications and the massive connections of IoT. Such capabilities have been made possible by the design models being configured in the new 5G new radio air interface such as the installation of a self-contained TDD subframe. The 5G new radio is particularly designed to enhance mobile broadband use (eMBB) with the aim of broadening the capacity of Internet usage and improving the general functionality of the 4G LTE technology. The 3GPP is the body that has been assigned to specifically design the 5G technology. It comprises of all branches in the communication network sector (Elleithy and Sobh, 2014).

10.4. MICROSERVICE ARCHITECTURE

Over the years the architecture of frameworks and designs have progressed drastically. Many new mechanizations, architectural patterns, and practices have emerged over the years. An example of the emergence of architectural patterns include microservices in the world of domain-driven design, continuation in delivery, platform, and infrastructure automation, scaling systems, polygon programming and persistence. Micro servicing is the process of bringing together the factors and elements that are changing because of the same reasons and separating those factors that are altered with other variables and at the same time developing, deploying, and independently maintaining the components. The services have been programmed to manage a specific task and together, they have the ability to solve complicated business difficulties through simple APIs as they can be able to communicate with other services.

10.4.1. Benefits of a Microservices Architecture

Because of how small a specific service is, designers have the ability to develop the services using teams from scratch and separating the services by service boundaries which enables for an efficient operation as it makes the scale up of the services in terms of development easy. When the manufacture of the services has been completed, the management is able to deploy the services independently of each other thus enhancing identification of hot services and modify them independently without having to alter other applications. The technology behind micro servicing also enables for error isolation. This is important because a service can be shut down in order to repair the error and at the same time another, services will continue operating fluently even at the time where the service stopped working. This has enabled designers to note and redeploy an entire application which leads to less efficiency in service delivery. With micro servicing, technology stacks are able to be identified and chosen on the basis of the functionality it needs to handle and this enhances efficiency because unlike the standardized, one-size-fits-all approach, resources can be wasted. This being a new technology, it is hard for computer engineers to incorporate it in their systems so there are organizations that are using certain principles when developing microservices (Saha, 2011). They include;

How to decompose: In this process developers need to understand vital business capabilities that provide value to end-users and the corresponding desired service that will be required to be defined. A high level of comprehension of business operations will be required in order to define services. For instance, online businesses how vast business capabilities such as order management, delivery management, inventory management, and procurement to mention but a few. A reliable service can then be designed once the business capability has been analyzed. During the design of services experts are grouped and every group deals with a specific service. This will help in stabilizing API boundaries.

Manufacture and deploying: Once the experts have already found the corresponding service needed to be designed from each business capability, suitable technology that will be used in solving a certain challenge is then assembles and the building process begins.

Design the individual services carefully: During the design process, the protocols which will be used in the interaction with the business capabilities should be clearly defined. Including the complexities and implementation details of the service is not necessary but service function needs to be clearly defined in order to show the client the kind of service which will be used to solve issues regarding a specific business capability. Inclusion of other complexities will make modification of the service hard as it will be challenging to determine the various parts of the service.

10.4.2. Decentralization

For organizations and businesses that are already testing and applying micro servicing models, they have decided to stick to one framework which is moving forward with the same people who developed the microservice as they are responsible in taking care of everything related to that service, there is no need of employing a third party or a support team to handle certain situations. An internal open-source framework can be configured in order to have the same function will. Using this approach any developer who wants to alter the schema of a service is able to check out the code, work on the feature and submit the PR. This will lead to saving of time as there will be no need of the developer waiting for the owner of the service to come and make the alterations. The library should contain clearly well-defined documentation regarding the steps needed to set up the service and the guidance for each service. This will enable other developers to be able to comprehend what needs to be done on the service and have the ability to work on the service. Open sourcing also motivates the developers to design a code that is of high quality because they know that other developers will use their codes and therefore, there is no room for making errors. Also, services can be collected from a central message bus and this will help in decentralizing things.

Routing of messages from various services are all being controlled by the bus. The main challenge with this system is that the bus keeps on getting more intelligent since more and more logic is being installed inside the central bus. This makes the bus to be well-versed and aware on the mechanics of the domain which makes altering of the schema extremely difficult and the system can lose coordination. What developers need to do is to regulate the amount of knowledge being fed to the central bus in order to make it less knowledgeable about the domain and enable it to handle the routing aspect only.

10.4.3. Deploy

Consumer written contracts for an API needs to be outlines and clearly defined in order to ensure there are no future breakdowns of your API in the event that changes have been made. The contracts clearly define the expectations and the specifications of clients and this will be a guide to the providers on the obligations they need to fulfill for each individual client. The specifications in the consumer-driven contracts need to be whole and complete in order for it to be deployed and before any alterations can be made on the services. It also enables the providers to know the link of a service to its specific business capability.

The common models being used in the deployment of microservices are multiple microservices per operating system (OS) and one microservice per OS.Multiple microservices per OS: Because this framework enables the host of each service not to be provisioned it has served time in automatic processes but the Independence of scaling and altering services is limited in this model. Dependable variables will be hard will get hard to be managed in this framework. Another challenge that can occur is unwanted side effects can be transferred to other running services which brings about difficulties in reproduction.

One microservice per OS: This framework was introduced in order to curb the challenges being experienced in the multiple microservices OS framework. Services in this framework have been well isolated therefore enabling developers to manage scaling and dependencies services independently. This operation can be very expensive but developers have designed a model where they utilize hypervisors where multiple virtual machines are positioned on the same host.

10.5. OPEN NETWORK SWITCHES

Open switches are defined as switches found in hardware and software components. Open switches can be altered independently and separately of each other. This will enable hardware components to support multiple OSs. This gives software developers an opportunity to rebrand an open switch, configure their own program, and sell it as a package.

10.5.1. Bare Metal Switches

This refers to an open switch system that operates with hardware components. Manufacturers and developers purchase the hardware components excluding the content and it is them who will load up the hardware device with the appropriate OS. This system has been used in building services for personal computers (PCs) and laptops for many years. After determining the type of applications that will be configured in the hardware device appropriate software is then determined and integrated. Taiwan is the fundamental manufacturer of bare metal switches with companies such as delta computer and alpha networks leading in its production. When manufacturers are purchasing the Bare metal switch, they also get a bootloader known as the open network install environment (ONIE) whose function is to enable the loading of an OS onto the switch. Some OSs that can be loaded using this technology include Cumulus Linux, Fastpath, and Switch Light. All these OSs essentially are commercial software and practical freeware in limited in the operations. It is mostly beneficial to commercial developers who want to create their own codes but it can't be deployed in the production network by itself (Saha, 2011).

10.5.2. White Box Switches

In the white box, you will find that the hardware and the software component have come together through the switch is still open because the integration of the OS and the hardware has not been done yet as is the case in black box. So, when purchasing a white box switch, it will contain a package, a bare metal switch and an OS.

10.5.3. Brite Box Switches

Brite is a shortfall of branded white box. This switch is made by an ODM and is often the same switch offered by the ODMs as their metal but it sports a front bezel with the brand name like Dell.

10.5.4. Merchant Silicon

Merchant silicon has played an important role in enhancing the functionalities of open switches be it bare metal, white box or britebox. This contrasts to ASICS which vendors have been using in the designing of high-end switches and routers. Although silicon is very beneficial in ensuring that there is tight integration of the vast feature set and the proprietary OS, you will find that the developers are releasing new generation chips after every 24 months because the production cycle is long and very costly. Silicon is not only being you in open switches but also closed switches. Companies such as Cisco and Jupiter are gradually introducing switches built on merchant silicon, e.g., Nexus 3000 and 9000. In the early 2000s, Sun Microsystems tried to tie the software very closely to their hardware. At the same time, there were other vendors like Dell and HP who are using ×86 based servers which made the functionality of Sun Microsystems to fail.

10.6. WIRELESS DATA LINKS AND COMMUNICATION FOR DRONES, UAV, UGVS, AND USVS

Commtact is a developing company that is struggling to advance the data link systems that will be ideal for critical communications in tactical unmanned systems. Examples of such systems include aerial vehicles, such as UAVs and drones, unmanned ground vehicles, and unmanned surface vehicles.

10.6.1. Mini Micro Data Link System (M2DLS)

This is an advanced digitized data link system. It is suitable for miniature and micro-sized UAVs and other unmanned platforms. It weighs about 100g. Using the gauss Ian shaped minimum shift keying digital modulation, the mini microdata link system (M2DLS) has the ability to provide full-duplex digital communication. This significantly reduces power consumption and at the same time maintaining a high data link performance with a high fade margin. This feature has a great compatibility with tactical unmanned systems that normally are lightly budgeted. With a range of up to 40 kilometers the M2DLS can download real-time images and videos LAN and serial data and information from a wide range of sensors. This optimizes the reliability and performance of tactical unmanned systems even under brutal conditions.

10.6.2. Advanced Mini Link System (AMLS)

Advanced wireless data link for sUAS and tactical UGVs: This is an advanced version of the data Link Systems specifically created to be used with mini UAVs and tactical UAS which are smaller in size. Just like the M2DLS, it is able to downlink real-time images and videos, LAN, and serial data and information from a wide range of sensors which are smaller in size. A duplex wideband has been enabled in this architecture and also error correction techniques plus communication techniques. Aircrafts now have the ability to operate without being supervised due to their high spectral efficiency and data rate selectivity being provided. Advanced wireless data link allows for ranges of up to 160 km which makes it conducive in the control of UAV and UGV missions.

10.6.3. Integrated Data Link Systems (IDLE MK-11)

Data link which provides a secure and ideal long-range UAV missions: The integrated data link system has specific design materials used to provide long endurance of unmanned aerial systems of heights that are medium and high-altitude areas. The integrated data link system has the ability to have full-duplex wideband, correction of errors techniques high-speed data transfer in the uplink and downlink channels. Integrated data link system creates a secure environment which enhances communication between an unmanned platform and the ground data terminal (GDT). Security comes about due to the centralization of control operations which can be installed on a vehicle or roof. Provided that the integrated data link system is within the range of sight, instructions from the GDT can be executed and it has the ability to downlink real-time video images, LAN, and serial data and information from a wide range of sensors. In terms of weight, the integrated data link system weighs about 2500 g and it has the ability to provide a scope of 250 km in operations. This is particularly significant for long-range UAV missions like search and rescue missions.

10.6.4. UVF/VHF Radio

Secure wireless data links for drones, UGVs, and USVS: The radio utilizes both analog and digital data link Systems Which have the capability of providing full-duplex audio and Ethernet data transmission for a wide variety of unmanned platforms. Such platforms include UAS, UGVS, and USVS. Using the frequencies transmitted by UVF and VHF, effective data transmission can be achieved which includes VoIP and air traffic control Communications with frequency bands ranging from 30 MHZ to 512 MHZ. Programs have been designed to manage and control the trans receiver where it's functions through the modulation and demodulation of both analog and digital transmission thus providing a wide horizon of functional options. Just like the integrated data link system, it weighs about 2500 g and this makes it suitable for installation and both ground and aerial platforms. It has the same range of 250 KM and this enables it to be significant in ISR missions. In the Marines, this frequency is used in ship to ship and ship to shore communications of vessels.

10.6.5. Secondary Link and UHF and FTS

Wireless data link for any class of unmanned aerial platform: This is an advanced version of a long-range half-duplex digital data link system. It has a weight of 60 grams making it suitable for a wide range of unmanned platforms. A narrow band digital simplex functionality is among its strongholds because it provides a lower rate communication through UHF. Because, it provides a wide range of data transmission, with ranges of up to 300 kilometers, As a result, it can be used as a primary link providing one communication channels for all unmanned vehicles. Intelligence can be backed up in the secondary link. Because of its light weight nature, it enhances performance of the system by providing security and low power consumption (Elleithy and Sobh, 2014).

10.7. QUANTUM COMPUTING

Quantum computers have the ability to perform quantum calculations and base their reasoning from calculating the likelihood of an object state before it is measured. Current computers use the computer language consisting of 1s and 0s to calculate logical operations. With the introduction of quantum computers, there is a huge potential to generate exponentially more data compared to the classic computers. When traditional computers are making logical operations, they base their decisions using the definite position of a physical state. Because of the binary nature of computer languages, operations are solely based on one of two positions. A bit is defined as a single state, such as "on" or "off". The approach in quantum computing is different because during operations the quantum state of an object is associated with a qubit. In the qubit state the computer shows the properties of a certain object before they are clearly defined. Some of the properties that can be detected are the polarization of a photon. Quantum computing does not give a clear position of an object; rather it creates a quantum state occurring in a mixed superposition. In the unmeasured quantum state the superposition of the object can be mingled with other objects creating a final object which has accurate mathematical formulas even though the outcome has not been clearly defined. Given that complicated mathematic formulas are applied in quantum computing, the superposition can be computed using special algorithms that can possibly take years to solve. These algorithms can solve great mathematical challenges, such as designing hard to break security codes (Elleithy and Sobh, 2014).

10.7.1. Types of Quantum Computers

Should a quantum computer to function properly, the algorithms need to hold the objects long enough in the superposition state in order to undertake important procedures on them. You will find that most objects in the superposition state lose that state through a process known as decoherence. This process makes the objects to be similar in measurements to the old classical bits. Decoherence occurs when the objects that are in the proposition state generally mix with materials that are a part of the measured system. A quantum shield is necessary in order to shield the objects to remain in their superposition states while at the same time making them easy to read. Although the quantum shield technology has not yet been developed, researchers already spent a lot of resources to design a more robust quantum process and create ways to improve the general performance.

The quantum computing technology is proving to be supreme from classical computer operations and companies, such as IBM and Google, are getting closer to creating accurate devices through the continuation of cramming more qubits together. Mixed reactions have been raised regarding the technology behind quantum computing as experts claim that there are hurdles in the framework that will be hard to overcome (Elleithy and Sobh, 2014).

10.7.2. Applications of Quantum Computing

Google performed tests on the quantum computing technology and can perform operations that could take classical computer thousands of years. Some of the fields that will significantly benefit from this technology include electronic materials discovery, solar capture, artificial intelligence, weather forecasting and climate change amongst many others.

10.8. DIAMOND SEMICONDUCTORS

In chemistry diamond is a metastable allotrope of carbon. Synthetic diamonds, which are more refined forms of diamonds, are used in Industries. The synthetic diamonds are developed through a chemical vapor deposition (CVD) process. Research shows that diamonds have the capability of producing a powerful power device. This is because of its special characteristics which include a wide bandgap of 5.45 eV, a high breakdown field of 10MV/cm inter-high thermal conductivity of 22W/cm. The high voltage electronic band gaps in devices is defined as wideband gap. Institutions are researching the latest technology. For instance, Waseda University in Japan recently presented a paper on a diamond FET for 1000-volt applications. The university is designing a diamond FET which undergoes a chemical reaction to become highly conductive. Using microwave plasma, the University of Waseda developed undoped diamond layer on top of a diamond substrate to make the diamond FETs. The CVD procedure is used in the creation process with thickness of 0.5. and a quarter meter being configured. Surface holes are created on top of the FET in order to create a conducive device. It can be a 2D hole gas and it is created by using an atomic layer deposition process to apply AI203 at 450°C.

The diamond age of electronics is becoming increasingly popular in industries trying to incorporate its usage in the production of objects. The physical and chemical properties of diamonds can revolutionize industries in terms of performance. Because of the strong covalent bonds that diamond possess, diamond has the ability to operate in extremely hot conditions without degrading in performance. It performs better than silicone, which is being used often in industries. Diamond has 22 times better heat transfer efficiency compared to silicone and thus, it can easily be cooled. Extreme voltages can be passed through diamond for a long time before it starts to break down implying that it has a greater tolerance to resistance. Diamond also contains electron holes which allows its electrons to freely move at a very fast rate. Some companies are already using diamond semiconductors which have proven to be more functional. Because of its properties, diamond-based semiconductors have the capability of heightening the power density which will lead to the design of fast, light, and simpler devices. In terms of environmental conservation, diamond performs a better job than silicon and can improve thermal performances within devices. The diamond semiconductors technology has a huge impact in industries. Automakers are planning to use the technology to power devices and control modules for electrical cars. At the same time, diamond semiconductors can elongate the battery performance of automobiles (Erol, Ufuk, and Tuna, 2005). Computer engineers are also applying the technology to optimize the usage of energy when data is being stored in cloud computer servers. Due to the fact that diamond semiconductors do not need large devices for them to be contained and it has a high energy-saving capability it paves way for the design of smaller devices such as microwaves, television, and digital cameras. In defense, scientists have proven that diamond semiconductors provide a greater range in reliability and Performance in operation even during extreme events. Diamond semiconductors facilitate first cloud integration for clients and businesses.

The benefits that come with using diamond semiconductors can give ideas to engineers to generate better devices that will probably solve unforeseen difficulties. The cost of financing cooling systems can be cut by half with the use of diamond semiconductors as it has the ability to reduce electronic wastage. People argue that using diamonds will be expensive because the mining processes are costly. On the other hand, evidence shows that lab-grown diamonds are very clean and affordable compared to natural diamonds. Diamond semiconductors have the capability of altering the whole electronic properties and create device structures more than 1,000 times smaller compared to silicon counterparts.

10.9. EXPANSION OF ARTIFICIAL INTELLIGENCE

The technology behind artificial intelligence is significantly gaining popularity in broad range of industries, organizations, and government sectors. In the current world, the applications of artificial intelligence have already shown its significance. Some of the applications involve facial recognition, language translators, and assistance such as Google Voice, Siri, and Alexa. Due to the unnoticed contribution of artificial intelligence in productivity, growth, and innovation in the business world, companies are increasingly harnessing the power of artificial intelligence in running their operations. Artificial intelligence was first brought to our attention in 1956 at a conference at Dartmouth College where researchers came with different scope of topics ranging from language simulation to learning machines. Artificial intelligence has gained momentum over the past two decades as scientist have developed advanced machine lea0rning algorithms, which are being used to harness the power of artificial intelligence effectively. We can also train bigger and complex models due to ongoing developments in computer hardware. The models are accessible to consumers with the help of cloud technology. For instance, autonomous vehicles use advancements in other fields, such as computer vision, mapping, satellite technology, sensors, and robotics and integrates these technologies to create a device that has artificial intelligence capabilities. Serious breakthrough is still needed by scientists in order to achieve the main objective that artificial intelligence is required to function. Artificial intelligence is required to act and function like a normal human being. Therefore, it should be able to tackle the general challenges in the same way humans do (Erol, Ufuk, and Tuna, 2005).

Excitement is associated with the technological advancement known as deep learning. An algorithm is created to enable a device to normally function is the same way as human neurons interact in the brain. Artificial intelligence can therefore be used to create a framework that consists of simulated interconnected neurons. Neural networks currently possess only three to six layers and a handful of neurons.

Deep learning networks have the capability of having over 10 layers with the number of neurons exceeding one million. Artificial intelligence has already created a handful of frameworks in machine learning which include supervised learning, unsupervised learning and reinforcement learning. Supervised learning is the most used model and works with available data and output variables which have been clearly defined. Training data is used in supervised learning frameworks because it assists the system to clearly differentiate and understand the relationship between provided inputs and outputs. Unsupervised data is similar to supervised data although it does not have labeled training data. Last but not least, in reinforcement learning a scoring system has been formulated and the model is trained to receive virtual rewards or punishments and using the scoring system to give a score. Machine learning through the use of artificial intelligence has come with a lot of limitations. One example of such limitations is the need of massive human capital in order to label the training data. Another limitation is the need to enhance the experiences so that it becomes human-like. Transfer learning which involves training a model on a particular job and immediately applying the trained knowledge to a similar but distinct activity is the potential solution.

Without a doubt, artificial intelligence can be used to improve the performance of businesses, especially in predictive maintenance area where analyzing large amounts of high-dimensional data can be performed quickly with deep learning. With this technology, businesses have the ability of detecting errors and anomalies that are easily ignored for example, during factory assembly lines. In supply chain management artificial intelligence can reduce the operational costs through improving fuel efficiency and optimizing routing of delivery traffic. With the improvement of speech recognition, artificial intelligence can lead to better customer service. The adoption of artificial intelligence in business practices is proving to be extremely beneficial and will lead to revolutionization of technology in future (Saha, 2011).

References

1. Banzal, S., (2007). Data and Computer Network Communication (pp. 39–67). New Delhi: Firewall Media.
2. Carne, E. B., (2004). A Professional's Guide to Data Communication in a TCP/IP World (p. 253). Massachusetts: Artech House.
3. Cowley, J., (2012). Communications and Networking: An Introduction (pp. 1–81). Berlin: Springer Science & Business Media.
4. Emilio, M. D., (2013). Data Acquisition Systems: From Fundamentals to Applied Design (pp. 1–99). Berlin: Springer Science & Business Media.
5. Gast, M., (2005). 802.11 Wireless Networks: The Definitive Guide (pp. 1–67). California: O'Reilly Media, Inc.
6. Gelenbe, E., Caglayan, M. U., & Tugcu, T., (2005). New Trends In Computer Networks (pp. 1–83). Singapore: World Scientific.
7. Gupta, P. C., (2006). Data Communications and Computer Networks (pp. 31–71). New Delhi: PHI Learning Pvt. Ltd.
8. Homero, Toral-Cruz, Albena, D. M., Miroslav, V., Kamaljit, I. L.,& Robert, B., (2015). Research Trends and Challenges for Network-Based ICT Systems. Retrieved from link.springer.com: https://link.springer.com/article/10.1007/s11277–015–2724–4 (accessed on 22

March 2020).

9. Dhotre, I. A.,& Bagad, V. S., (2008). Data Communication (p. 276). New Delhi: Technical Publications.
10. Ibe, O. C., (2017). Fundamentals of Data Communication Networks (pp. 1–17). New Jersey: John Wiley & Sons.
11. Jaffe, D. J., (2004, July 1). The Challenges of Network Technologies. Retrieved from computerweekly.com:https://www.computerweekly.com/feature/The-challenges-of-network-technologies (accessed on 22 March 2020).
12. Jiang, S., (2018). Wireless Networking Principles: From Terrestrial to Underwater Acoustic (pp. 1–101). Berlin: Springer.
13. Khaled, E.,& Tarek, S., (2014). New Trends in Networking, Computing, E-learning, Systems Sciences, and Engineering (pp. 1–101). Berlin: Springer.
14. Marko, P., Ivan, C.,& Peter, K., (2016). Challenges of Information and Communication Technologies Usage in E-Business Systems. Retrieved from intechopen.com: https://www.intechopen.com/books/e-business-state-of-the-art-of-ict-based-challenges-and-solutions/challenges-of-information-and-communication-technologies-usage-in-e-business-systems (accessed on 22 March 2020).
15. Meadow, C. T., (2002). Making Connections: Communication Through the Ages (pp. 1–31). Maryland: Scarecrow Press.
16. Pal, A., (2013). Data Communication And Computer Networks (pp. 1–79). New Delhi: PHI Learning Pvt. Ltd.
17. Prasad, K. V., (2004). Principles of Digital Communication Systems and Computer Networks (pp. 13–73). Massachusetts: Cengage Learning.
18. Quirke, B., (2000). Making the Connections: Using Internal Communication to Turn Strategy Into Action (p. 286). London: Gower Publishing, Ltd.
19. Rackley, S. A., (2011). Wireless Networking Technology: From Principles to Successful Implementation (pp. 1–69). Netherlands: Elsevier.
20. Robertazzi, T. G., (2017). Introduction to Computer Networking (pp. 1–80). Berlin: Springer.
21. Saha, D., (2011). Next Generation Data Communication Technologies: Emerging Trends: Emerging Trends (pp. 1–65). Pennsylvania: IGI Global.

22. Siddiqui, S., (2005). Roaming in Wireless Networks (pp. 1–31). Pennsylvania: McGraw Hill Professional.
23. Tarmo, A.,& Ville, J., (2014). Introduction to Communication Networks (pp. 19–61). Massachusetts: Artech House.
24. Vijay, J., Ghanshyam, S., Manish, T., & Antonio d'Alessandro, (2019). Optical and Wireless Technologies: Proceedings of OWT 2018 (pp. 1–100). Berlin: Springer.
25. White, C., (2015). Data Communications and Computer Networks: A Business User's Approach (pp. 1–61). Boston: Cengage Learning.

INDEX

Printed in the United States
By Bookmasters